Captivity and Sentiment

Reencounters with Colonialism: New Perspectives on the Americas

editors (all of Dartmouth College)
Mary C. Kelley, AMERICAN HISTORY
Agnes Lugo-Ortiz, LATIN AMERICAN STUDIES
Donald Pease, AMERICAN LITERATURE
Ivy Schweitzer, AMERICAN LITERATURE
Diana Taylor, LATIN AMERICAN AND LATINO STUDIES

Frances R. Aparicio and Susana Chávez-Silverman, eds. *Tropicalizations: Transcultural Representations of Latinidad*

Michelle Burnham, *Captivity and Sentiment: Cultural Exchange in American Literature, 1682–1861*

Colin G. Calloway, ed., *After King Philip's War: Presence and Persistence in Indian New England*

Captivity

&

Cultural Exchange in

Sentiment

American Literature,

1682–1861

Michelle Burnham

Dartmouth College

PUBLISHED BY UNIVERSITY PRESS OF NEW ENGLAND

HANOVER AND LONDON

Dartmouth College

Published by University Press of New England

© 1997 by the Trustees of Dartmouth College

First paperback printing 1999

Printed in the United States of America

5 4 3 2

CIP data appear at the end of the book

Contents

Figures

Acknowledgments

The effects of innumerable exchanges are inscribed throughout this book. I pay tribute to some of those exchanges here, if only as a way of acknowledging my continuing indebtedness. Neil Schmitz, Ken Dauber, Deidre Lynch, and Bill Warner were among the earliest and best readers of this project, and I am grateful for their advice and encouragement. Of its most recent readers, I thank particularly Don Pease and Mary Kelley for their careful and helpful responses to the manuscript, which has benefited much from their comments. Many readers responded helpfully to sections of this project at various stages in its development; I thank especially Nancy Armstrong, Dwight Atkinson, Paula Backscheider, Bob Daly, Tim Dykstal, Jim Holstun, Susan Howe, and Stacy Hubbard for their responses and suggestions. Some of the ideas in this book were presented as lectures at Auburn University, and I appreciate the exchanges and dialogue generated there among colleagues and graduate students. Taylor Stoehr helped set me on my way at the very beginning and read the manuscript with care later on; I know that I would have done well to adopt more of his excellent suggestions. And without the members of our Buffalo reading group, this book may never have come into existence; many thanks to Gail Brisson, Eric Daffron, Anna Geronimo, Julia Miller, and Juliana Spahr.

I have been fortunate in receiving a research grant-in-aid from the Office of the Vice President for Research at Auburn University, which enabled me to travel to The Newberry Library in Chicago, and a summer research grant from the College of Liberal Arts at Auburn University. I am grateful also to Dennis Rygiel for granting me the release time necessary to complete the project. Phil Pochoda at the University Press of New England has been generous in his support and enthusiasm for this project. Finally, thanks to Dick Burnham and Ulla Burnham; Nicholas Burnham and Gisela Ballard; and Christina, David, and Julia Strickler. And to Chip Hebert, who asks the best questions.

Earlier versions or portions of three chapters in this book have been published elsewhere. I thank *Early American Literature* (*EAL*) for permission to reprint sections of chapter 1 that first appeared as "The Journey Between: Liminality and Dialogism in Mary White Rowlandson's Captivity Narrative" in *EAL* 28:1 (1993) 60–75. A version of chapter 6, titled "Loopholes of

Retreat: Harriet Jacobs' Slave Narrative and the Critique of Agency in Foucault," appeared in *Arizona Quarterly* 49 (1993) 53–73. I thank the Arizona Board of Regents for permission to reprint portions of that essay here. Chapter 2, "Between England and America: Captivity, Sympathy, and the Sentimental Novel" also appears, in slightly different form, in *Cultural Institutions of the Novel,* edited by Deidre Lynch and William B. Warner (© 1996 Duke University Press. All rights reserved).

October 1996   M.B.

Captivity and Sentiment

INTRODUCTION

I know not, reader,

whether you will be moved

to tears by this narrative;

I know I could not write it

without weeping.

—Cotton Mather,

Decennium Luctuosum

(1699)

*T*HE IMAGE OF Cotton Mather weeping over the stories of colonial Anglo-Americans held captive by Indians and his subtle injunction that readers do the same provokes the simple question with which I began this project: why does captivity, particularly the captivity of women, so often inspire the sentimental response of tears? From the biblical image of the captive Israelites weeping on the banks of a river in Babylon to the sentimental media coverage of Americans held hostage in the Middle East, the representation of captivity has invariably, it seems, been accompanied by tears—and perhaps more by the tears of spectators than by those of the captives themselves. Moreover, those tears historically have signaled a sensation of belonging that is felt as pleasurable, quite in spite of the representation of suffering that inspires it. This book repeatedly turns to moments and texts in early American cultural and literary history in which the figures of captive women have elicited this ambivalent sentimental response. It repeatedly finds that what is at stake in the fate of these figures is nothing less than the reproduction of the nation.

Most explanations of sympathy ignore its element of pleasure and accordingly miss its profound ambivalence. The easiest way to explain sympathy, for example, has been to invoke the seemingly obvious mechanism of spectatorial identification: if we are moved by scenes of confinement and homelessness, it is because we imagine ourselves in the place of the suffering captives. This formula has been repeated from at least Edmund Burke's 1757 claim that "sympathy must be considered as a sort of substitution, by which we are put into the place of another man, and affected in many respects as he is affected" (41), to Philip Fisher's recent description of sympathy as "equations between the deep common feelings of the reader and the exotic but analogous situations of the characters" (118). But like tears themselves, this explanation blurs rather more than it clarifies. More specifically, by focusing on the affective relation of similarity between the captive and her audience, it obscures the complex exchanges between the captive and her alien captors. In this respect, the traditional understanding of sympathy repeats the same strategies of narratives and novels of captivity. Like the media portrayal of hostage crises, captivity literature constructs and reinforces a binary division between captive and captor that is based on cultural, national, or racial difference. Since captivity typically takes place in colonial contexts of cultural as well as military warfare, this rhetorical opposition serves to justify the political and social antagonism that both propels and results from the sentimental representation of captivity.

One aim of this book is to expose critically this strategic element of captivity literature but also to complicate it by examining a further dynamic obscured by the paradigm of sympathy outlined above by Burke and Fisher. One symptom of this hidden dynamic is the fascination, the almost subversive pleasure, with which audiences have responded to captivity scenarios. After all, a surprising number of the texts studied here—from Mary Rowlandson's captivity narrative to *Uncle Tom's Cabin*—were once popular literature, even extraordinary best-sellers. Why and how does captivity literature function as escape literature, and what might the sentimentality of these texts tell us about the terms of such escape? What is the source of the pleasure that underwrites sympathetic response?

The following chapters pursue such questions by examining texts published in North America from the seventeenth through the nineteenth centuries that depend on a central and sympathetic figure of a captive woman. The genres studied are not always easily distinguished from one another and indeed, their shared political and affective strategies indicate exchanges between them that are muted by efforts to contain them within coherent generic boundaries. What brings together the colonial American captivity narratives, Anglo-American sentimental novels, and African American slave narratives studied here is their mutual engagement in a project much like the one Cotton Mather invokes in the epigraph above: provoking their readers to cry for their captive heroines. One key to the cultural logic that supports this response of tears is suggested by the categories in which we place these texts, since describing them requires adjectives that articulate a complex network of political and social intersections: "colonial American," "Anglo-American," "African American." It is at—or more precisely, across —such intersections that I locate the sentimentalism of these texts, for their "moving" qualities are inextricably linked to the movements in and by the texts themselves across various borders. In their narrative content as well as in their circulation as print commodities, these texts traverse those very cultural, national, and racial boundaries that they seem so indelibly to inscribe. Captivity literature, like its heroines, constantly negotiates zones of contact such as the "frontier," the Atlantic Ocean, the master/slave division, and the color line.

These borders invoke the specific and intersecting histories of colonial relations in North America, just as the notion of "contact zone" more broadly does. I take the term from Mary Louise Pratt, who defines it as "the space of colonial encounters, the space in which peoples geographically and historically separated come into contact with each other and establish ongoing relations, usually involving conditions of coercion, radical inequality, and intractable conflict" (6). Ethnohistorical studies likewise remind us that the exchanges that take place across these early American zones of contact are framed and transected by the practice of and resistance to colonialism.[1] But it is Homi Bhabha's theory of interstitiality that points to the specifically political possibilities contained within these sites of colonial contest, for such "'in-between' spaces provide the terrain for elaborating strategies of selfhood—singular or communal—that initiate new signs of identity, and innovative sites of collaboration, and contestation, in the act of defining the idea of society itself" (*Location* 1–2). Narratives and novels of captivity demonstrate that crossing transcultural borders exposes the captive to physical hardship and psychological trauma. But they also reveal that such crossings expose the captive and her readers to the alternative cultural paradigms of her captors. In collision with other, more dominant paradigms, these emergent hybrid formations can generate forms of critical and subversive agency, both within and outside the text.

These popular texts accordingly function as escape literature because their heroines so often indulge in transgressive behavior or enact forms of resistant agency, not in spite of their captivity but precisely as a result of it.

The tears that so often accompany accounts of female captivity both mark and mask that agency; sentimental discourse at once conceals the movement across such boundaries and legitimizes the transgressive female agency produced by it. When writers from Cotton Mather to Susanna Rowson to Harriet Beecher Stowe invite their readers to cry, they allow them the disavowed pleasure of indulging in unlegislated escape. But they also invite their readers into a national community that is experienced affectively precisely because its claim to integrity (whether geographical or moral) depends on remembering to forget the border transgressions and colonial violence that have secured it.[2] Chapters 1 and 2 trace exchanges between, respectively, settler and native populations and imperial and colonial English people in the colonial era. Indian captivity narratives emerge during this period, circulating the subversive possibilities of cultural exchange and enlisting those possibilities in the reproduction of a national community. Narratives about women, in part because their aggressive acts generally required more careful justification and posed more danger of subversion than those of men, acquired a particular cultural appeal. This ambivalent trope of female captivity becomes refigured in later historical periods to serve—and sometimes to resist—the representational and affective imperatives of American nation-building in popular sentimental novels of the revolutionary period (chapter 3), frontier romances of the Jacksonian era (chapter 4), and abolitionist literature of the decade preceding the Civil War (chapters 5 and 6).[3]

The traditional formulation of sympathy as an identification with those suffering figures whom we are or could be like obscures these ambivalent sites of agency and their colonialist context by positing a model that reifies and segregates cultural, national, and racial identities. Literary histories and the categories they produce frequently do much the same thing. American studies, for example, has only recently begun to reassess and critique its exceptionalist foundations by examining the ways in which national and local categories are constructed, revised, and reinvented in a complex of transnational and cross-cultural relations.[4] This project contributes to that reassessment by situating captivity literature within its intercultural context and by establishing its affectivity as a function of that context. By doing so, it also interrogates the specifically sentimental appeal of the exceptionalist myth. Like the texts examined here, exceptionalist narratives of American literature and culture have historically obscured their colonialist origins and the production of cultural difference within them.

Earlier I gestured toward an alternative model for understanding sympathetic tears as a cover for the physical and imaginative violation of borders of difference. Captivity scenarios and sentimental response are in these terms mutually constitutive, dependent on the specifically colonial confrontations that produce them. This formulation resists the onetime convention of treating captivity narratives and sentimental fiction as two separate and distinct traditions whose eventual merger signaled the decline of the former. Captivity narratives have been described as degenerating—once they became influenced by eighteenth-century English novels of sensibility—from earlier, less fictional, and more religiously oriented texts into texts aimed at "commercialism" (VanDerBeets, *Held Captive* xxviii), written by "the hack writer gone wild" (Pearce 16), and filled with "brutality, sadomasochistic and titillating elements, strong racist language, pleas for sympathy and commiseration," and depictions of women as helpless "frail flowers" (Namias 37). But the tendency to locate the source of this influence in the purportedly English origins of the novel hints that, in some accounts at least, a more specifically nationalist anxiety might inflect this narrative of corruption and diminishment. After all, captivity narratives have been consistently characterized as "uniquely American" (Levernier and Cohen xxvii), as the "first distinctively American literary genre" (Lang, "Introduction" 21) and as a site in which "a particularly American discourse regarding our historical identity" (Fitzpatrick 3) was articulated.[5] The more insistently the line of distinction between genres and the line of exception between continents is drawn, however, the more cloaked become the critical interstitial spaces between them.

Recent studies have moved toward understanding the more sentimentalized captivity narratives as productive of critical cultural possibilities rather than corruptive of aesthetic or national standards, and they therefore usefully revise the story of "progressive degeneration" (Ebersole 101) imposed by earlier critics on the genre. Christopher Castiglia, for example, persuasively argues that, by virtue of their very implausibility, sentimental captivity tales allowed women writers to articulate for themselves and their readers otherwise unimaginable feminist alternatives.[6] Emphasizing instead the religious function of reading practices, Gary Ebersole reminds us that the sentimental portrayal of captivity inspired a somatic experience in its contemporary readers that worked to assure them of their own moral virtue (117–29). For all their differences, these two accounts have in common a privileging of the emotional relation established between the white female captive and her implicitly white (and largely female) audience, a focus that follows the definition of sympathy shared by Edmund Burke and Philip Fisher as an identification based on resemblance. But as I suggested earlier, that relation ignores the Amerindian captors who formed the backdrop and support for these sentimental equations and who frequently became the victims of that equation. These texts put into circulation critical and feminist materials, but those materials depend on the cultural surplus generated in exchange with groups that are simultaneously slated for destruction, removal, or exploitation. For these reasons, the validation of sentimentalism must be wary of repeating sentimentalism's own concealment of the "conditions of coercion, radical inequality, and intractable conflict" (Pratt 6) that characterize colonialist borders.

In this context, Laura Wexler's critique of Victorian America stands out for its attention to sentimental culture's well-camouflaged practice of violence, especially on those "others" who failed to meet its standard of feeling and selfhood. As much as it legitimized those who managed to "accommodate to its image of an interior," sentimental fiction depersonalized those who could not (17). Wexler's analysis, developed in response to arguments by Philip Fisher and Jane Tompkins on behalf of sentimental fiction's subversive political potential, indicates that radical claims made on behalf of that fiction have overlooked its practice of "tender violence." This insight calls for a skepticism toward the critical tendency to sentimentalize sentimental literature, a skepticism that chapter 4, for example, develops more specifically by investigating how frontier romances and political rhetoric in the 1820s worked to reproduce the contexts of imperialism and nationalism from which they derived their affective support.[7] At the same time, however, this study seeks to locate moments of critical resistance enabled by hybrid formations generated within scenarios of cultural exchange. In order to locate and identify those formations, the deconstruction Wexler performs on sentimentalism's falsely maintained opposition between public and private must be extended beyond the domestic national borders within which her analysis remains. Just as captivity narratives have been positioned within a rhetoric of exceptionalism, American sentimental novels have been read within isolated national and cultural contexts, encouraging a persistent lack of attention to the ambivalent products of the contact zone, where cultural difference emerges amid colonial exploitation.

This paradigm extends back at least to Leslie Fiedler's *Love and Death in the American Novel,* a text notable not only for its often cited castigation of sentimentalism but for its development of a theory of American literature around the materials of captivity narratives. Fiedler locates "what is peculiarly American in our books" (n.p.) in the culture-crossing adventures of frontier heroes like Daniel Boone and Natty Bumppo. What makes "the American novel . . . different from its European prototypes" (11) is its story of the white male's flight from the woman-centered home into the wilderness inhabited by dark men. What finally enables the "Americanness" of American literature to be realized, according to this account, is the successful exorcism of the artistically enfeebling influence of sentimental novels. Fiedler's fleeing frontier heroes are therefore mirrored in the flight of "American" novelists and critics away from the "sentimental travesties" (89) written by Susanna Rowson and Samuel Richardson, as Nina Baym first noted in her classic article on "how theories of American fiction exclude women authors" ("Melodramas"). The myth of exceptionalism is therefore founded on a gesture that, by aligning sentimental fiction both with women and with Europe, at once masculinizes and isolates American literature. The explosion of scholarship on women writers and sentimental fiction that accompanied and followed Baym's critique has continued to interrogate and challenge that gendered division.[8] But this important body of scholarship has given less challenge to the nationalist division and its segregationist effect. In fact, the isolationist foundations of American literary history have been as often reinforced as they have been dismantled by the inclusion of this once marginalized body of literature. As a result, the transnational and intercultural origins of sentimental discourse and the very reliance of sentimentality on the kinds of colonial relations associated with contact zones have continued unacknowledged.

In her influential defense of sentimental fiction, for example, Jane Tompkins makes a case for its conformity to existing theories of American literature, arguing that critics have falsely described these novels as "turning away from the world into self-absorption and idle reverie" (143). Thus, a novel like *Uncle Tom's Cabin,* she contends, focuses on the home merely as "the prerequisite of world conquest" (143); no less than contemporary domestic advice manuals, Stowe's novel harbors an "imperialistic drive" to "coloniz[e] the world in the name of the 'family state' under the leadership of Christian women" (144). This redescription might qualify sentimental fiction and the women who wrote it for inclusion within various theories of American literature from which they have been silently exiled, including Sacvan Bercovitch's study of the uniquely American jeremiad or definitions that insist on the expansionist imagination within American books.[9] At the same time, Tompkins's description accurately, if uncritically, points to the ways in which sentimental fiction can participate in a project of cultural and religious imperialism that has not only domestic but global pretensions.[10] However "American" a novel like *Uncle Tom's Cabin* may be, for example, to isolate it within national borders is to miss its colonizing transcontinental reach into Liberia and the implications of that reach for abolitionism and racial ideology within the United States (implications examined in chapter 5). The moving bodies of captive women documented in the books studied here are inscribed by tensions between, on the one hand, their service to national or cultural reproduction and, on the other, the threats they pose to such reproduction. It is precisely this irresolvable tension between national agents and minority agency that sentimental discourse adjudicates. As chapter 3 maintains in its discussion of republican motherhood, agency's ambivalent oscillation between autonomy and dependence is implicit in the very origins of U.S. political formations and their sentimental constructions of national belonging.

In his own act of exorcising sentimentalism, Leslie Fiedler makes a confession that betrays a different sort of difficulty posed by writers of sentimental novels like Susanna Rowson, one that has nothing to do with his own overt concerns with standards of aesthetics or masculinity. These writers, he explains, "sometimes moved back and forth between the old country and the new with an ease which distresses the classifier" (67). *Captivity and Sentiment* is concerned with the interstitial sites marked precisely by these two paired indicators: the distress of classifiers and the mobility of bodies. While critics have sometimes placed captivity literature and sentimental literature in contest with each other on a field defined and critiqued in terms of gender, that field has been consistently surrounded, as it were, by an isolationist fence that has blurred the relations of contestation that take place on and across its containing borders. As chapter 2 argues, bringing eighteenth-century stories of female captivity into transcontinental dialogue highlights the arenas of friction and exchange that exceptionalist paradigms of American studies, like sentimental nationalism, conceal. The texts studied in this book often resolutely inscribe the boundaries on which isolationism and exceptionalism depend, but attending to their transgression of those same borders encourages them also to circulate as the unwitting bearers of cultural difference within American literary and national histories.

Captivity and Sentiment locates agency at those overlooked sites of cultural difference. The category of agency has been an ongoing source of concern within cultural studies, in large part as a result of the dilemma posed by the model of agency and its containment associated with the work of Foucault. That model posits a relationship between subject and structure that operates on the trope of captivity, as Foucault's interest in institutions of confinement like the prison, the clinic, and the asylum might suggest. The prospect of subjects incapable of escaping from or altering the political and cultural structures in which they are confined has generated, as if in sympathy for those subjects, a substantial and wide-ranging body of critical response. Chapter 6 turns to this conceptual border, the dividing line between subject and structure, in order to demonstrate that debates about agency have faltered by leaving this boundary intact. It is the hybrid and unpredictable effects of cultural exchange documented in Harriet Jacobs's slave narrative that brings into relief this fissure and its political possibilities, overlooked equally by the Foucauldian analysis of agency and its Lacanian critique. Practicing the colonial strategies of resistance that Homi Bhabha positions within the eclipsed regions of interstitiality, Jacobs's narrative exposes the limitations to the sentimental sense of national belonging so often mobilized by the tradition of captivity literature within which it is written. The example of Harriet Jacobs in the final chapter illustrates that critical agency is generated in sites of exchange and also that such agency purchases a measure of its efficacy by exploiting the very structures of confinement from which it enables bodies to escape. The resistant and unrecuperable surplus of cultural difference always left over by the process of cultural exchange finally speaks to the crucial necessity of identifying what sentimentality hides as well as what it allows.

The conclusion turns to two examples, Briton Hammon's obscure eighteenth-century slave narrative and the popular 1991 science fiction film *Terminator 2,* which illustrate what can get lost behind the blinding veil cast by tears. It argues for sustaining an interculturalism that would engage sites of exchange between and within texts, alongside and within multiculturalism's sometimes sentimental emphasis on traditions defined and distinguished by coherent cultural, racial, or national categories. The intercultural spaces that sometimes go unremarked between those categories tell a history of colonialism in North America, a history in which both cross-cultural captivity and sentimental discourse have their origins. In turn, these ambivalent colonial arenas call for a more critical assessment of the role of sentimentalism in U.S. nationalism. They also call for an increased attention to the ways in which those representations a spectator most identifies with, is most moved by, have been, in Gayatri Spivak's words, "secured by *other* places" (269).

Chapter 1

CAPTIVITY,

CULTURAL CONTACT,

AND COMMODIFICATION

MARY WHITE ROWLANDSON'S 1682 captivity narrative begins with her careful recollection of the violent scene of Indian attack on her Lancaster, Massachusetts, home, where she watches her own imminent fate rehearsed as nearby houses burn and their inhabitants are killed or taken captive. "At length," she writes, "they came and beset our own house, and quickly it was the dolefullest day that ever mine eyes saw" (118).[1] For two hours, she estimates, the Indians "shot against the House, so that the Bullets seemed to fly like hail; and quickly they wounded one man among us, then another, and then a third" (118–19). She watches her sister and her nephew die, while a bullet passes through her own side and wounds the daughter she carries in her arms. When the Rowlandson house is set on fire, she is forced to take her children and depart, with "the fire increasing, and coming along behind us, roaring, and the Indians gaping before us with their Guns, Spears, and Hatchets to devour us" (119). Mary Rowlandson's abandonment of her "roaring" home and her entrance into the hands of the "gaping" Indians retrospectively marks her transition into a physical and cultural homelessness that would resist psychological and ideological closure long after her experience of Indian captivity came to an end.

Within a short time after this raid but in what seems an immeasurable cultural distance, Rowlandson would be sewing shirts for and declining tobacco from the Wampanoag sachem Metacom, whom the English called King Philip. King Philip's War erupted in June 1675 and was followed by a series of surprise raids like this February 10 one by Narragansett Indians on the frontier settlement of Lancaster. A number of southern New England tribes had joined with Metacom's Wampanoags to resist the effects of growing Euro-American hegemony in the region, including diminished land, contests over political power, and property disputes.[2] But because the Indians typically took English captives away with them after skirmishes such as the Lancaster one, the conflict between these two cultures was often represented in terms of another kind of property: human property. Captives served as tools of economic negotiation and as figures of political and religious significance as they circulated between the New England tribes and the New England colonists. The body of the captive, exchanged as an unusual sort of commodity between two social and military antagonists, consequently told a history in which often contradictory economic, cultural, and religious signs were articulated.

Rowlandson's narrative ends with a tone of calm and a noticeable absence of descriptive detail, in striking contrast to its opening representation of the violent attack on Lancaster. Two woodcuts in a 1771 edition of Rowlandson's narrative nicely illustrate this stylistic shift from her narrative's first frantic scene to its rather orderly and routine conclusion. The first portrays the fearful chaos of the Lancaster raid, as figures raise their arms in grief and flight from a collection of burning houses (fig. 1). A second woodcut that appears near the end of the narrative portrays the captive calmly discussing the terms of her ransom with the Indians Tom and Peter (fig. 2).[3] Rowlandson barely records her return to the Puritan community and does not mention at all her reunion with her husband and children. Instead, she closes the narrative with a list of providences that retroactively expose God's plan to test severely but ultimately deliver the Puritan project in New England.

This interpretive framework is consistent with that supplied in the preface to her book, which is signed "Ter Amicam" and has been attributed to Increase Mather. Mather's preface reinforces the theological significance of Rowlandson's experience by presenting her story as a singular example "of the wonderfully awfull, wise, holy, powerfull, and gracious providence of God," which should "be exhibited to, and Viewed, and pondered by all, that disdain to consider the operation of his hands" (114).[4] If Rowlandson experienced conversion through captivity, Mather implies, then her readers should experience conversion as a result of reading about her captivity: "Reader, if thou gettest no good by such a Declaration as this, the fault

FIG I.   Woodcut of the raid on Lancaster, from *A Narrative of the Captivity Sufferings and Removes of Mrs. Mary Rowlandson* (Boston, 1771). Photo courtesy of Edward E. Ayer Collection, The Newberry Library.

must needs be thine own. Read therefore, Peruse, Ponder, and from hence lay by something from the experience of another against thine own turn comes, that so thou also through patience and consolation of the Scripture mayest have hope" (117). In Mather's view, the vivid details offered in scenes like the opening description of Indian attack would, if read properly, inspire this edifying result.

FIG 2. Woodcut of the captive Mary Rowlandson with the Indians Tom and Peter, from *A Narrative of the Captivity Sufferings and Removes of Mrs. Mary Rowlandson* (Boston, 1771). Photo courtesy of Edward E. Ayer Collection, The Newberry Library.

It is difficult to know, however, whether readers responded as Mather insisted they should. His preface was eliminated from later editions of the narrative, and Rowlandson's initial self-proclaimed statement of purpose emphasizes not the conversion to spiritual propriety but the relation of a personal history: "and that I may the better declare what happened to me during that grievous Captivity," she writes, "I shall particularly speak of the severall Removes we had up and down the Wilderness" (121). Rowlandson's narrative retroactively attempts to collate and comprehend the meaning of her unprecedented cultural circulation as a commodified captive. She lived and traveled with her Algonquin captors in the New England wilderness for nearly three months, and the narrative she wrote upon her return records her extraordinary experience of cultural contact. For the most part, that contact was characterized by perpetual conflict, for the captive was daily forced to confront the incommensurability between the English culture she left behind and the Algonquin one she was forced to inhabit. This Puritan Englishwoman's extended habitation within the radically alien culture of her Indian captors necessarily makes her narrative a history of transculturation and of a subjectivity under revision.

Such conflict and its effect on the texture of Rowlandson's account has become, for recent readers, the most fascinating aspect of her text, and the instant popularity of her narrative suggests that seventeenth-century readers also responded to those elements in her story that set it apart from much of the literature available in Puritan New England.[5] Indeed, the circulation of her text is no less important than Rowlandson's own circulation. Her book was one of the most popular in seventeenth-century New England and was read widely in both the old and the new worlds. Charles H. Lincoln suggests that "[n]o contemporary New England publication commanded more attention in Great Britain or in America" (110) than her narrative, and Frank Luther Mott lists the book as the first prose best-seller in America (20). The first edition of her narrative was reputedly exchanged between so many hands that no copy of it survives.

This link between Rowlandson's experience and her culture's fascination with it is perhaps best expressed in the irony that what may have been the first example of escape literature in America was a narrative about captivity. Even as the Puritans and the Algonquins negotiate the possession of this captive-commodity, Rowlandson's text, in its effort to "the better declare what happened to me," documents her own attempt to negotiate between Puritan and Algonquin cultural practices. This entangled exchange produces tensions and contradictions in her narrative, such as the difference between the urgently narrated opening scene of fire, bloodshed, and death and the composed complacency of those concluding passages acknowledging the work of providence. Such contradictions in turn carve out transgressive spaces that resist definition by or accommodation within either Algonquin or English cultural paradigms, spaces that therefore unwittingly escape dominant Puritan ideology and theology. The dangers and possibilities of cultural exchange within the colonial contact zone would generate literary and political strategies associated with the secular genre of the novel, within whose sentimental discourse scenarios of captivity and escape would continue to be explored and exploited.

The Mirror of Typology

Mary White Rowlandson was the wife of Lancaster's Puritan minister, the daughter of the town's wealthiest original landowner, and the mother of three surviving children. Other than these familial relations, almost nothing is known of Rowlandson's life before her captivity. When she peered from her Lancaster home onto the scene of "gaping" and "devouring" Indians, what did this New England woman know about those men and women who were to become her captors? Given the language barrier and the Puritan aversion to the Papists, it is unlikely that she was familiar with the representations of Indians in earlier captivity narratives written by French Jesuits and Spanish conquistadors. English people were forbidden to live with the Indians (Vaughan 208–9), but Indians were sometimes employed as servants or apprentices in New England homes or businesses, and there is evidence to suggest that the Rowlandson household contained at one point such an Indian servant.[6] These indentured Indians were usually Christianized, and they constituted a group for whom Rowlandson clearly had little affection or respect, for in her narrative she singles out betrayals of the English by various "Praying-Indians" (152) and particularly remarks on the "savageness and bruitishness [*sic*] of this barbarous Enemy, I [aye], even those that seem to profess more than others among them" (122).[7]

When Puritan New Englanders like Rowlandson happened to employ or meet individual Indians, they were likely to be such Christianized Indians who, at least since the Pequot War several decades earlier, had been increasingly compelled to abandon their traditional economies (Salisbury, *Manitou* 238). Furthermore, the religious typology that structured Puritan hermeneutics encouraged the colonists—especially during periods of warfare—to perceive the Indians as agents of Satan, designed to tempt and test the election of individual Puritans and the integrity of the New England project as a whole.[8] It is clearly by way of such typology that Mary Rowlandson orders and understands her own experience with her captors. In the introductory section of her narrative, for example, before it becomes structured into a series of "removes" that recount Rowlandson's stages of travel through the wilderness, she compares the destruction she has witnessed to the misfortunes of Job, whose possessions were destroyed by agents of Satan as a test of faith. Of the thirty-seven inhabitants of her household, Rowlandson notes, twelve were killed, twenty-four taken captive, and "one, who might say as he, Job 1.15, *And I only am escaped alone to tell the News*" (120). In similar fashion, Mather in his preface likens her trial "to those of Joseph, David and Daniel" (114).

Rowlandson refers to the Indians in these first few pages as "murtherous wretches," "bloody Heathen," "merciless Heathen," "Infidels," "a company of hell-hounds," "ravenous Beasts," and "Barbarous Creatures" (118–21). During the first night of her captivity, she observes "the roaring, and singing and danceing, and yelling of those black creatures in the night, which made the place a lively resemblance of hell" (121). Such descriptions are consistent with typologically informed perceptions of the Indians such as those offered in contemporary accounts of King Philip's War,[9] and the Puritan Rowlandson repeatedly casts her experience in terms of both specific and general biblical precedents. In this context, Rowlandson's captivity represents a version of the Babylonian or Egyptian captivity of the Israelites at the same time that, as David Downing notes, she "presents her captivity as an image of the unredeemed soul in the hands of the devil" (256).

Typology ideally operates through a structure of equivalence, in which events in scripture reflect and foretell the outcome of events in the world, just as figures and incidents in the Old Testament prefigure those in the New Testament. This process, which Erich Auerbach refers to as figural interpretation, requires the substitution of a biblical event or person with an earthly event or person, "in such a way that the first signifies not only itself but also the second, while the second involves or fulfills the first" (73).[10] Typology's central mechanism, therefore, is something like a mirror, allowing one set of events to be substituted for another provided the two bear some reciprocal resemblance. Once made, that substitution facilitates the prediction of secular history by providing a model within which to interpret the significance of historical outcomes. If Mary Rowlandson's trial mirrors that of the captive Israelites, then her own good piety coupled with God's providence should lead her to redemption. As Auerbach explains, "an occurrence on earth signifies not only itself but at the same time another, which it predicts or confirms, without prejudice to the power of its concrete reality here and now. The connection between occurrences is not regarded as primarily a chronological or causal development but as a oneness with the divine plan, of which all occurrences are parts and reflections" (555). History becomes mediated through and is made comprehensible by its analogy to scripture, just as the figures of William Bradford and John Winthrop in Cotton Mather's *Magnalia Christi Americana* are representative types that allegorize New England's history even as they repeat the histories of Moses and Nehemiah. Once the initial typological substitution is made, the Puritan struggle in the New World comes to seem no less inevitable than its eventual success.

Early criticism of Rowlandson's narrative tended to highlight her use of typology and, as a result, to place her text within an orthodox Puritan literary and theological tradition.[11] More recently, however, this narrative has gained interest and status as a text that unwittingly breaks with and even subverts that tradition. This subversion, however, does not result from Rowlandson's misuse or abandonment of typology. It occurs rather because her use of typology begins to fracture, to fall in upon itself. Increasingly, toward the end of her narrative, where her recourse to scriptural quotations and analogies multiplies, typological relations become unable to contain the accumulation of details and events she has recorded. The assumed equivalence between her categorical knowledge grounded in Puritan English culture and her daily experience gained among the Indians begins to collapse. The simple substitution of experience for knowledge and of the Algonquin cultural practices she encounters for her Puritan assumptions and beliefs about the Indians becomes suspended in a moment of negotiation that resists the closure that typology would impose on it. And because substitution fails, succession fails; the anticipated outcomes predicted by typological relations are not only delayed, but they risk nonarrival. The integrity of Puritan epistemology and the teleology of history stall at this moment of undecidability, when the mirror of typology begins to reflect distortions.

Those distortions result from Rowlandson's liminality, from her partial and stunted transculturation to Algonquin tribal life; they mark the subjectivity effects of her experience of cultural exchange. The influence of her unprecedented cultural mobility on her text and on the Puritan English society in which that text circulated has been underestimated in critical discussions of this narrative, which for the most part have assigned contradictions in the narrative to Rowlandson's psychological trauma rather than to her cultural circulation. At least since Richard Slotkin's early analysis of the discrepancies in Rowlandson's narrative technique, critical attention has focused on what is often referred to as the two "voices" in this text,[12] a narrative dichotomy whose most striking effects occur in the moments when Rowlandson's description of her participatory experiences contradict the interpretive conclusions she draws from them, when her record of an Indian's sympathy and generosity nevertheless leads her paradoxically to declare the universality of Indian savagery and barbarity. These are precisely those moments of inequivalence, those moments of typology's reflective failure.

Because there is absolutely no acknowledgment of such failures in the text itself, it is difficult to determine whether its author and its earliest readers were fully aware of these contradictions. There is nothing in either Rowlandson's prose or Increase Mather's preface to indicate an awareness of the dissonance between her portrayal of the Indians as savage and cruel and her descriptions of individual Indians who are kind and sympathetic. How then are we to explain the emergence of this representation of the Indians as humans, as a culture rather than as a type, within a text that cannot articulate such a possibility? How do these figures escape their containment, their own captivity, within Puritan ideology? Mitchell Breitwieser locates this "realism" in a conflict between the individual psychology of its author and the demands of her Puritan culture, arguing that Rowlandson's unsuccessful attempts to repress her grief enable "a human Indian figure [to] come into view at the margin of perception" (132).[13] Yet the absence of "human" Indians from other captivity narratives, an enormous number of which were told or written by grieving mothers whose infants died during captivity, suggests that such trauma cannot fully account for the realism of Rowlandson's text. It is necessary to consider as well the significant effects of transculturation, the inevitable exchanges of language, material goods, modes of behavior, and ideological orientations that characterize the scene of Indian captivity. In this context, Mary Rowlandson's captivity narrative stands out not because of her experience of grief but because it records so many of these kinds of transactions. The recollective language of her text reveals the effects of cultural liminality, of a functional adaptation, however partial, to Algonquin tribal life. Rowlandson's psychic disorientations, therefore, indicate the anxiety of adjustment to an alien culture as much as they signify a response of grief at the loss of a familiar one, and it may in fact be this transculturation as much as her mourning that Rowlandson feels she must repress. In other words, when typological equivalence fails or falters, it signals the activity of other forms of exchange.

The Friction of Exchange

Rowlandson acknowledges her commodity status as a captive, her simultaneous use value and exchange value for her captors, when she observes that her mistress, Weetamoo, a Pocasset Indian married to the Narragansett sachem Quinnapin, refused to lend her to another Indian for fear of losing "not only my service, but the redemption-pay also" (151). The practice of captive-taking predates European contact, when, as Colin Calloway notes, captives were usually either adopted or tortured to death as a way of replacing or avenging the death of a family member lost in war. That practice persisted but was also revised within the new colonial economy that emerged between natives and settlers, when a developing market value for European captives prompted Indians to begin selling them for ransom ("Uncertain Destiny" 195). Although hardly a commodity in the sense that a gun or a piece of gold is, in this hybrid colonial economy the captive nevertheless circulated as an object of trade subject to some of the same cross-cultural translations and investments that inscribed other commodities. In periods of warfare, captives became one of many common objects of exchange between Europeans and Indians, who, despite the lack of a shared language or culture, had always participated extensively in trade with each other. Specific accounts of exchanges between them illustrate, however, that certain values could not and need not be so easily agreed upon. When they were acquired by the Indians, for example, items such as gold pieces were perforated and strung onto wampum necklaces, and gun barrels were sawn off so that they could be played as flutes or whistles. Copper kettles were sometimes cut up into arrowheads or game pieces (Axtell, *European* 256), and sometimes placed on the heads of the dead, while stockings were used as tobacco pouches (Sturtevant 86–87). When Henry Hudson gave the Delaware Indians iron hoes, they wore them about their necks until sailors who arrived the next year taught them how to make handles (Axtell, *European* 256).[14] As Alden Vaughan suggests, the Europeans' desire for land and their practice of placing beaver pelts on their heads may have struck the Indians as equally absurd (329). Though it did not produce the practice of taking captives, colonialism did produce the market for captives, just as it produced the market for these other goods. And by situating the Indian captive within this arena of exchange between cultures, the fluctuating movements and values prompted by that exchange come vividly into relief.

Rowlandson notes that although her master is the Narragansett sagamore Quinnapin, she was "sold to him by another Narrhaganset Indian, who took me when first I came out of the Garison" (125) in Lancaster. Although she does not mention the terms of that first sale, her record of it indicates a relatively common phenomenon of Indian captivity in colonial America: captives often underwent a series of exchanges and owners, sometimes traded within the tribe and sometimes between tribes. Her son Joseph, for example, after tarrying too long during one visit with his mother, angers his master who "beat him, and then sold him. Then he came running to tell me he had a new Master" (144). This serial process of successive exchanges established through relations of equivalence is overshadowed in Rowlandson's narrative by the protracted negotiations leading up to her eventual ransom, when as a commodity she is substituted for another whose value she mirrors.[15] Her narrative in fact stands as a record of the precarious status of the captive-commodity within the suspended period and the hybrid space that precedes her removal from the borderland of cultural exchange.

If Rowlandson's narrative brings our attention to this moment, it also requires that we extend the concept of exchange to include not merely economic transactions but also cultural and linguistic transactions. The traditional as well as the coerced mobility of the Algonquins necessarily brought them into frequent contact with foreign groups, encouraging not only the exchange of products but the assessment of values that are not merely economic. The work of anthropologists in general and of ethnohistorians of colonial North America in particular attest to the existence and significance of such exchanges.[16] The trade of goods is only one aim or result of cultural contact; education or religious conversion were often equally predominant goals, and changes in language, attitude, or behavior were as frequently their effects. James Axtell calls this process "cultural warfare" (*Invasion Within* 4), and indeed these other forms of exchange—social, ideological, linguistic—reveal the conflict that underlies any seemingly placid process of exchange, for such transactions are frequently unsolicited, accidental, even violent and are seldom entered into with the pleasure one might associate with the marketplace of commodity exchange. As a result, these transactions indicate the friction at the center of any act of exchange.

This friction characterizes the suspended moment of substitution; it marks the struggle between cultures, languages, or commodity owners for power, predominance, or profit. In the process the friction can produce emergent forms, new linguistic or behavioral modes that come to occupy a space *between* the cultures or languages that frame them. The friction of cultural conflict opens up spaces that escape and frequently transgress those structures whose contact produces them. My analysis of Rowlandson's text focuses on precisely this site of conflict and exchange, where the process of substitution has commenced but is not yet complete, where the stasis of negotiation forestalls the movement of succession. This liminal site, this hinge that both separates and joins two collaborators who are at the same time opponents, is the site of the captive. Within such a space and at such moments in the process of exchange, the captive is effectively between owners, between cultures, between identifiable values. As long as negotiation continues, the relation of equivalence that determines economic value—and cultural values—remains unestablished.

Once negotiation ceases and the course of a transaction is complete, each commodity becomes something else, for the process of substitution and succession necessarily produces continual transformation, the change within exchange. As commodities change hands, the commodity itself changes, becomes inscribed by the friction of exchange. When the commodity exchanged is a human subject, such inscription can not only alter the subject itself but can disturb or confuse the discourse and culture that finally incorporate it. If subjectivity, like value, is formed through relations of equivalence with others,[17] then circulation within a foreign system of value(s) necessarily reassesses and revises that subjectivity, just as value is reassessed and revised when commodities are put into circulation. Once value has been determined and substitution has taken place, the friction of exchange appears absorbed within the seeming stability of commodity ownership or of cultural coherence but not without having created a potential out of which new types, new subjectivities, and new positions for resistance and power can emerge. Thus, with the eventual exchange of Mary Rowlandson for twenty pounds, her suspended cultural identity and liminal subjectivity appear resolved; she is purchased by her husband and reclaimed by Puritan New England. The seeming simplicity of such a transaction belies, however, the residual inscription of her body, her text, and her subjectivity by the experience of Indian captivity.

In other words, cultural exchange produces a supplement, an extraordinary kind of surplus. The cultural or ideological surplus resulting from the circulation of the captive is profoundly ambivalent; it constitutes not a differential that leads to addition but an "additional" that signifies difference. The production of this cultural supplement is the production of cultural difference, in the sense Homi Bhabha gives it: cultural difference "addresses the jarring of meanings and values generated *in-between* the variety and diversity associated with cultural plenitude"; cultural difference inhabits "that *intermittent time,* and *interstitial space,* that emerges as a structure of undecidability at the frontiers of cultural hybridity" ("DissemiNation" 312; emphases added). Thus, the surplus left over after the event of cultural exchange is like the "'difference' of cultural knowledge that 'adds to' but does not 'add up'" and therefore "is the enemy of the *implicit* generalization of knowledge or the implicit homogenization of experience" (313). This supplement inhabits that contested space marked out by the act of exchange, a space often characterized by an extreme anxiety. Such anxiety, evident in Rowlandson's text as well as in Increase Mather's preface to it, highlights by concealing the fact that this surplus can threaten to disrupt the apparent homogeneity and stability of the system that absorbs it. I am interested here, then, in what the stories of captives tell us about the economics of cultural exchange and about what might be called the cultural anthropology of captivity as a kind of economic exchange.[18] It is precisely such cross-cultural exchanges that can produce a surplus able to contest and destabilize the presumed autonomy and homogeneity of monocultural systems.[19]

Liminality and Transculturation

Indian captivity, as it was documented in colonial America, was an occasion for the simultaneous invention and destruction of the self. The captive occupies a liminal position, suspended in the cleavage that divides one cultural paradigm from another, and this tenuous and anxious status necessarily inflects the discourse of the recently redeemed captive. The anthropologist Victor Turner positions liminality as the second of three stages in rites of initiation, as the margin or threshold between separation from a community and reaggregation into it (196).[20] Unlike Turner's model, however, Rowlandson's experience of liminality is not a process that takes place within a single culture but one that places her between two separate and distinct cultures, a site produced by colonialism. Far from reproducing the recognizable patterns of social ritual, her dramatic and traumatic event of liminality oscillates between two systems of belief and ritual in a constant condition of the unexpected. By faithfully recording the resultant interactions and conversations between herself and the Indians, Rowlandson's captivity narrative reveals the challenge these exchanges and dialogues posed to Puritan ideology. This text's narrative dichotomy and its ideological contradictions are grounded in the linguistic and cultural exchanges that make up so much of the detail of Rowlandson's story.

The captive's journey separates her from English culture, the Puritan community, and the domestic family. The division of her narrative into "removes" enhances the sense that with each successive departure the captive becomes increasingly distant from her own culture and moves further and further into a wilderness familiar only to her Algonquin captors. That separation necessarily produces changes in the captive's behavior, attitudes, and subjective sense of self, changes evident in her detailed record of the gradual process of transculturation she undergoes over the twelve weeks of her captivity. Resistant as she is at first to Indian food, she grows accustomed to it, and while it was at first "very hard to get down their filthy trash," by the third week that which "formerly my stomach would turn against" became "sweet and savoury to my taste" (131). Although she remains all but deaf to her captors' humor, she does become increasingly sensitized to the intricacies of Indian cultural expression. Early in her captivity Rowlandson hears an account of a female captive who, along with her child, complained of homesickness so frequently that the Indians finally "made a fire and put them both into it" (129), a story she relates with unqualified horror and fear. Much later in her narrative, when the Indians tell her that they have roasted and eaten her son, she skeptically dismisses the tale after "consider[ing] their horrible addictedness to lying, and that there is not one of them that makes the least conscience of speaking the truth" (141).

Her skill in sewing and knitting allows Rowlandson to begin to assume a distinct role within the Indian community.[21] Not only does her production of clothing, stockings, and hats increase her interaction with the Indians, but it gives her a significant position within their economy. She is paid for her work, and she reintroduces that payment back into the tribe, either by trading for other goods, sharing her edible earnings, or simply offering her payment—"glad that I had anything that they would accept of" (136)—to her master. Several times, Mary Rowlandson refers to the Indian camp as "home" (136), and she notes that one particularly dreary campsite was blessed with nothing but "our poor Indian cheer" (129). Her inconsistent use of pronouns likewise reveals an often confused cultural identification. During the seventh remove, for example, she begins by associating herself with the Indians: "After a restless and hungry night there *we* had a wearisome time of it the next day." However, as the group arrives at "a place where English cattle had been," at "an English path" and "deserted English fields," it is the objectified Indians who take "what *they* could" from the forsaken land (although Rowlandson admits that "myself got two ears of Indian corn"). At the end of this scene she suddenly identifies herself instead with the English, claiming that the stolen corn would serve as "food for *our* merciless enemies [the Indians]," though she goes on to conclude that "that night *we* had a mess of wheat for *our* supper" (132–33, emphases added), including herself again among the Indians.

In two of the later removes, Rowlandson betrays the extent of her immersion in Indian society. During the seventeenth remove, after a day of travel, she remembers that "we came to an Indian Town, and the Indians sate down by a Wigwam discoursing, but I was almost spent, and could scarce speak" (148). Such a claim suggests that the captive would on other occasions "discourse" with the Indians, but was too "spent" to participate this time. Similarly, during the nineteenth remove, when the captive is called to a counsel, she notes that she "sate down among them, as I was wont to do, as their manner is" (151), again suggesting a comfortable understanding of at least the basic tribal customs and language. Though the Indian language is transcribed only once (148), Rowlandson repeatedly refers, both directly and indirectly, to conversations between herself and the Indians. These conversations reveal a development in Rowlandson's ability to converse with her captors, as well as a growing complexity of interaction that involves both a greater mutual interest and a greater shared hostility.

Rowlandson's first recorded dialogue with her captors is characterized by the mutual suspicion that marks their earliest exchanges, for in response to the Indians' request that she "[c]ome go along with us," Rowlandson extracts a promise that if she complies she will not be hurt (120). Later that first night the Indians deny her request to sleep in an abandoned English house, insisting that she share their conditions rather than continue to "love English men still" (121). By the third remove, however, an Indian makes a remarkable concession to her own cultural requirements by offering her a Bible and promising that she will be permitted to read it, while in the seventh remove another Indian is visibly intrigued by her willingness to eat horse liver, which, Rowlandson recalls, "I told him, I would try, if he would give a piece, which he did" (132–33). These two exchanges alone signify a fascinating process of growing cross-cultural recognition, if not one of culture blending, that was hardly operative at the outset of her captivity. Meanwhile, her relationship with her master, Quinnapin, develops to the point where he "seemed to me the best friend that I had of an Indian," while that with her mistress, Weetamoo, degenerates to such a level that Rowlandson's complaints and requests are met with slaps, denials, and an "insolency [which] grew worse and worse" (139). By the thirteenth remove, the captive's emergent ability to negotiate the cultural and linguistic divide between herself and her captors allows her to serve as a mediator and perhaps as a translator between the new English captive, Thomas Read, and the Indians, who were "all gathered about . . . asking him many Questions." When Read, "crying bitterly," tells Rowlandson his fears that he will be killed, she "asked one of them, whether they intended to kill him; he answered me, they would not" (142). This remarkable exchange suggests that Rowlandson had a capacity to communicate with the Indians that Read, for one, lacked.

The narrative's language of recall and its record of linguistic exchanges reveal that Rowlandson's immersion in Amerindian culture places her in a culturally liminal subject position that is no longer commensurable with, though by no means alien to, the Puritan and English subjectivity with which she entered captivity. However, as transculturated as Mary Rowlandson becomes and as much regard as she grows to assume for her Indian master, she hardly becomes Indianized and certainly does not find a replacement for her domestic ties among the Indians. While many Anglo-American captives were adopted and underwent a process of cultural integration by ultimately joining the tribes that took them captive, Rowlandson remains in a resistant liminal state, that "no-man's land betwixt and between" (Turner 41) one cultural paradigm and another. Later captives, like Eunice Williams and Mary Jemison, married Indian men, spent the remainder of their lives as members of the Indian tribal community, and repeatedly refused pleas to return to white settlements. Their illiteracy and, in Williams's case, loss of facility with the English language leave their experiences a difficult matter of historical reconstruction.[22] Amid that silence, Rowlandson's narrative offers one account of such exchange and the friction that characterizes it.

Mary Rowlandson recorded her experience as a captive in the postliminal period following her return to Puritan society, and her narration of past events is inflected both by a residual cultural liminality and by the dominant Puritan culture from which she was removed and to which she returned. In retrospect, her captivity seems to her a type of spiritual pilgrimage during which her sanctity and election were tested, "in which the Lord had His time to scourge and chasten me" (167). Yet it was not only the individual Puritan Mary Rowlandson who was tested during this journey; her discourse was tested as well. By the time she wrote her narrative, the daily challenge that Amerindian culture posed to that discourse had receded, and her Puritan worldview—like her family—had been largely restored. Yet the challenge to New England Puritan discourse, as remote as it may have seemed to Mary Rowlandson once she was ransomed and to the English once they have won King Philip's War, is nevertheless recorded in the intercultural dialogue inscribed in her best-selling narrative. The very urge to write of her experience in order to "the better declare what happened to me" attests to her memory's resistance to easy containment within available Puritan modes of understanding, perhaps in part because her experience of transculturation led her to encounter examples of female political and economic autonomy that transgressed the roles for women defined by her own society.

Transgression and the Anxiety of Motherhood

Mary Rowlandson's captivity narrative entered public circulation only with some degree of anxiety. Despite his explicit conviction that this text contains an important and exemplary lesson in piety, Increase Mather's preface is littered with apologetic justifications for its publication. Not surprisingly, these anxious apologies collect around the issue of gender. Mather seems to want to protect this female author from aspersion and to deliver her from rumor. "I hope by this time," he writes, "none will cast any reflection upon this Gentlewoman, on the score of this publication of her affliction and deliverance" (115). He claims that "this Gentlewomans [*sic*] modesty would not thrust it [her narrative] into the Press" except at the insistence of "[s]ome friends" (115), and he therefore insists that "[n]o serious spirit, then (especially knowing any thing of this Gentlewoman's piety) can imagine but that the vows of God are upon her. Excuse her then if she come thus into publick, to pay these vows" (116). It is as if, by describing circulation in the spiritual terms suggested by the act of "paying vows," Mather hopes to detract attention from the circulation of both Rowlandson and her narrative.

Mather's apologies signal a common seventeenth-century anxiety in New England about the conjunction of publicity and women, an anxiety exemplified by Anne Bradstreet's brother when he responded to the publication of her poetry by claiming that "[y]our printing of a Book, beyond the custom of your sex, doth rankly smell" (Parker 63; qtd. in Koehler 31) and by the Puritan authorities in their earlier condemnation and exile of Anne Hutchinson. The public mobility of women led to suspicions of, if not accusations against, their virtue. Such rumors also characterized the response to Mary Rowlandson's captivity and redemption, for one of the several narratives of King Philip's War published in London in 1676 claims that

> There was a Report that they had forced Mrs *Rowlinson* to marry the one-eyed *Sachem*, but it was soon contradicted; For being a very pious Woman, and of great Faith, the Lord wonderfully supported her under this affliction, so that she appeared and behaved her self amongst them with so much courage and majestick gravity, that none durst offer any violence to her, but on the contrary (in their rude manner) seemed to shew her great respect. (*New and Further* 5)

Clearly there was some speculation—on both sides of the Atlantic and long before the publication of her narrative—about this captive's virtue. Such speculations are hardly surprising considering that circulation by women has as often been perceived as a threat to society as the exchange of women has been called the fundamental basis of it. What is surprising is that no public record, to my knowledge, announces such speculations about Rowlandson without dismissing them in the same sentence. This example might be taken to illustrate a remarkable rule: transgression by female captives repeatedly escapes the kind of censure that accompanies so many other kinds of female transgression; transgression within captivity is always, sometimes quite amazingly, legitimated. One critic argues that Rowlandson escapes censure because she appears to accept the patriarchal arrangement of Puritan society and to adopt the commensurate role of Puritan goodwife (Davis 50). This assessment fails to note, however, that Rowlandson's narrative teeters on the very edge of telling an entirely different story about women, quite in spite of its explicit acceptance of the Puritan social order.

Mary Rowlandson's was the first captivity narrative written in English, and it was also the first book originally published in New England that was written by a woman.[23] Her narrative is unique not only for its account of cultural exchange but because it delivers an early and rare female voice to the textual documents of Puritan America. It is therefore necessary to be attentive to the gendered accents that inflect the cultural dialogue between Puritan and Indian inscribed in her text. Her narrative not only records a specifically Puritan Englishwoman's view of her Algonquin captors but documents her assumption of a role among them that is a radical alternative to available roles for colonial New England women. If the cultural surplus contained in this text registers an incipient critique of Puritan ideology, it also harbors a potential feminist critique of Puritan society. Again, this surplus is largely concealed, since the narrative does not overtly stage these critiques so much as it unwittingly performs them by putting the material for such critical positions into circulation. In this case, that material resides in the contrast between Rowlandson's goodwife status in patriarchal Puritan society and her status as independent producer-exchanger within the Indian community, revealed in the careful depiction of her daily life among the Algonquins. If the effects of Rowlandson's cultural circulation sometimes escape their containment by scripture, typology, and conventional seventeenth-century literary forms, the effects of her circulation as a Puritan woman threaten to escape her insistent and anxious self-definition as a mother and as a dependent Puritan wife.[24]

The experience of captivity involves a constant oscillation, not only between Puritan and Indian subjectivities but between a whole series of self-doublings. One of the most fascinating of these is Mary Rowlandson's simultaneous occupation of the noncirculating position of the mother and the exchangeable one of the captive. Following Levi-Strauss, Luce Irigaray argues that Western patriarchal society "is based upon the exchange of women" (*This Sex* 170), who circulate as commodities between men. Irigaray goes on to divide these "women-as-commodities" into the categories of private use value and social exchange value, represented by the figure of the mother and the virgin. The mother's status is analogous to private property, unavailable for exchange; whereas the virgin who awaits exchange on the marriage market represents, like the captive, pure exchange value. Rowlandson's status as both mother and captive introduces to this model a complicating revision that locates resistance within the confining patriarchal order outlined by Irigaray.

From the very beginning of her narrative, Mary Rowlandson defines herself as a mother. She writes that at the approach of the attacking Indians "I took my Children . . . to go forth and leave the house," but her escape is cut off by a barrage of bullets, one of which penetrates "the bowels and hand of my dear Child in my arms" (119). The ensuing captivity effectively begins for Rowlandson with a violence directed against her motherhood, for she claims that "[t]he Indians laid hold of us, pulling me one way, and the Children another" (120). The early part of her narrative focuses on Rowlandson's concern for her wounded daughter Sarah, whom she continues to carry in her arms. After Sarah's death, Rowlandson's concern immediately shifts to her other two children, who are held captive among different but nearby groups of Indians. She struggles to maintain contact with them, and even when that contact becomes impossible, she continues to worry over their physical and spiritual welfare. Captivity thus removes Rowlandson's children from her sight and subjects them to the surveillance of the Indians. Her dead daughter Sarah is taken and buried without her knowledge, while her other children are subjected to the discipline of distant and alien others. Rowlandson laments the absence of her children, claiming that "I had one Child dead, another in the Wilderness, I knew not where, the third they would not let me come near to"; but she also expresses anxiety that she "should have Children, and a Nation which I knew not ruled over them" (126). Her motherhood has been usurped and her maternal supervision over her children incapacitated.

Yet Rowlandson's maternity is not erased so much as it is held in suspension. As she represents it, her maternal gestures appear to her captors as ineffectual and senseless as her orthodox Puritanism. In response to her wounded daughter's incessant moaning, her captors warn her that "your Master will knock your Child in the head" (125); and when she goes to visit her daughter Mary after Sarah's death, "they would not let me come near her, but bade me be gone" (126). Because the Indians appear not to understand, or at least do not respond properly to, Rowlandson's maternal or religious gestures, those gestures inevitably fail to produce their intended effects. In the terms of the model proposed by Irigaray, Rowlandson's use value is effectively suspended along with her motherhood. From the perspective of the Puritan society from which she has been abducted, her maternal use value becomes eclipsed by a reinstated exchange value, for as soon as she is taken captive, Rowlandson is quite literally put back on the market. Because the captive must be purchased by her Puritan husband from her new Indian master, she becomes once again a commodity for exchange between males. Thus, Mary Rowlandson undergoes, as a captive, a symbolic *revirginalization* in the sense that she once more becomes an object of exchange, and this shift is evident in her home culture's patent concern over her virtue.[25]

Indeed, Rowlandson's narrative betrays its own concern with the threat to the exchange value of female captives, even or especially to captives who are mothers. At one point Rowlandson relates a story about a pregnant woman whom the Indians reputedly "stript . . . naked, and set . . . in the midst of them; and when they had sung and danced about her . . . they knockt her on head" (129). Perhaps in response to such tales as well as in defense of rumors about her own virtue, Mary Rowlandson more than once insists that "not one of [the Indians] ever offered me the least abuse of unchastity to me, in word or action" (161). Clearly, Rowlandson is defending less her captors than herself from the accusations of seduction, or even rape, that she expects from her own society. Such defenses of her chastity might also be seen as a means through which Rowlandson maintains her exchange value. Her captors force her to estimate that value when they call her into an Indian council and ask her to declare "how much my husband would give to redeem me" (151). Her own price quote is then duly delivered to Boston, as part of the negotiations between her Indian owners and her Puritan husband over the sale and repurchase of the recommodified Mary Rowlandson.

Yet while she is constituted as a passive commodity in relation to the two cultures between which she circulates, Rowlandson's record of her daily life among the Algonquins reveals her participation in a radically independent role. After Mary Rowlandson crosses the Connecticut River with her captors to join King Philip's crew, mention of her economic activity among the Indians begins to abound. She notes, for example, that

> During my abode in this place, Philip spoke to me to make a shirt for his boy, which I did, for which he gave me a shilling: I offered the mony to my master, but he bade me keep it: and with it I bought a piece of Horse flesh. Afterwards he asked me to make a Cap for his boy, for which he invited me to Dinner. . . . There was a Squaw who spake to me to make a shirt for her *Sannup* [husband], for which she gave me a piece of Bear. Another asked me to knit a pair of Stockins, for which she gave me a quart of Pease: I boyled my Pease and Bear together, and invited my master and mistriss to dinner. (135)

Such examples support Laurel Thatcher Ulrich's claim that "Rowlandson survived because she knew how to use English huswifery in the services of her captors" (227). Yet while the skills Rowlandson employs may be those of the English housewife, her structural deployment of those skills moves away from the Anglo-American model and toward conformity with the Amerindian culture in which she was living.

Colonial American women were by no means exempt or excluded from economic activity; on the contrary, they performed vital production and management functions in the household and frequently bartered goods precisely as Mary Rowlandson does. Nevertheless, a married woman's role as producer was always conditioned by her legal subordination to her husband, and even though her position in the household was integral and valued, it was always one of an assistant or "helpmeet" to the patriarch of that household. When a Puritan woman assumed complete management of her husband's business or homestead during his absence or after his death, it was perceived not as a permanent control but as a kind of deputized authority that she would relinquish in the event of his return or her remarriage. Marriage may have been a colonial New England woman's primary means of economic improvement, but marriage hardly constituted economic independence. "To talk about the independence of colonial wives," as Ulrich notes, "is not only an anachronism but a contradiction in logic," since to be a wife was to be defined legally and economically in terms of one's husband, in whose name property was held and to whom the wife's income legally — if not always in practice — belonged (37–46). Mary Rowlandson is probably performing a very familiar social gesture, then, when she offers Philip's payment for the shirt to her master. Although he rejects the money, insisting that she keep it, she offers her next two payments in the form of a meal and later gives to her master a knife that she receives in exchange for a shirt, "glad that I had any thing that they would accept of, and be pleased with" (136).

Yet Rowlandson's efforts to contribute her earnings to the household of her Indian master gradually diminish, and her economic activity takes on an increasing autonomy. Later in her captivity she accepts an Indian's request to reknit a pair of stockings only on the condition that she be released from her master's wigwam, where she has been put under house arrest for speaking and supposedly conspiring with another English captive. She barters her next series of garments for a hat, a silk handkerchief, and an apron for herself. The activities Rowlandson performs were probably familiar ones, but the structural framework of independent producer-exchanger within which they are performed is a marked change from the role of Puritan goodwife that she occupied when she was taken captive.

Unfortunately, it is difficult to determine with convincing accuracy how characteristic this new role might have been for women in the southern New England tribes with whom Mary Rowlandson traveled. After King Philip's War, the remaining population of those tribes largely dispersed among other tribes to the north or west or underwent significant transculturation through contact with and conversion by Euro-Americans. These Indians left, of course, no written texts, and a certain amount of historical simplification and error inevitably compromised characterizations of their domestic and tribal economies. Historical evidence does show, however, that Algonquin tribes were, if not matriarchal, certainly far less patriarchal than Puritan New England. While land in Anglo-American families was owned by the husband, most Indian property was owned by families and was usually under the control of the Indian women who farmed it and inherited rights to it (Sturtevant 167). Moreover, evidence of the practice of female political power and of matriarchal kinship systems has been found among southern New England tribes (Salisbury 41). Laurel Thatcher Ulrich claims that "[a]mong [Rowlandson's] many losses was a role shift from mistress to maid" (228), but that loss is accompanied by a potential gain in the shift to a culture in which "[w]omen were mistresses of their own bodies" (Jennings 49).

Mary Rowlandson never explicitly admits that such an alteration has taken place in her status, much less stages a critique of Puritan gender roles by overtly valuing her unusual economic independence. Nevertheless, all but one record of her trading activity is immediately followed by a request or an attempt to see her son, the only child with whom she has been able to maintain contact. After feeding her master and mistress dinner with her first earnings, Rowlandson, "[h]earing that my son was come to this place . . . went to see him" (135); almost immediately after exchanging a shirt for a knife, she "asked liberty to go and see" (136) her son; following another exchange of a shirt for some broth, she asks an Indian for news of her son, since "I had not seen my son a pritty while" (140); and not long after trading some stockings for some groundnuts, "my Son came to see me, and I asked his master to let him stay awhile with me, that I might comb his head, and look over him" (144).[26] This pattern suggests that her participation in independent acts of economic exchange may have generated an anxiety over the displacement of her motherhood, manifested by the immediate and impulsive assertion of her maternal identity following representations of her activity as producer-exchanger.

If her narrative exhibits an insistent maternalism at those moments that record her economic autonomy, it exhibits fierce hostility at those moments that record the autonomous authority of her Indian mistress. Margaret H. Davis suggests that while Rowlandson submits to the authority of male Indians, she resists that of female Indians "because her training as goodwife assigns her the position of mistress in her household, equal to female peers and head of servants and younger women" (55). The Rowlandson household did contain an Indian servant, which doubtless influenced the captive's attitude toward her captors. But significantly, the Indian who lived with the Rowlandsons was male, and Mary Rowlandson seems otherwise resigned to her status as servant to Quinnapin and Weetamoo, whom she calls "master" and "mistress," traditional appellations by which New England servants referred to their employers. There is clearly something more than goodwife training or even jealous competition for the attention of her master at work in her depictions of her Indian mistress. The narrative tells us little of Weetamoo's social status other than describing her as "King Phillips wives Sister," a description Lincoln supplements in a footnote by explaining that she was the widow of Alexander, Philip's brother, and that she was called "the Queen of Pocasset" (125). In fact, Weetamoo was what New Englanders called a "squaw sachem" (Leach 5). The sachem occupies the position of highest authority in the Indian community, and Weetamoo, though nominally subject to Philip, had elected to combine her Pocasset tribal forces with the alliance forming under Philip, and shared leadership responsibility with him during the war. Weetamoo probably joined the Narragansetts in August 1675, and at least by the time of the Lancaster raid in February 1676 she was, Leach notes, "the wife of sachem Quinnapin of the Narragansett tribe" (164).

Narratives of King Philip's War, such as the 1676 *Present State of New-England,* frequently refer to an unnamed "*Squaw Sachem* (i.e., a Woman Prince, or Queen) who is the Widow of a Brother to King *Philip*" (unpaginated). None of those narratives, however, makes the connection between this powerful Indian leader, who believed that her first husband was poisoned by the English,[27] and Mary Rowlandson's recalcitrant mistress. Rowlandson certainly never mentions such a connection nor, rather incredibly, does Leach in his history of the war. However, Leach's evidence of Weetamoo's remarriage to Quinnapin affirms that it was precisely this pair with whom Rowlandson journeyed as captive and servant through the New England wilderness. The political identity of Weetamoo suggests that Rowlandson's hostility may be in response to the example of a woman whose power and status exceeded that of most of her male company, including her husband, Quinnapin, and far exceeded that imaginable by a woman in Puritan society. It is Weetamoo who refuses to eat the dinner Rowlandson cooks for her master and mistress "because I served them both in one Dish" (135), it is Weetamoo who "gave me a slap in the face" (139) when Rowlandson complains of the load she was made to carry, and it is Weetamoo who incenses Rowlandson by deciding to turn back from the direction in which the group is traveling (139). When Rowlandson refuses to give a piece of her apron to Philip's maid, Weetamoo "rises up, and takes up a stick big enough to have killed me, and struck at me with it" (142).

Rowlandson clearly dislikes this woman, not simply for her power but for her social status, for she singles Weetamoo out from her master's "three squaws" as a "severe and proud dame . . . bestowing every day in dressing her self neat as much time as any of the Gentry of the land: powdering her hair, and painting her face, going with Neck-laces, with Jewels in her ears, and Bracelets upon her hands: When she had dressed her self, her work was to make Girdles of Wampom and Beads" (150).[28] The captive recognizes that she, like the decorative jewels and makeup, is a sign of her mistress's social status and wealth, for she observes that "Wettimore thought, that if she should let me go and serve with the old Squaw [another of Quinnapin's wives], she would be in danger to loose, not only my service, but the redemption-pay also" (150). This comment also conveys crucial information about domestic economic relations among the specific Algonquin women with whom Rowlandson lived, for it indicates that each of Quinnapin's wives holds property separately. Furthermore, if Weetamoo is in danger of losing her servant's value to another of her husband's wives, Quinnapin at best jointly owns with his wife the captive and her value.

A record of Weetamoo's appearance in a Plymouth court in 1659 confirms this evidence of her property ownership. She entered a complaint then, and again in 1662, against her first husband, Wamsutta (or Alexander) "for having sold, six years previously, some lands which she claimed belonged really to her, and for which he had never paid her her share" (*Some Indian Events* 21). Furthermore, another colonial record contains a letter written by a "Merchant of Boston" claiming that Weetamoo "is as Potent a Princess as any round about her, and hath as much Corn, Land and Men at her Command" (*Some Indian Events* 21)—details consistent with other evidence of matrilinearity among the Narragansett (Sturtevant 193).

Whether Rowlandson recognizes the extent of Weetamoo's power as a sachem or not, she is certainly aware that this woman exercises autonomous authority and accumulates social wealth. The very excessiveness of her hostility to her mistress suggests that the example of Weetamoo disturbed her, not just because she was one of countless Indians who exercised power over a captive Englishwoman but because she was a woman with power over men. By contrast, the captive's representation of powerful male Indians such as Philip or Quinnapin is marked by a distinct regard if not explicit affection. The example of Weetamoo, like the example of Rowlandson exercising her own economic independence, might have had subversive potential in the Anglo-American culture where this narrative circulated. Such subversion is disabled by the hostility and anxiety that tends to revise or mask any explicit critique of Puritan gender roles that this text might have inadvertently staged. Yet her strategic assertions of an anxious motherhood and her unaccountable aggressiveness toward a powerful Indian female, who might have unconsciously and disturbingly reflected Rowlandson's own newfound autonomy back at her, mark the site of a surplus in her narrative, a surplus that has been generated by her experience of cultural exchange and that resists containment by the legitimating force of her recuperation into Puritan society.

On the one hand, captivity puts Mary Rowlandson into circulation as a passive object of exchange; on the other hand, captivity allows Rowlandson an economic independence that permits her a kind of temporary escape from patriarchal subordination. The female captive is, in Irigaray's terms, subject to male specul(ariz)ation, "[a] hinge bending according to the exchanges" (*Speculum* 22) of men; but as an autonomous agent of exchange, Rowlandson threatens to *unhinge* the basis of a male-controlled economy and symbolic order. Mary Rowlandson's captivity is both an inscription of Puritan patriarchal law and an escape from it. The mother/virgin dichotomy that, for Irigaray, marks the male-controlled economy of desire collapses within the transcultural scene of captivity and opens a feminist space within the dominant patriarchal order.

Yet what becomes of that temporary producer-exchanger role exemplified by the captive once the doubled self reintegrates as a result of patriarchal redemption? Mary White Rowlandson returns to Massachusetts and records her experience in an effort to "the better declare what happened to me during that grievous Captivity" (121). She writes a text that six years after her return from captivity enters the marketplace as a commodity, and it does so between the texts of two men. A preface written by the religious patriarch Increase Mather precedes her own text, and a Fast Day sermon written by her husband, Joseph Rowlandson, follows it. It is as though the printed book mirrors Rowlandson's condition as a body exchanged between males. Nevertheless, the publication of her book also puts into circulation a record of female escape from commodification from within commodification. By doing so it generates possibilities for a strategic feminist critique not accounted for in the restrictive marketplace that Irigaray inherits from Levi-Strauss. These critical social possibilities, set loose by the cultural surplus of Rowlandson's narrative, furthermore characterize the content of what would later come to be called the genre of the novel.

Dialogism and the Novel

The protofeminist content of Rowlandson's narrative, like its inconsistent and multiple narrative voices, results from the series of exchanges prompted

by her captivity among Algonquin Indians. But if her partial transculturation necessarily removes her from the cultural practices of seventeenth-
century Puritan New England society, it also moves the form of her captivity narrative away from traditional seventeenth-century literary genres.
Critics who have, quite correctly, aligned her narrative with such familiar
Puritan genres as the spiritual autobiography, the conversion narrative, and
the jeremiad nevertheless concur that, while these generic structures inform
Rowlandson's text, no one of them sufficiently describes it. Some consequently have claimed that it constitutes its own genre; others separate individual narratives into smaller, already established genres, and still others
define it as multigeneric.[29]

Any definitive generic categorization of this text runs the risk, however,
of repeating Rowlandson's own anxious and insistent self-alignment with
those values and categories, such as the Puritan goodwife and orthodox Puritanism, valued by and identified with the community from which Indian
captivity removed her. What gets overlooked thereby is that her narrative's
particular significance for genre studies lies precisely in its resistance to standard classification.[30] Her text accommodates her individually experienced
paradigm crisis only by moving between and forming combinations from
among several traditional narrative forms, and as a result available vehicles
of representation necessarily become distorted or revised. Emphasizing her
use of recognizable genres such as the sermon is therefore like emphasizing
her use of typology: while both observations are accurate, both tend to align
her narrative with a project of recuperating and reproducing dominant cultural forms and values, rather than with provoking an inadvertent crisis or
schism within them. Rowlandson's narrative certainly relies on such legitimating forms, but it also puts into circulation a cultural friction that challenges and disrupts those forms. If redefining genres or creating new ones
will not resolve the question of how to classify Rowlandson's text, it is because captivity narratives—like the captives who wrote them—occupy a
space suspended between coherent generic forms. That space is not only
one aligned with the genre of the novel but one created by the practice of
colonialism.

While many earlier critics frequently claimed that captivity narratives
fulfilled a novelistic need in a society otherwise devoid of such amusements,
more recently these texts—and Rowlandson's in particular—have been explicitly aligned with the genre of the novel.[31] This classification would seem
to resolve the dilemma the captivity narrative has long posed to traditional
generic categories. Bakhtin, for instance, posits as the origin of the novel a
scene of contact between two dramatically different classes and languages.
The heteroglossia that results from such contact is, for Bakhtin, the fundamental characteristic of the novel form, which dialogically incorporates a

variety of languages and genres. Rowlandson's text certainly exhibits the linguistic and cultural dialogism that would characterize it as a type of proto-novel since it mixes the discourse of an orthodox Puritan woman, the discourse of that Puritan woman undergoing the process of transculturation, and conversations between that woman and individual Indians who speak an entirely different language. But like Turner's model of liminality, Bakhtin's description of the novel sets the scene of dialogic conflict between classes within a single culture rather than between two separate and distinct cultures. This latter site is specific to the history of colonialism in New England, which inevitably resulted not only in violent conflicts between native and settler populations but in the kinds of contested cultural exchanges recorded in Rowlandson's captivity narrative.

Despite such notable exceptions as John Eliot and Roger Williams, by the time of King Philip's (or Metacom's) War few Puritan colonists in New England lived in close contact with substantial groups of Amerindians, and even fewer knew their language. By the 1670s, those Indians who inhabited Anglo-American communities tended to do so as individuals in socially and economically subordinate roles (Sturtevant 177), such as the Indian servant in the home of the Rowlandsons. In fact, Rowlandson repeatedly records her fear and astonishment at seeing enormous numbers of Indians together, as though she had no idea that they existed in such quantities. Upon her arrival at one Indian town her surprise and terror is palpable: "Oh the number of pagans (now merciless enemies) that there came about me" (124). At another temporary abode she remarks that "[t]he Indians were as thick as trees: . . . if one looked before one, there was nothing but Indians, and behind one, nothing but Indians, and so on either hand, I my self in the midst" (132). When she meets King Philip and his crew, she "could not but be amazed at the numerous crew of Pagans that were on the Bank" (134).

As the lone Christian Englishwoman at these gatherings, her assumptions about national distribution, and hence about cultural power over what for her was New England, become threatened by a sudden and terrifying reversal. The colonialist hierarchy that Mary Rowlandson carried with her into captivity threatens to topple when this Puritan Englishwoman stood "alone in the midst" of such large numbers of Indians. Indeed, it is at one of these sudden meetings with a large crew of Indians that, Rowlandson remembers, "my heart began to fail: and I fell a weeping which was the first time to my remembrance, that I wept before them" (134). The captive's tearful response here indicates not only grief or trauma but a frightening realization that English supremacy is less stable and English victory less assured than this Englishwoman once believed. These tears mark precisely one moment when typology threatens to fail, when the promise of Puritan history foretold by the biblical history of the Israelites stumbles over the surplus generated by cultural exchange. That promised narrative, an imperialist one of national and religious victory, encounters resistance.

Significantly, the moment at which she first breaks down and openly weeps before them occurs in the context of Indian laughter. It is striking that what seems most to unnerve and upset Mary Rowlandson about the Indians—far more than the bundle of bloodied Puritan garments in one Indian's wigwam, for example—are their laughter and celebrations, which she records with some consistency. When she is denied permission, during her first night of captivity, to sleep in an abandoned house, she receives the amused but unappreciated Indian response of "what will you love English men still?" Instead she is forced to witness an Indian victory celebration and to hear "the roaring, and singing and danceing, and yelling of those black creatures in the night" (121). When she falls from a horse during their journey, "they like inhumane creatures laught, and rejoyced to see it" (123). Later in her captivity, during a particularly clumsy river crossing "the Indians stood laughing to see me staggering along," resulting in "teares running down mine eyes" (147). The sudden appearance after this incident of a band of Indians "dressed in English Apparel," surely suggesting an English military loss, simply "damped my spirit" (148) in comparison. Mary Rowlandson hears and records the sometimes humiliating, sometimes ironic laughter of the Indians, although she is, of course, incapable of sharing in it or even of recognizing such moments as comic. She remains deaf, for example, to the subversive humor of the Indians' boasting that "they had done them [a defeated English military company] a good turn, to send them to Heaven so soon" (160).

What is remarkable about such passages is not that Rowlandson records them—after all, she inserts them in order to illustrate her captors' insensitivity and inhumanity—but that they so consistently portray the Indians with a complexity and a detail utterly absent from other representations of Amerindians in colonial New England literature by Puritans. Descriptions such as these never explicitly intrude onto Mary Rowlandson's consistently unmodified assertions that the Indians are cruel, savage, barbarous heathen who act as instruments of Satan. A challenge to that belief, however, is inscribed linguistically in the dialogue she records, and that challenge disrupts the stable operation of religious discourse and national ideology in this text. The Indians laugh, and the gap between their world and their captive's can suddenly be defined in culturally complex ways rather than in terms of typological oppositions. As a culturally liminal figure, Rowlandson's perception of the Indians as types is coupled with the detailed observations necessary to her survival within this strange culture. Algonquin ceremonies, which she considers meaningless if not absurd, are nevertheless intimately described; their dress, their eating habits, their mourning practices, even the vanity of an Indian woman, are all recorded so that "I may the better declare what happened to me." There is no real need, then, to document in detail the domestic restoration of her family at the end of her narrative, not because it is an event without importance but because it is an event whose ritual significance she already understands.

Transgression erupts in Rowlandson's captivity narrative precisely where the logic of Puritan discourse breaks down. The acts of exchange that she records threaten the stability of Puritan ideology and its typological economy of equivalence. Moments of Indian laughter, celebrations and rituals performed by groups of Indians, an Indian's gift of an English Bible to the captive, Quinnapin's query to Rowlandson of "When I washt me? I told him not this month, then he fetcht me some water himself, and bid me wash, and gave me the Glass to see how I lookt" (150): these are all events that Rowlandson struggles to incorporate into the structures of typology and providence that organize Puritan discourse. In her interpretation the laughter and dances are tests of her spiritual fortitude, and the acts of generosity are divine providences, the sudden intercession of God—operating through Indian figures—on her behalf. Yet an accumulated cultural surplus provokes a resistance within this simple exchange of act for type. The five "remarkable passages of providence" that she catalogs at the conclusion of her narrative are beset by a similar failure to add up convincingly. These providences are in fact most remarkable as providences that favor the Indians, which Rowlandson is able to appropriate for herself and the English military only by an awkward process of reversal that continually threatens to collapse in upon itself, by a fudging of accounts that can barely conceal its own flawed math. This substitutive failure is all the more evident as a result of both Rowlandson's and Increase Mather's desire for its success, for it is only with the success of substitution that historical succession can proceed, Rowlandson's redemption can be secured, and the promise of the New England project be fulfilled.

The publication of her narrative circulates within the larger Puritan society two often incompatible and inequivalent discourses, in which the representation of the Algonquins in Rowlandson's liminal discourse exceeds and escapes their representation in her orthodox Puritan discourse. That inequivalence creates possibilities that, for Bakhtin, define the novel: "an acute feeling for language boundaries (social, national and semantic)," a fracturing of the "absolute fusion of ideological meaning with language," the ability of a culture to become "conscious of itself as only one among *other* cultures and languages," the emergence of "speaking human beings" from behind the "words, forms, styles" of national language forms (370). Puritan ideology's typological image of the Indian must suddenly confront a "speaking human" Indian.

As this chapter has demonstrated, Rowlandson's readers were confronted with a series of new and radical possibilities in her narrative. Those possibilities were nevertheless sufficiently recuperated or obscured to allow Increase Mather to advertise her text as a vehicle for reinforcing the dominant social, political, and theological codes that her narrative otherwise appears to challenge or upset. This unusual fracturing or doubling within her text has the effect of representing more than one version of the subject Mary Rowlandson, and that complexity and inconsistency point toward the representation of self associated with the novel. As Deidre Lynch argues, what characterizes the novel form is less the expression of "a singular interiority" than "a contradictory relation between personal truths and the forms that make them publicly apprehensible, between actual and stipulated mental states." It is therefore in this "lack of fit between multiple accounts of the self" (142) that the subjectivity associated with the novel is located. When the Indians laugh at Mary Rowlandson, for example, her discomfort seems rooted in part in a sense that the comical figure they perceive is not equivalent to her own self-perception. Rowlandson's captivity narrative puts not only multiple accounts of herself—as Puritan goodwife and mother, as independent producer-exchanger—into circulation among a transatlantic reading public, but it circulates also competing versions of Amerindian culture. If this gives the representation of the captive a sense of incipient psychological depth, it likewise gives to Algonquin culture unprecedented dimensions of cultural breadth and depth.

Mary Rowlandson's captivity narrative was originally published with her first husband's last sermon, a jeremiad delivered on Fast Day to his Puritan congregation in Wethersfield, Connecticut. By binding together a minister's sermon exhorting the community to fast with a narrative in which the minister's wife struggles daily against literal starvation, the first editions of this book may have enhanced its plea for a resurgent Puritan piety. The eventual disappearance of Joseph Rowlandson's sermon from subsequent editions suggests in retrospect what its Puritan readership probably already felt: Mrs. Rowlandson's narrative achieved the effect that Puritan ministers had long been striving to instill in their congregations. *The Possibility of God's Forsaking a People Who Have Been Near and Dear to Him,* the title of the Reverend Joseph Rowlandson's final sermon, may well have seemed a more tangible and threatening possibility in the wife's literal experience than in the husband's weekly sermon. As Derounian suggests ("Publication" 255), the readers of Rowlandson's captivity narrative probably derived as much secular fascination from it as they did religious inspiration.

It is also likely, however, that Rowlandson's *Narrative* itself was one of the forces that helped to create those more secular reading interests through its liminal generic form. Rowlandson is able to contain and make sense of her unusual experience only by combining elements of the various narrative structures available to her, yet the narrative dialogism of her text exceeds the sum of that combination, just as elements of her experience among the Algonquins escape her effort to understand "what happened to me during that grievous Captivity." Within this text's conservative theological message is a dialogic and cultural surplus that escapes through the seams of the act of substitution. The genre combination Rowlandson practices is like the transgressive "additional" generated by the friction of exchange: it adds to but will not add up. The Puritans purchase Mary Rowlandson, and the Algonquins receive twenty pounds, but this transaction is hardly as clean and simple as it appears. However effectively this captivity narrative circulated an appeal for renewed piety, it could not help but circulate an appealing story of cultural escape. Richard Slotkin has suggested that captivity by Indians was virtually the only acceptable way for a Puritan to experience the otherwise forbidden wilderness and the Indian culture that inhabited it (*Regeneration* 100). Edward M. Griffin (47) and Christopher Castiglia (4) note that, for many female captives, release from the Indians frequently promised only a return to captivity in another form—as a domestic wife and mother in Puritan New England. As these compelling readings suggest, the captivity narrative offered readers a transgressive account of legitimized escape from dominant social and moral norms.

Narratives like Mary Rowlandson's, which recalled such experiences of cultural exchange, expose the possibility of an ambivalent and unquantifiable value that, in Homi Bhabha's words, "adds to" but does not "add up." The "additional" generated by the friction of cultural exchange produces a difference that would allow Mary White Rowlandson's captivity narrative, without changing a word, to be advertised as a story neither about God nor about an exemplary figure of piety but about the individual Mary White Rowlandson, a figure that readers would come not only to identify *as* a virtuous type but to identify *with* in a relation of sympathy. Cotton Mather, less than twenty years after his father published the preface to the first Puritan captivity narrative, tells the audience of one of the last Puritan captivity narratives that its instructive value is signified by its reader's involuntary need to cry for the suffering captive.[32] The captive returns from the colonial borderland of cultural exchange as an individualized but also a transculturated subject, developments essential to the sympathetic identification on which sentimental discourse depends. Indeed, it would be the emergent sensitivity to the transgressive surplus in narratives like Rowlandson's that would necessitate sentimental discourse and its veil of tears. Narratives like hers inevitably revealed the boundaries of the Anglo-American Puritan culture that consumed them, probably moving its readers to desire both a redrawing and a crossing of those boundaries. Such ambivalent desires would continue to define captivity narratives, which, over the following century, begin to look more and more like sentimental novels precisely as a result of their struggle to contain such transgressive elements and the mobility that produced them.

Chapter 2

BETWEEN ENGLAND AND AMERICA: CAPTIVITY, SYMPATHY, AND THE SENTIMENTAL NOVEL

URING HER 1676 captivity by Algonquin Indians in the New England wilderness, Mary Rowlandson turns, in one of the numerous scriptural references that mark her 1682 narrative, to a particular psalm: "I fell a weeping which was the first time to my remembrance that I wept before them. . . . now may I say as, Psal. 137.1. *By the rivers of Babylon, there we sate down: yea, we wept when we remembered Zion*" (134). On the other side of the Atlantic and over half a century later, the captive heroine of Samuel Richardson's 1740 *Pamela* invokes the same tearful psalm:

I remembering the 137th Psalm to be a little touching, turned to it, and took the Liberty to alter it to my case . . .

When sad I sat in B——n-hall,
All watched round about,
And thought of every absent Friend,
The tears for Grief burst out. (127)

If these two captive women were moved to tears by their experiences, their accounts of captivity inspired a correspondent sympathy in their readers. Indeed, audiences were apparently captivated by these two books: both Rowlandson's narrative and Richardson's *Pamela* were transatlantic best-sellers, appealing to popular reading tastes in colonial New England as well as in England.[1] That popularity has been accounted for by the fact that these texts offered their audiences the highly desirable combination of a sensational and adventurous plot with moral and religious instruction, thereby inspiring not only tears but pious reform in their readers. We have seen how Mather's preface to Rowlandson's narrative, for example, uses the occasion of her recent captivity and of continuing Indian warfare to encourage religious conversion among readers. He insists that her particular account "makes deepest impression upon the affections" (116) and that her example of piety "deserves both commendation and imitation" (115). When Mather instructs readers to "Peruse, Ponder, and from hence lay by something from the experience of another against thine own turn comes" (117), he anticipates that seventeenth-century Puritans, by imagining themselves in the captive's place, might strive to resemble the converted and reformed Rowlandson.

By the time Richardson made a similar argument for *Pamela,* however, novels were regularly being condemned as morally damaging, and for virtually the same reason that Mather had praised Rowlandson's earlier narrative: the capacity to inspire sympathetic identification in readers. Because moralists and educators assumed that sympathy led to imitation, they believed that readers would be encouraged to repeat the transgressive adventures of the novelistic heroes and heroines with whom they identified. Eighteenth-century novelists and romance writers therefore strategically attempted to position their work in such a way as to evade condemnation within this model of reader identification. In 1705, for example, Mary de la Rivière Manley explained that the responses of "Fear and Pity" propel readers to imitate novelistic examples, since "we in some Manner put ourselves in the Room of those we see in Danger; . . . and the fear of falling into like Misfortunes, causes us to interest our selves more in their Adventures" (35). She proceeded to argue that her *Secret History of Queen Zarah* would "instruct and inspire into Men the Love of Vertue, and Abhorrence of Vice, by the Examples propos'd to them" (38) in the text. Not until Richardson, however, would this defense result in the profound combination of critical success and moral validation awarded to *Pamela.*

The eighteenth-century regulation of novel reading also operated within this paradigm of identification paired with imitation. Thus, Maria and Robert Edgeworth, who in their 1801 *Practical Education* discouraged young women from reading novels, nevertheless deemed *Robinson Crusoe* suitable because, they assumed, young women were simply incapable of imitating the appealing adventures and solitary travels of Defoe's hero (Armstrong, *Desire* 16–17). When Richardson successfully articulated his first sentimental novel as a deliberately ethical project, he did so not by disabling identification but by exploiting it. The instructive efficacy of *Pamela,* like that of Rowlandson's narrative, was theoretically inseparable from its ability to inspire affective sensation, for it was supposedly by sympathizing with these virtuous and pious heroines that readers were moved to imitate their exemplary behavior. It was precisely as a result of this sympathetic exchange between reader and text that Richardson could imagine English readers becoming a community of ethical individuals in response to the examples represented in his novel.

Eighteenth-century sentimental novels like Richardson's may operate within such a system of imaginative exchange, but they also develop within a context of other exchanges across cultural, national, and continental boundaries. The Atlantic Ocean is one such crossed and uncrossed border, an expanse that is implicitly invoked as a border whenever the labels "English" and "American" serve to define distinct and coherent literary traditions. Yet as Ian K. Steele has pointed out, the Atlantic is as much a conduit facilitating connection as it is a barrier encouraging insulation. This relation was perhaps even more acknowledged in the eighteenth century when, Steele notes, "[a]ny informed adult living within the English Atlantic empire in 1739 knew that the Atlantic Ocean was traversed regularly, whether or not that person had crossed it. This same person also knew that the North American continent had never been crossed by anyone" (273). Popular texts such as colonial "American" captivity narratives and "English" sentimental novels also regularly crossed this border. The exchanges and transgressions within and between these two kinds of texts are fundamental to the development and function of sentimental discourse during this period. The moving qualities of books such as Rowlandson's and Richardson's depend not only on their stories of transgressive mobility but on the movement of the texts themselves across the border of the Atlantic, the watery margin that at once sealed and held open the ambivalent relation between the American colonies and the British empire. The popularity of these two accounts of female captivity and their associated moral legitimacy is ultimately a measure of the degree to which they successfully obscured those transgressive elements.

Border Crossings

Like novelistic discourse, nationalist discourse relies on the profoundly affective experience of sympathy. From Ernest Renan's early claim that "nationality has a sentimental side to it" (18) to Homi Bhabha's recent assertion that the nation is a form of "cultural identification" ("DissemiNation" 292–93) with a deeply affective dimension, discussions of nationalism insist on the substitutive empathy of identification. When Benedict Anderson links the nation with the novel, he does so precisely through this feature of identification. Not only do nationalist and novelistic discourse both emerge simultaneously in the eighteenth century, but, he argues, both rely on a new conception of temporality comparable to what Walter Benjamin calls "meanwhile," in which disparate and distant individuals are perceived to exist simultaneously. According to Anderson, it is in this open, transverse time associated with the novel, where separate characters live coincidental lives linked by a single narrative, that readers become able to imagine the community of the nation. New World creoles came to conceive of themselves as contemporaneous national communities, as "Americans" or "Brazilians," for example, by reading about and imagining the existence of others who resembled themselves, a phenomenon facilitated by the development of print capitalism and the growth in literacy and in print languages. This sentimental experience of imagining others whose experiences are similar to, if not interchangeable with, one's own—experiences such as the journeys taken by Creole functionaries along particular routes or "the shared fatality of trans-Atlantic birth" (57)—therefore becomes coincident with a feeling of stable national identity. Novel reading provided a way for these otherwise unrelated individuals to learn of their common experiences and thus "to visualize in a general way the existence of thousands and thousands *like themselves*" (77; emphasis added). To this extent, for Anderson as well as for Richardson, the imagined community created through sympathetic identification is a community constructed and held together on the basis of resemblance or likeness.

The movement of printed texts across regional, social, and cultural boundaries is the indispensable condition for producing such an imagined community and the identification on which it is founded. This movement has its analogue in the process of sympathy, which requires a crossing of the boundary between reader and text. One might therefore expect to find the earliest formations of both the novel and the nation in a text notable for its own mobility as well as for its ability to move readers. Nancy Armstrong and Leonard Tennenhouse, in their analysis of the "origins" of the English novel and European nationalism, find precisely such a text in the colonial American genre of the captivity narrative.[2] An experience of virtually incessant mobility is recorded by Mary White Rowlandson in her narrative of captivity among the New England Indians, which chronicles her violent abduction in the 1676 raid on Lancaster and her subsequent trials, both physical and spiritual, as she journeys with her Algonquin captors through the wilderness. But it is the movement of the text itself, which traveled from the American colonies to England and found active readership on both continents, that is central to Armstrong and Tennenhouse's argument. By encouraging its readers to "care about" an unimportant Englishwoman and her sufferings, they claim, Rowlandson's captivity narrative constructs an imagined national community through the process of reader identification. Just as the abducted captive is "poignantly aware that survival depends on her ties to" (395) her increasingly distant Anglo-American community, the narrative "asked its readers [in England] to imagine being English in America" (394). Because the isolation of the Englishwoman in captivity among non-English people emphasizes her national difference, it enables readers to imagine their own position within a national community through identification with her.

The radical differences between the European captive and her Amerindian captors may have encouraged English readers to identify with Rowlandson, but those differences are presumably also what fascinated them so about her story. The circulation of Rowlandson's popular text across the boundary between colonial outpost and imperial center is therefore subtended by Rowlandson's own circulation across the even more profound cultural boundary between colonial Anglo-American society and tribal Algonquin Indian society. As Armstrong and Tennenhouse accurately note, the captive must sustain her ties to English culture in order eventually to reintegrate with the community she left behind. But securing that return also requires that Rowlandson develop relations within the Algonquin community she inhabits for nearly twelve weeks. The establishment of these latter ties complicates the model of reader identification on which Benedict Anderson's discussion of nationalism relies. Ultimately, Rowlandson's account calls into question the kind of imagined community produced by reader identification.

Throughout her captivity, Rowlandson continually asks her captors if and when she will be sold; and when asked by them "how much my husband would give to redeem me," she struggles to come up with a sum large enough not to "be slighted" by the Indian sagamores and small enough to "be procured" by her husband (151). Such dialogues reveal the captive's awareness that her return is contingent upon a mutually agreeable act of exchange between her Algonquin master and her Puritan husband. But if Rowlandson's return depends on both these parties, her survival depends almost entirely on her captors. As the previous chapter documents, she must learn to travel in Indian fashion through the wilderness, to recognize Algonquin words and customs, to barter for Indian food, and to tolerate it once it is given to her. Her narrative documents not only her early resistance to such alien customs but her increasing familiarity with and practical acceptance of them. To this extent, it is not Mary Rowlandson's Englishness at all that de-termines her survival during captivity but precisely the degree to which she abandons her Englishness in the process of transculturation.

In other words, as a captive, Rowlandson occupies a position of cultural liminality rather than one of cultural integrity. That liminality requires that one ask what the readers of this captivity narrative identified with when they identified with Mary Rowlandson. While her narrative undoubtedly led readers in England to imagine "being English in America," it is equally likely that it led English readers on both sides of the Atlantic to imagine the possibility of not being English at all, to imagine a liminal or hybrid, if not an Indian, cultural identity. Indeed, the captive's experience of transcultura-tion, which is everywhere evident in her narrative, undoubtedly contrib-uted to the book's unprecedented public appeal. This narrative implicitly critiques the assumption that readers can identify only with figures whose culture, race, or nationality resembles their own, for to identify with Row-landson is necessarily to identify both with her English difference from the Indians and with her difference from English culture through her participa-tion in Algonquin society, both with her insistent Englishness and with her departure from it. Readers confronted and responded to the multiple ver-sions of self, signaled by the resultant sense of singular interiority, produced by the captive's exchange across the colonial space of the contact zone.

When Rowlandson's narrative was originally advertised in the American edition of *Pilgrim's Progress,* it was called a "pathetically written" story, a phrase that in the seventeenth century meant "movingly written" (Derou-nian, "Publication" 244). What is moving about this narrative is precisely the fact that Rowlandson herself is always moving even while disclaiming that movement. Pathos inhabits the disjunction between the cultural iden-tity that Rowlandson so insistently asserts and the textual evidence that contradicts this assertion. Franco Moretti has argued that "[t]ears are al-ways the product of *powerlessness*" and that "[t]hey presuppose a definitive estrangement of facts from values, and thus of any relationship between the idea of *teleology* and that of *causality*" (162). This very tension is apparent in the scene in which Mary Rowlandson herself is first moved to tears. When the captive arrives at an Indian village and finds herself the lone Christian among a "numerous crew of Pagans" who "asked one another questions, and laughed, and rejoyced over their Gains and Victories," she "fell a weep-ing which was the first time to my remembrance, that I wept before them" (134). Rowlandson's Puritan reliance on typology and its promise that, like the captive Israelites, she too will be delivered from affliction clearly en-counters a threat at this confrontation with the quantitative strength of the Indians. Rowlandson weeps at that moment when what should happen may not happen, when values and facts fail to coincide. Likewise, her readers are moved at those moments when what Rowlandson *claims* to be—a coherent English subject and a model Puritan goodwife—coincides least with what she *appears* to be: a mediating subject who participates in the tribal economy, is able to conform to Indian social practices, and has a command of at least the basics of Algonquin language. The captive professes an identity whose fixity is belied by the unstable and mobile process of identification that supports that identity.

Rowlandson's narrative points toward a model of identification that emphasizes disjunction and disavowal rather than resemblance and imitation. It challenges the notion that sympathetic identification constitutes an equivalent and seamless exchange in which individuals imaginatively substitute themselves for others "like themselves," a formulation that assumes rather than explains the sentimental affect that characterizes the narrative of novels and nations. Why should identification produce sympathetic tears even as it produces a coherent community? The tears that are so often a sign of sentimental identification—of the successful establishment of this relation of apparent equivalence—result, I suggest, not from the seamless substitution of self for other but from the necessary margin of inequivalence produced by such an exchange. In other words, what is sentimental about the imagined communities novels create is the obscured fact that they are not based on likeness.

The psychoanalytic model of ambivalent identification that underlies Homi Bhabha's description of national narrative accommodates this inequivalence, which Anderson's discussion overlooks. For psychoanalytic theory, to align identification with imitation or resemblance is to miss what Bhabha calls its "dialogical or transferential" character, since any identification with a likable image or feature is always "constituted through the *locus* of the Other" ("DissemiNation" 313), performed on behalf of a gaze from the perspective of which that image is seen as likable. Two seemingly incompatible but nevertheless interdependent relations constitute this process: an imaginary or specular identification with that which the subject is (or wants to be) like and a symbolic identification with that which the subject is not (and often does not want to be) like. The first is an identification with an appealing image—with, for example, the image of the suffering English captive piously reading a Bible and yearning for home. The second is an identification with the displaced location from which that image appears as appealing—with, in Rowlandson's narrative, the liminal position of cultural and national indeterminacy. Furthermore, readers are compelled to identify with the former only by identifying with the latter, since the image of Rowlandson's coherent Englishness takes on particular value only from the locus or perspective of her transgressive liminality. The circular movement between these two modes of identification generates a disjunctive gap between them, a gap that is concealed beneath the construction of fantasy.[3] For Anderson, the national identity of subjects arises from their identification with similarities, with others "like themselves." Here, identity is instead a retroactively determined effect of naming that works to erase any identification with difference.

This model of a doubled identification can account for the sentimentality of novels and nations in a way that identification understood as pure resemblance or imitation cannot. For the "moving" effect of novelistic and nationalist discourses results from the dialectical movement of identification across the gap or border between resemblance and its failure. The tears generated by sympathy function as a veil that masks the incommensurability between these two levels of identification, obscuring difference within the fantasy of sameness and commonality. This liminal gap of inequivalence marks, for Bhabha, the site of subjective agency, a site for the articulation of cultural difference and minority resistance. But that agency veiled by affective sensation can also constitute a violence aimed at difference, deployed in the service of preserving and reproducing a community based on resemblance. Such forms of active agency are commonly disavowed and concealed by the passive sensation of "being moved." In this sense, sympathy is a movement that insistently denies its own activity, a border crossing that conceals its own transgressiveness.

As objects in motion across various borders, both Rowlandson and her text are in perpetual danger of going astray, a possibility that is suggested by Rowlandson's need to insist that she has returned physically and ideologically unviolated to her Anglo-American community.[4] Her narrative consistently disavows the transgression it documents. That disavowal is repeated by the model of identification that Armstrong and Tennenhouse borrow from Anderson, a model that allows the imaginary substitution of the English reader for the wholly English captive, to constitute a balanced exchange that leaves no disabling remainder. The liminal space of transculturation within Rowlandson's narrative suggests that the operation of identification cannot be reduced simply to a function of mere resemblance or likeness but must account for the moments at which resemblance slips and equivalence fails. The narratives of female captivity published in the century following Rowlandson's reveal that it is precisely at such moments that identification acquires its affective property, its sentimentality. Although Rowlandson patiently awaits her deliverance from captivity, even choosing to "wait Gods time" (161) rather than accept one Indian's offer to help her escape, later captives often betrayed less faith in typology and divine providence. In the disjunctive moments when teleology's promise of what should happen failed to conform to causality's account of what was happening, those captives were sometimes prompted actively to escape from their captors. There-fore, to investigate the function of sentimentality within the discourses of the novel and the nation, it is necessary to pay attention to the strategies of later captivity narratives, to determine what happens when their captive heroines move across cultural frontiers, and to ask why readers are moved to tears by their stories.

Captivity and Escape

The popularity of Rowlandson's narrative and its ideological usefulness in an era of persistent Indian warfare and waning Puritanism prompted the publication of hundreds of editions and numerous collections of captivity narratives, both factual and fictional, throughout and beyond the following century. By the late eighteenth century many of these texts—like the 1787 "Panther Captivity" and Ann Eliza Bleecker's 1793 *History of Maria Kittle*—are virtually indistinguishable from sentimental novels.[5] Such developments clearly result in part from the incorporation of structural and stylistic ele-ments from novels like Richardson's, which were among the most popular books read in the American colonies. But this consistent development can-not be explained solely by the later adoption of novelistic elements, since the production of readerly sympathy serves a crucial function in the strate-gies of captivity narratives; indeed, some of the earliest narratives already rely on the sympathetic relation between reader and text that only later marks sentimental novels. My interest here is not in chronologically privi-leging one of these genres over the other but in determining the political implications of their production of sympathy around the scene of female captivity. To do so requires placing these two narrative forms in a dialogic transatlantic context, where, during the eighteenth century, they clearly overlapped. As Armstrong and Tennenhouse suggest by linking Rowland-son's narrative directly with Richardson's *Pamela,* the captivity narrative and the sentimental novel were in cross-continental dialogue from the be-ginning. By reinitiating this exchange, I aim to expose the gap that these texts' sentimentality works to seal—the gap between an identification with the captive's virtuous and passive suffering and an identification with her transgressive and active agency. Although many eighteenth-century narra-tives of male captivity were often as sentimental as those of women,[6] I focus on the latter here because they more tellingly reveal the function and strat-egy of such affect. In these narratives sentimentality works through reader identification to mask the agency of women held captive, an agency whose often startling violence encouraged colonial practices of genocide against

Amerindians. At the same time, sentimentality works to reproduce performatively the Euro-American community, a process facilitated by the fact that so many captives were also mothers.

Captivity narratives nearly always begin with the moment of Indian attack, and the descriptions of these attacks incessantly focus the reader's attention on the abduction or death of infants. It has been estimated that at least one-fifth of the women taken captive from New England were either pregnant or had just given birth (Ulrich 205). While no evidence exists to suggest how many of those who published their stories were among that one-fifth, the number of narratives that begin with a woman being hauled into captivity from the delivery bed is staggering enough that any reader comes to expect this opening image. When the Indians carry away Elizabeth Hanson with her four children, the "youngest child but fourteen days old," Hanson claims that the Indians "immediately before my face knocked its brains out" (232). Mehetable Goodwin's Indian master "violently Snatcht the Babe out of its Mother's Arms, and before her Face knockt out its Brains" (Mather, *Decennium* 210); Hannah Dustan's captors literally pull her out of the bed in which she had only days earlier given birth, and "e'er they had gone many steps, they dash'd out the Brains of the Infant, against a Tree" (Mather, *Decennium* 264). Clearly, this stylized scenario was both politically effective and potently affective, and later narratives capitalize on its sentimental potential. When the Indians arrive at the home of Frances Scott, Scott's young daughter "ran to her Parent, and, with the most plaintive Accents, cried, 'O Mamma! O Mamma! Save me!' The Mother, in the deepest Anguish of Spirit and with a Flood of Tears, intreated the Savages to spare her Child; but with a brutal Fierceness, they tomahawked and stabbed her in the Mother's Arms." These narratives insistently subtract the captive mother's capacity to act in response to the violence against her family that she is forced to witness. Frances Scott's narrative even inserts details that further enhance the captive's passivity: the Indians instruct the mother to remain firmly in one place while her children are killed, and they subsequently throw the corpses onto the floor "near the Mother" (9).

If the children of female captives happen to escape such early deaths, they are often immediately separated from their mothers.[7] Mary Rowlandson claims that in the turmoil of the attack on her home, Indians were "ha[u]ling Mothers one way, and Children another" (143), and she expresses outrage over the fact "that I should have Children, and a Nation which I knew not ruled over them" (147). Jemima Howe, separated from her nursing infant, insists that "the Indians, I suppose on purpose to torment me, sent me away to another wigwam which stood at a little distance, though not so far from the one in which my distressed infant was confined but that I could

plainly hear its incessant cries and heart-rending lamentations" (Drake 147).[8]
Jean Lowry records the successive removal of her five children from her and
asks "What could be more distressing to a tender hearted Mother?" (11) than
to know that "the fruit of my Body . . . should be brought up in Paganism"
(14). Rachel Plummer's much later narrative recounts a similar incident in
language that is even more explicitly sentimental. Plummer believes that the
Indians deliberately "brought my little James Pratt so near me that I could
hear him cry. He would call for mother, and often was his voice weakened
by the blows they would give him. I could hear the blows. I could hear his
cries; but oh, alas, could offer him no relief" (338). Repeatedly, the captive
mother is portrayed as an unwilling spectator made to watch or overhear
the violent murder or abuse of her child. Her sympathetic suffering is enhanced by her enforced lack of agency. Philip Fisher has identified with sentimentality precisely such "moments when action is impossible," for "[t]ears
represent the fact that only a witness who cannot effect action will experience suffering as deeply as the victim" (108). The position of witness held
by grieving mothers in these narratives is shared by the captivated and sympathetic reader, who, like the mother, can only passively endure this emotional scene.

The event of captivity is followed by an almost incessant mobility, as the
captive must travel with the Indians into and through the wilderness. Within
this entirely alien culture, Anglo-American assumptions, behavior, and morality invariably misfire and fail to elicit the responses they are accustomed
to producing. While such failed gestures include pleading and fainting, the
most common one is weeping. Massy Harbison explains that she "never
wept" while being forced to watch her children murdered and scalped because "it is more than probable, that tears at those seasons of distress, would
have been fatal in their consequences; for savages despise a tear!" (41). Cotton Mather writes that the worst hardship captives must endure is being
made to watch "their Friends made a Sacrafice [*sic*] of Devils before their
Eyes, but be afraid of dropping a Tear from those Eyes, lest it should, upon
that provocation, be next their own Turn, to be so Barbarously Sacrificed"
(*Decennium* 208). Later he notes that "when the Children of the English
Captives Cried at any Time . . . the manner of the Indians was, to dash their
Brains against a Tree" (*Decennium* 213). The captive's tears may lead to death,
but as they do so they translate directly into tears of sympathy in the reader,
as Mather's concluding words suggest: "*Nescio tu quibus es, Lector, Lecturus
Ocessis; Hoc Scio quod Siccis scribere non potui* [I know not, reader, whether
you will be moved to tears by this narrative; I know I could not write it
without weeping]" (*Decennium* 213).[9] As early, then, as 1699, tears in captivity narratives signal not only the sympathy of English captives for one an-

other but, even more significantly, the reader's vicarious sympathy for the suffering captives—a response that explicitly distinguishes them from the unsympathetic Indians.

These strikingly recurrent narrative elements all insist on the captives' Christian and English difference from their captors, and they insistently encourage reader identification with that difference. Because the experience of captivity, however, entailed crossing the cultural frontier into Amerindian society, it often resulted for many of these captives in more startling forms of transgression. These transgressions amounted not to differences from the Indians but to differences from the English, since survival frequently necessitated abandoning Anglo-American cultural traditions, social and legal standards, and gendered codes of conduct. Captivity was, in this sense, a profoundly ambivalent experience, not only for the captives but for their readers. Often the same narratives that circulated horrifying accounts of victimization also circulated fascinating stories of escape from dominant social and moral norms. In fact, the act of escape from captivity was frequently the most ambivalent element in these narratives, since it was at once a heroic instance of female bravery and an often extraordinary act of female violence.

What is most remarkable about such stories is that they were so easily and readily legitimated by the very culture whose standards they blatantly transgressed. The white captive of the Indians most often returned to her community not as a criminal or as a threat to the social order but as a heroine and an exemplar of it. The strategies of sympathetic identification that we have seen at work in these narratives are central to this cultural legitimation. The increasingly sentimental discourse these narratives employ manipulates the transgression occasioned by captivity into a heroism that over the course of the eighteenth century would become more and more explicitly associated with nationalism. Narratives of female captivity fulfilled this nationalist function particularly effectively, largely because so many of the women taken captive were mothers whose bodies quite literally reproduced the nation and therefore had to be preserved. By encouraging readers to identify with the captive mother, these narratives attempt to veil her violent act of agency beneath the urgency of this reproductive necessity.

This strategy is evident in the famous captivity of Hannah Dustan, which Cotton Mather incorporated into no fewer than three of his publications between 1697 and 1702.[10] Mather clearly intended the narrative to serve as anti-Indian propaganda and at the same time to encourage Christian piety in his readership. Yet what is most remarkable about this brief account is its use of sympathetic identification with a captive's motherhood to sanction a lawless act of female violence. Mather's attempt to conceal the ambivalence of that identification by denying its transgressiveness provides a model for the operation of sentimentality in both novelistic and nationalist discourse.

When Indians attack and enter Hannah Dustan's home in a 1697 raid, her husband is absent; she is taken from her lying-in bed, made to watch her newborn infant murdered before her eyes, separated from the rest of her family, and dragged through miles of wilderness by her Indian captors. Mather's narrative enhances the captive's fear of both ideological and physical violation by "those furious tawnies." Her Indian captors, converted to French Catholicism, will not allow her to say her "English" prayers, and they tell her that when they arrive at an Indian village she "must be Stript, and Scourg'd, and run the Gantlet through the whole Army of Indians" (*Decennium* 265).

The ritual of the gauntlet, in which an assembled file of Indian villagers beat the captives with sticks and rocks as they ran through them, frequently triggered fears of rape, since the captives were sometimes (or at least imagined that they would be) forced to disrobe and run naked.[11] It is apparently this frightening threat to her own body that leads Dustan to persuade her midwife and a young boy captive with her to assist her in killing and "cutting off the Scalps of the Ten Wretches" while they sleep. The captive's deed dangerously resembles—in its method of attacking sleeping victims, the use of Indian tomahawks, and the practice of scalping—the same Indian threats it was an attempt to escape from. Mather easily justifies Dustan's murder of her Indian captors, however, by insisting that "being where she had not her own Life secured by any Law unto her, she thought she was not Forbidden by any Law to take away the Life of the Murderers, by whom her Child had been Butchered" (*Decennium* 266). The captive's active violence is explicitly sanctioned by the violence she has passively witnessed and endured, and it is more specifically sanctioned by the conditions of motherhood and threatened female sexuality.[12]

Mather's emphasis on these conditions attempts to subordinate the unavoidable possibility of the reader's identification with the act of female agency itself. From its beginning the narrative places the reader into the position of the passive mother who must witness the destruction of her home and children. But this specular identification is supported by another identification, for it is precisely from the perspective of her transgressive act of violence that the image of Dustan as a passive victim acquires its forceful appeal. This necessarily doubled identification produces an inconsistency—in this case, a yawning gap—between the image of the innocent English mother and her incredible act of "Indianized" aggression. What is ultimately affective about this story is the imperfectly sealed margin between these two identifications, between a sympathetic grief for the mother's loss and a sympathetic approval of her aggressive compensation for that loss.[13] Affect fills the space of that disjunction, and in doing so it converts the subjective agency of the captive into (and conceals it within) the passive sensation of being moved.

Indian captivity stories like Dustan's often served to justify genocide, and Cotton Mather clearly appropriates her example to support and encourage anti-Indian sentiment and action. But Mather's careful explanation of Dustan's motivation and his strategic veiling of her own aggression suggest that her act may have represented as much of a threat as it did a response to one. Clearly, this Puritan goodwife's murder of ten Indians was unusual enough to require explanation. Laurel Thatcher Ulrich explains that although colonial American women were generally expected to respond to battle or captivity with submission and piety, actions like Dustan's might have been validated simply by the absence of her husband, for whom Dustan would have been acting as legitimate proxy (179). But even if such conditions sanctioned Dustan's refusal to submit to Indian captivity, the condition of coverture, which subjected seventeenth- and eighteenth-century New England women to legal, economic, and civic representation by their husbands, rendered wives captive in another sense—to a patriarchal authority that virtually required female obedience as a duty (Ulrich 6–7). In this context, Dustan's act of violence was not only unusual enough to require explanation but also radical enough to require containment by Mather's discourse.

The necessity and the function of Mather's affective representation of her experience become evident in comparison with the best-known instance of female violence in New England before Dustan's legendary escape. Four years before he publicly celebrated Dustan for killing ten Catholicized Indians, Cotton Mather publicly condemned Elizabeth Emerson, Hannah Dustan's unmarried sister, for allegedly killing her newborn twins. Dustan received reward money in exchange for the Indian scalps, was invited to visit at the home of Judge Samuel Sewall, and became something of a celebrity. Emerson was tried, convicted of murder, and hanged.[14] Mather's responses to these two events certainly mark the differences between Indians and English infants as victims of violence, but the relation between the two agents of violence suggests why Mather emphasized Dustan's reproductive motherhood and why that emphasis effectively obscured the very elements of female aggression that, in her sister's case, were considered most threatening and punishable.

At the same time that he applauds Hannah Dustan's action, Mather demonizes her Amerindian victims. In this way, the narrative of her captivity, which circulated in an era of French and Indian warfare, works to construct an explicit border between the Protestant Anglo-American community and the outside threats to its coherence and identity, and it does so by constructing an impassable border of difference between the English captive and her Frenchified Indian captors. Like Rowlandson's narrative, Mather's account insistently denies that the captive herself violates that border. By forging an explicit identification with Dustan's motherhood, by asking in a sense that its readers imagine themselves as mothers, the text produces an imagined community and emphasizes the necessary reproduction of that community. Yet this identification, this crossing between reader and text, also involves a transgression that it denies. Only by acknowledging the ambivalence that surrounds her act of agency and readers' response to it can we account for how Dustan's narrative could produce an imagined English community in one century and an imagined American community in another.

By the nineteenth century, Hannah Dustan's story had become an example of a specifically American national valor and of a heroism that is encoded not by the doctrinal law of the state but by the sentimental law of motherhood. Robert B. Caverly, who published *Heroism of Hannah Duston* in 1874, offers Dustan as an inspirational national heirloom to the living descendants of "old New-England mothers" (14) and cites her heroic escape as the originary moment of the colonies' eventual rise to independence. He includes in his book a genealogical list of her thirteen children and compares her story to that of Hannah Bradly, who in 1736 shot one Indian and killed another by pouring a tub of boiling soap over his head when he entered her home. He notes that Bradly, like Hannah Dustan, "left numerous progeny" and that her "descendants are to be found in New England almost everywhere" (57). The monument erected in her honor represents a seven-and-a-half-foot figure of Dustan "with uplifted tomahawk, in the act of executing the courageous, tragic exploit" (*Complete Description* 22), which the statue commemorates; and the inscription carved into the monument virtually insists on her long-lasting reproductive value by describing her as one "of our ancient mothers" (Caverly 379). Mather's strategy of justification was still being repeated by the end of the nineteenth century, when Charles Corning's account of the event offers "the horrors of the fire-side massacre at home," "the agony of beholding innocent infants dashed against rocks or impaled on sharp stakes," and "the vengeance of outraged womanhood" as explanation for how "civilized women and mothers" could "become more savage than the savages themselves" (38). Significantly, Corning's account concludes with a reminder that because Dustan was the source of "an active prosperity, who have done well their part in the making of New England," she should be remembered as "a stern, unyielding matron" rather than as "the prototype of the fabled Amazon" (39).

Collections of captivity narratives began appearing in the late eighteenth century and continued to be published throughout the nineteenth century. Examples such as John Frost's 1854 *Heroic Women of the West* often followed a principle of inclusion that favored stories of maternal heroism such as Hannah Dustan's. Likewise, the 1825 edition of Massy Harbison's narrative has appended to it the story of Mrs. Merrill's defense of her Kentucky home from Indian attack in the 1790s. Mrs. Merrill is described as a "heroic mother" who "in the midst of her screaming children and groaning husband, seized an axe and gave the ruffian a fatal blow" (62). After repeating this act on the next four Indians who rush toward her, a retreating Indian reportedly exclaims that "the squaws have taken the breach clout and fight worse than the *Long Knives*" (63). The conclusion to Harbison's own narrative assures its readers that her sufferings resulted in "successful issue; as they tended to give fresh impulse to those who were already engaged in the conflict, and to engage others in it" (44).

Narratives such as these clearly work to reproduce their readers as an imagined national community, but they simultaneously produce an identification with the female transgression that a national rhetoric of maternal reproduction works to conceal. The affective appeal of these narratives can only be understood in terms of this dual identification. Sentimentality sutures the gap between these two levels of identification, as John Frost's introduction to his collection suggests: "The heroism of woman is the heroism of the heart. Her deeds of daring and endurance are prompted by affection. . . . Captured and dragged away from her home [she] endures fatigue, braves danger, bears contumely, and sometimes deals the death-blow to the sleeping captors, to save the lives of her children. Such is woman's heroism" (iii–iv). These aggressive mothers are, in Frost's conventional formulation, less agents than victims who are passively moved to action by maternal feeling. The sympathetic tears that accompany the captive's reentrance into her community reaffirm the coherent identity of that community only by pretending to erase her incommensurable agency. As Franco Moretti has claimed, the blindness produced by tears "enables us *not to see*. It is a way of distracting us from the sight of what has upset us, or rather of making it disappear" (179). The operation of sympathy, like the experience of captivity, must be seen as transgressive in both senses of the word—as a crossing that is inevitably asymptotic and that within its remaining and irreducible space always retains the potential of going astray.

Sympathy and the Novel

The heteroglossia that, for Bakhtin, characterizes novelistic discourse is not only an internal characteristic of the genre but an external condition for its production: novels appear out of the exchanges that traverse those zones of contact where cultures and nations chaotically cross.[15] Colonial American captivity narratives document the radical cultural contact that takes place on such a border, and their further passage across the border of the Atlantic puts the narratives themselves into dialogic contact with other texts. This

ceaseless mobility suggests that novelistic discourse emerges not in fixed locations or static moments but within a constant movement *across* borders. If
sympathy is a movement that obscures its own activity, then novels are transcultural and transnational products that sentimentally obscure those crossings. By reading Rowlandson with Richardson, Armstrong and Tennenhouse reenact a crucial transatlantic exchange, one that significantly revises
Eurocentric narratives of the novel. Sentimental novels like those of Richardson, however, insist on an equivalent notion of identification, which
Armstrong and Tennenhouse adopt when they argue that Richardson's
Pamela—like its forebear, the captivity narrative—creates a coherent national community. By reading Rowlandson through Richardson, reading
the captivity narrative as a sentimental novel, they overlook the transgressive level of identification that operates not only in captivity narratives but
in sentimental novels. The identification with difference becomes obscured
beneath the fantasy of a coherent community of Englishness, much as the
tears produced by captivity narratives veil the potential danger of an identification with the captive's agency. If instead of reading captivity narratives
in the way that Richardson insists sentimental novels should be read, we
read sentimental novels in the way outlined by the examples of captivity
narratives above, the sympathetic identification on which those novels' reproduction of an imagined community relies appears far more ambivalent
than Richardson made it out to be.

Richardson's preface to *Pamela* insists that its readers, by being "*uncom-
monly* moved" by the incidents in the novel, will imitate its heroine's example of virtue and piety. The letters from readers that follow his preface con-
firm their sympathetic engagement with Pamela's suffering, but they also
reveal an identification with the least virtuous aspects of her behavior. One
anonymous letter claims that the novel's "Incidents are so natural and interesting that I have gone hand-in-hand, and sympathiz'd with the pretty
Heroine in all her sufferings" (6). But when this reader details those incidents that most engaged him, he claims to have identified not with Pamela's
passive suffering but with her active attempts to escape from that suffering:
"I have interested myself in all her Schemes of Escape; been alternately
pleas'd and angry with her in her Restraint; *pleas'd* with the little Machinations and Contrivances she set on foot for her Release, and *angry* for suffering her Fears to defeat them" (6). In other words, what moves this reader
are the moments of Pamela's own mobility, specifically those moments
when she uses deceptive "Schemes," "Machinations," and "Contrivances"
actively to escape from her confinement and from her captor, Mr. B.

In fact, while Pamela Andrews may be a paragon of female virtue, modesty, and benevolence, her entrance into a condition of captivity leads her
into a practice of deception that resembles her captor's behavior more than

it adheres to her own principles of ethical conduct. She arranges a forbidden correspondence with Parson Williams, hides the pages of her journal, lies about her plans and motives, sneaks through the window while her guard Mrs. Jewkes sleeps, and attempts to escape over the garden wall. Like the heroines of captivity narratives who transgress their own moral standards by imitating their captors, Pamela learns this strategic trickery from Mr. B himself, who claims "I believe I must assume to myself half the Merit of your Wit, too; for the innocent Exercises you have had for it from me, have certainly sharpen'd your Invention" (202). Unlike the unquestionably immoral actions of her captors, however, the captive's deception is implicitly innocent, and it is innocent because it is legitimated by the condition of captivity itself. She momentarily subverts her own standards of conduct only in a grander effort to uphold those standards, and this logic of legitimation, which is also Cotton Mather's logic, obscures and dilutes her transgressive actions.

Pamela worries to her parents early in her captivity that she will become "an Intriguer by-and-by; but I hope an innocent one!" (118) and prays for the success of "my dangerous, but innocent Devices" (149). When Mr. B later places her before a mirror, he exposes the gap between her evident innocence and honesty and the concealed "Tricks and Artifices, that lie lurking in her little, plotting, guileful Heart" (162). These latter qualities, which he discovers by reading her journal, are secrets that the mirror will not reflect. But it is precisely this gap between Pamela's virtue and her artifice, between the image the mirror reflects and the information her pages reveal, that finally transforms Mr. B when he reads the "very moving Tale" (208) that is her narrative of captivity. The inconsistency between these two modes of identification are evident in Mr. B's explanation of his reform to Pamela's father: "tho' she is full of her pretty Tricks and Artifices, to escape the Snares I had laid down for her, yet all is innocent, lovely, and uniformly beautiful" (255). The sentimental affect that Mr. B experiences while reading her journal works to suture the irreconcilable gap between two planes of identification; Pamela's active agency is disavowed by the reader's passive sensation of "being moved."[16] The prefatory letter from Aaron Hill, added to the second edition of the novel, offers Pamela's effect on her master as a model for the text's effect on its reader: "Not the charmer's own prattling Idea struck so close to the Heart of her Master, as the Incidents of the Story to the Thoughts of a Reader" (17).

Through this process of readerly sympathy, *Pamela* aims to reproduce a moral English community outside the text; it ideally transforms its readers into reformed Mr. Bs and virtuous Pamelas. This couple becomes, in effect, the textual parents of a nation distinguished by its "Example of Purity" from the vices of "a neighboring Nation; which now shall have an Opportunity to receive *English* Bullion in Exchange for its own Dross, which has so long passed current among us in Pieces abounding with all the Levities of its volatile Inhabitants" (5). This letter to Richardson imagines that the novel itself circulates as though it were English currency, a piece of "our Sterling Substance" whose inherent morality prevents it from *"frenchify-[ing]* our *English* Solidity into Froth and Whip-syllabub" (7). If the novel supposedly produces and preserves a particularly English integrity and value in its audience, the resolution of its plot performs the same function within the novel. Mr. B's authentic marriage to Pamela averts not only the immoral but the economically unproductive possibility that if she "should have a dear little one, it would be out of my own Power to legitimate it, if I should wish it to inherit my Estate; . . . as I am almost the last of my Family, and most of what I possess must descend to a strange Line, and disagreeable and unworthy Persons" (230). Indeed, following the conclusion of Pamela's journal, Richardson assures us that, like the heroic mothers of contemporary captivity narratives, "[s]he made her beloved Spouse happy in a numerous and hopeful Progeny" (409). This assurance of reproduction with which the novel ends retroactively veils the agency that preserved the maternal body of the captive; the transgressive actions of the heroine are virtually washed away in the flood of tears produced by the sympathetic community within the novel and reproduced in the virtuous English community outside it. What the affect signaled by sentimental tears enables us not to see, in *Pamela* as well as in contemporary captivity narratives, is the efficacy of subjective agency.

That blindness has an efficacy of its own, particularly in the era of British warfare with the French and Indians during which *Pamela* was published. The novel's fantasy of a distinctively English community was no doubt particularly appealing to both continental and colonial English readers during this period, but it concealed an ambivalence capable of disrupting that community. When Esther Edwards Burr read Pamela's narrative of captivity in 1755, she was virtually immobilized at her home in New Jersey, afraid to travel to see her parents in Stockbridge or her friends in Boston because of the ongoing war. Burr records in her journal—written as a series of letters to her friend Sarah Prince—her response to *Pamela,* along with her concern over "the state of our Nation and the French Nation, and how probable it was that the French might overcome in their desighns [*sic*] to this Country" (76).[17] Her responses to the novel and to the war, however, are equally ambivalent. Although she argues that Richardson "has degraded our sex most horribly, to go and represent such virtue as Pamela, falling in love with Mr. B. in the midst of such foul and abominable actions" (99), she later claims that Pamela "was more than woman—An *Angel imbodied* [*sic*]" (105). When she complains about "what a tender Mother undergoes for her children at such a day as this, to think of bring[ing] up Children to be *dashed against the stones by our barbarous enemies*—or which is worse, to be inslaved by them, and obliged to turn *Papist*" (142), her fears are torn between the local violence of the war and the national and religious implications of an English defeat. Her journal reveals the literal fear of captivity and the accompanying fear of mobility felt by New Englanders, especially by New England mothers. At the news of increased fighting she claims that "no body stirs no more than if it was impossible" and exclaims: "*Wo* [*sic*] to them that are *with Child,* and to them that give suck in these days!" (177). Upon finally attempting a delayed journey, Burr reasons that "if the Indians get me, they get me, that is all I can say" (223). Such conditions probably made reading *Pamela* and Indian captivity narratives particularly affective for New Englanders, and the sense of national community such texts created was no doubt consoling in an era when the borders of that community were challenged by both the French and the Indians.

Yet it is impossible to account for the political function of Richardson's novels and of sentimental captivity narratives within the later rhetoric of the American revolution against Britain without acknowledging their readers' more subversive identification with the captive heroine's transgressive actions. As Jay Fliegelman has argued, the later American reception of both *Pamela* and *Clarissa* tended to translate the heroine's "act of disobedience into a heroic rebellion" (*Prodigals* 130). The American Revolution appropriated these captive Englishwomen less as models of passive virtue than as victims whose suffering legitimated their active agency. Richardson's captive heroines, like Hannah Dustan, came to represent America itself as a "woman on the verge of bringing out a new and virtuous generation" (*Prodigals* 122). The very texts, therefore, that enable the community of the nation to be imagined are also texts that enable the disruption and reconfiguration of community to be imagined. This possibility is occluded by the reduction of identification to simple resemblance and by the assumption that nationalist and novelistic sentiment is a function of that resemblance. Sentiment appears rather at those moments when resemblance fails, and it appears as the blinding veil of tears that both masks and marks an unaccountable border of difference.

Nation and Identification

If sentimental novels offer the consoling illusion of a community based on resemblance, then it is no surprise that such novels enjoyed their greatest popularity in the eighteenth century during periods of crisis in national coherence. The publication of *Pamela* in England in 1740 ushered in the cult

of sentimentality that remained popular until the 1780s, a period characterized by a series of military conflicts with the French and Indians that challenged and established the borders of the British Atlantic empire. Significantly, after the American War of Independence, the popularity of these
novels quickly declined in England in concert with the general cultural devaluation of sentiment. It was precisely at this time, however, that sentimental novels began to flourish in America and to flourish as specifically
American novels. William Hill Brown's epistolary novel, *The Power of Sym-
pathy,* published in 1789, was advertised as "the first American novel" and
still remains the text most often nominated to that status. Brown's novel
contains a series of letters between Myra Harrington and Mrs. Holmes on
the function and course of female education, in which Mrs. Holmes warns
her charge that "the books which I recommend to your perusal are not always applicable to the situation of an *American* lady" (77). She explicitly develops this critique of English literature and implicitly calls for an American
national literature when she remarks that the ridicule of educated women
"is evidently a *transatlantic* idea, and must have been imbibed from the
source of some *English* novel or magazine" (80). Mrs. Holmes goes on to
recommend American-authored books characterized by "sentiment, morality and benevolence" (81) but marked also by nationalist themes: Noah
Webster's *Grammatical Institute,* Joel Barlow's *Vision of Columbus,* and Timothy Dwight's *Conquest of Canaan.* If these texts are preferable, it is because
"*English* books" are "filled with local descriptions, which a young woman
here [in America] is frequently at a loss to understand" (77). The assumption undergirding Mrs. Holmes's claim is that the sympathetic identification that makes novels a form of moral education is hindered by the absence
of a national identity shared by both reader and text.

Such assumptions, together with the persistent critique that American
novels were poor imitations of British models, fostered a palpable anxiety in
nineteenth-century America about producing and defining a distinct national literary tradition. The sentimental legacy of American exceptionalism
continues to characterize the institution of American literary criticism.
From F. O. Matthiesen's *American Renaissance* to David S. Reynolds's *Beneath the American Renaissance,* American literary criticism has repeatedly
defined its object of study by distinguishing what is unique about literature
that is produced in a place called America. The critical labels most often attached to American literature are also ones commonly affixed to the American nation: a commitment to democracy, the pursuit of freedom, the presence of the frontier.[18] While these definitions aim to construct a separate
but equal literary tradition, they also confine American literature, American
culture, and even American writers within a totalizing identity by asserting
a kind of sympathetic resemblance between them. As a result, American lit-

erary history becomes isolated from the transnational and transcultural contexts in which it inevitably takes shape.[19]

The undeniably affective appeal of exceptionalism suggests that its claim to distinctive and stable identity works only by obscuring mobility and difference. Indeed, the exceptionalist argument contains an ambivalence arising from the fact that it can only be from an external perspective—from the position of a European or British literary tradition, for example—that the uniqueness of American literature comes to seem so appealing. As Nina Baym points out, nineteenth-century reviewers defined "American" literature only by constant reference to English examples from which it purportedly differed (*Novels* 242). National literary traditions can be imagined as coherent, as structured on a principle of commonality, only by imagining the border between them to be fixed and uncrossed. By obscuring the movement and exchange of texts across borders like the Atlantic, exceptionalist theories tend to reproduce those texts' sentimental fantasies of coherent national communities. These porous borders or frontiers are, however, precisely where Bakhtin locates the dialogism of novelistic discourse and where Homi Bhabha focuses his study of the ambivalence of nationalist discourse. The narrative duplicity that characterizes the nation and the novel must also be recognized in the process of identification by which their discourses create imagined communities.

The strategies of sympathetic identification within sentimental captivity narratives and novels elucidate the function of the "sentimental side" that Renan attributed to nationalism. If sentimental novels appear not within a static national topography but only in a context of exchange across colonial cultural and national borders, then the process of identification on which that genre relies must accommodate the relation between individuals who lack, rather than share, commonality. The inevitable limitation of resemblance is concealed within the fantasy of a community based on resemblance—an imagined community that is sentimental precisely to the extent that it lacks resemblance. Perhaps what the novel and the nation most deeply share, then, are these ambivalent relations between subjects who are, in fact, not alike. By repeating the strategies of discourses that insist on equivalence, exceptionalism reproduces the fantasy of resemblance and community and perpetuates its concealment of the sometimes violent agency that preserves the imagined body of the nation, that "mother country" that reproduces itself through the ambivalent strategies of sympathetic identification. Captivity narratives and sentimental novels of the revolutionary era would exploit such gendered representations in order to mobilize anti-British aggression. But as the next chapter argues, popular postrevolutionary sentimental novels elaborate the ways in which the dilemmas of agency suddenly faced by women were shared by citizens of the new republic.

Chapter 3

REPUBLICAN MOTHERHOOD
AND POLITICAL
REPRESENTATION IN
POSTREVOLUTIONARY
AMERICA

T HE TITLE PAGE of the 1773 edition of Mary White Rowland-son's captivity narrative featured a woodcut that depicts the captive defending her home by aiming a disproportionately large gun at four armed Indians. This illustration is, of course, consistent neither with the details nor the agenda of the text itself, since the captive left her burning home with a child, not a gun, in her arms and is more easily imagined reading a Bible or sewing a shirt than shooting a rifle at her captors. The title of this tenth edition, *A Narrative of the Captivity, Sufferings and Removes of Mrs. Mary Rowlandson,* also abandons the religious emphasis of the original, and its subtitle singles out from the many "remarkable Events" of her captivity the provocative claim that she was "treated in the most barbarous and cruel Manner by those vile Savages" (fig. 3). "The Sovereignty and Goodness of God" is no longer the subject of nor the redeeming agent in this edition; in-stead, its subject is the individual Mary Rowlandson, who is retroactively

A
NARRATIVE
OF THE
CAPTIVITY, SUFFERINGS AND REMOVES
OF
Mrs. *Mary Rowlandson,*

Who was taken Prisoner by the INDIANS with several others, and treated in the most barbarous and cruel Manner by those vile Savages : With many other remarkable Events during her TRAVELS.

Written by her own Hand, for her private Use, and now made public at the earnest Desire of some Friends, and for the Benefit of the afflicted.

BOSTON:

Printed and Sold at JOHN BOYLE's Printing-Office, next Door to the *Three Doves* in Marlborough-Street. 1773.

1773

FIG 3. Title page, *A Narrative of the Captivity, Sufferings and Removes of Mrs. Mary Rowlandson* (Boston, 1773). Courtesy, American Antiquarian Society.

imagined aggressively defending herself and her home against the violence of her Indian captors.

The American revolutionary era saw a remarkable renewal in the popularity of Rowlandson's text; an unprecedented seven editions of her narrative appeared in the 1770s alone, after having been reissued only once—in 1720—since its original year of publication.[1] This sudden interest in her story during a decade in which the colonists increasingly saw themselves as the victims of British oppression suggests that her narrative circulated as an example of such oppression, and the newly added woodcut reinforces such a reading. But the inconsistency between this secular, politicized reception of her text and the religious emphasis of the narrative itself is in another sense suggestive of the profound transformation of print culture and of the public's relation to print that took place within the century since the narrative was first published.

The shift from the 1682 image of a pious Mary Rowlandson delivered from captivity by the hand of God to the 1773 image of Mary Rowlandson aiming a musket at her captors was facilitated by the emergence of a critical public sphere. Michael Warner has argued that in Puritan New England printed texts circulated as vehicles of a stable and divine authority that individuals internalized through the private process of reading. Print, in other words, did not confront authority; it imprinted authority. But with the development in the mid-eighteenth century of what Jürgen Habermas calls a public sphere, print discourse became a public tool for the emancipatory resistance to authority rather than the source of an uncontested authority (Warner 19–20). Habermas argues that because this autonomous public sphere mediated between civil society and the state it was capable of criticizing and regulating both domains, which were newly separated from each other as a result of a developing market economy of exchange. The public sphere therefore became a space in which private individuals engaged in rational and critical discussion that aimed to produce public opinion. In revolutionary America, such discussions centered on the colonies' relation to British authority, and the critical public sphere clearly played an instrumental role in building popular consensus for an armed resistance to Britain. Captivity narratives like Rowlandson's not only circulated an appropriate image of colonial oppression but also provided an effective rhetoric for imagining and justifying colonial resistance.

In fact, as Greg Sieminski has pointed out, the pictorial staging of Rowlandson's confrontation with the Indians in this woodcut directly parallels that of Paul Revere's incendiary popular engraving of the 1770 Boston Massacre. The text accompanying both illustrations also reinforces those parallels. In Revere's illustration the citizens of Boston are fired on before the State House by British soldiers, who are described in the accompanying

FIG 4.   Paul Revere, *Bloody Massacre perpetrated in King-Street, Boston . . .* , *1770.*
Courtesy, American Antiquarian Society.

poem—much as the Indians are in the subtitle of the Rowlandson text—as
"fierce Barbarians grinning o'er their Prey" (fig. 4).[2] Like the woodcut, Revere's engraving propagandistically distorts the event it pictures, since the
British troops were reputedly provoked by the belligerent Bostonians. But
as Jay Fliegelman argues in his reading of the engraving, such distortions
were paradoxically attempts to more faithfully depict the scene with psychological rather than factual precision. If both these illustrations misrepresent the event they portray, they do so to represent more authentically the

public's affective response to it (*Declaring Independence* 76–78). Mimetic distortion becomes, in eighteenth-century rhetoric, the necessary tool of emotional accuracy.

Fliegelman's study significantly supplements Michael Warner's claim that participants in the public sphere were defined negatively, by the absence of any particular personal characteristics or status. Warner notes that persons entering print discourse are characterized only by the abstract quality of virtue, which "comes to be defined by the negation of other traits of personhood" and as the "rational and disinterested concern for the public good" (42). Fliegelman insists that this rationalist "principle of negativity" remained, throughout the eighteenth century, in constant dialectical tension with an antirationalist emphasis on sentiment and a persistent tendency to define individuals by their personal sensibilities. Such a tension is evident in printed artifacts such as Rowlandson's captivity narrative and Revere's image of the Boston Massacre, which clearly influenced public opinion not just by appealing to abstract reason but by appealing to personal sympathy. Indeed, the affectivity of such texts strategically aimed to provoke active agency in the public, since an audience that is emotionally moved by an image of violent oppression, it was assumed, would actively move to resist such oppression (Fliegelman, *Declaring Independence* 76–78). One might almost read Mary Rowlandson's aggressive response to her captors in the woodcut as the designed effect of Paul Revere's earlier, affective illustration of colonial captivity.

The consensus-producing function of the public sphere therefore relied as much on the operation of sympathy as it did on the faculty of reason, and few images inspired a more sympathetic response in revolutionary America than that of a captive female. The publication of captivity narratives dramatically increased in the decade before the war, older captivity narratives were suddenly reprinted, and the captive heroines of Samuel Richardson's sentimental novels became popular symbols of the tyrannized colonies. But like the 1773 refiguration of Mary Rowlandson—on whom the image of a more violently aggressive captive such as Hannah Dustan seems to be grafted—Pamela and Clarissa were not simply appropriated in revolutionary America as passive victims but were reimagined as active agents of heroic rebellion (Fliegelman, *Prodigals* 89). The captive female was a central, if ambiguous, figure in the revolutionary rhetoric that manipulated public opinion for acts of resistance and ultimately armed revolt against Britain.

Colonial women, as well as men, responded in active ways to this rhetoric. Women often organized and led collective opposition to British authority in the form of consumer boycotts of British-manufactured goods, petitions publicly declaring support for an armed resistance, or mob riots that proceeded through the streets of cities like Boston. Once the war began, they produced goods and provided services for the army, often traveling with the troops as nurses, cooks, or companions. Some served as spies or smugglers, and a few women even achieved mythological status as soldiers who fought in the war by disguising themselves as men. This politicization of colonial American women has led some critics to suggest that the revolutionary era initiates a progressive shift in the role and status of women, indicated by the postwar surge in the importance and influence of mothers and female educators. Far more critics argue, however, that female participation in the public sphere was only an accommodation to the temporary wartime absence of most men and that any political or economic power women exercised during the war swiftly disappeared with its end. These critics, too, point to the postwar obsession with maternal influence and education, but they do so in order to emphasize the containment and repression of female power by the domestic role of the influential mother, rather than the continuation and extension of female power within that role.[3]

These studies emphasize the material shift in the status of women from the revolutionary to the early republican era but have tended to pay little attention to the discursive status of gender in the rhetoric of justified revolt that dominated the critical public sphere. On the other hand, studies of revolutionary rhetoric or of the public sphere in America have paid little attention to women. These oversights have left unexamined the relationship between the imagination of power in the postwar cult of republican motherhood and emergent constructions of the practice of national power in the new republic. In fact, in the decades after the war the image of the American nation as the embodiment of republican virtue begins to become intertwined with the image of the virtuous mother as the embodiment of the American nation. Ruth Bloch has argued that, as a result of transatlantic influences from the contemporary discourses of Protestantism, Scottish moral philosophy, and literary sentimentalism, definitions of virtue shift during the revolutionary era toward a more private and passive formulation that was explicitly associated with women (53). I suggest further that one might track this emergent link between American national identity and the maternal in the rhetoric of the revolution and its trope of female captivity. America's changing relation to power during the last decades of the eighteenth century was often articulated through the figure of the captive female, an image that circulated widely in the print culture of the public sphere—that contact zone between civil society and the state. Captivity narratives and sentimental novels of captivity published in the last two decades of the eighteenth century reveal that this rhetoric had profoundly ambivalent implications for the practice of female agency. Linda Kerber's study of women in the American republic echoes Joan Landes's claim for France that the republic "was constructed against women, not just without them" (12). But contemporary novels such as *Miss McCrea, Charlotte Temple,* and *The Female Review* illustrate that, in America at least, the republic was also, if paradoxically, constructed in the image of a woman.

Captivity and Revolutionary Rhetoric

The rhetoric that incited and justified colonial American rebellion against Great Britain generally invoked and elaborated one or more of three recurrent analogies: the relation between a slave and a master, that between a child and a parent, and that between a captive and a captor. According to the first trope, George III was a ruthless despot who aimed, through a widespread British conspiracy, to enslave the American colonies and to deprive them of their freedom. In the second, Britain was an irrational and tyrannical patriarch who denied his mature American child the right to economic and political independence. The third figure drew on the biblical image of the captive Israelites, as well as on popular Indian captivity narratives, to suggest that Britain—like the Egyptians or the Amerindians—was liable violently to threaten and destroy the domestic tranquillity of the colonists it held captive. Thus, the arrival of a standing army in Boston was seen as an act that rendered Boston a captive city; and when that army shot several youths in the Boston Massacre of 1770, the parallels to captivity narratives became increasingly highlighted, as the similarities between Revere's engraving and the woodcut of Rowlandson make clear.[4]

These three popular tropes often overlapped or coincided with one another as they appeared in the multitude of pamphlets, broadsides, sermons, and narratives of the revolutionary era. The relative interchangeability of these images depends on their mutual representation of a particular relation of power. Each trope relies for its rhetorical effect on a structural opposition between threatened freedom and abusive power, and each encourages and legitimizes colonial revolt on the basis of that opposition. The antinomy underlying these various rhetorical constructions originated, according to Bernard Bailyn, in the Whig theory of power, in which an unremitting aggressive force of domination systematically and inevitably destroys liberty. This Whig conception of power and freedom, adopted by the American revolutionaries, derives in turn from classical republican theory, which posits an incessant dialectic between corruption and virtue. According to this model, virtue is defined as the individual's ability to participate actively in civil society and to suppress private interests in favor of the public good. In this tradition of political theory, which J. G. A. Pocock traces, such virtue is in constant struggle against corruption, where corruption is the condition of dependence and passivity—including, for example, the dependence of

colonial Americans on standing British armies who are to act on their behalf—brought about by the failure of virtue. The colonies' declaration of independence is, in these terms, an assertion of and a call for the active performance of their virtue in response to the British monarch's corrupt abuses of
power.

The dichotomous power relation that these analogies construct is frequently gendered, particularly in the tropes of captivity and the family. Despite, for example, the emphasis on Britain's patriarchal oppression in studies of American revolutionary rhetoric, the texts these studies explore almost
always characterize Britain as the mother, not the father, of the colonies.
While Bernard Bailyn identifies in the political pamphlets of the period a recurrent use of the word *slavery* to describe the relation between Britain and
her colonies, nowhere does he mention the even more frequent occurrence
in those same pamphlets of the word *mother* used to describe that same relation.[5] These pamphlets elaborate on this association by referring to Britain
not simply as a mother to her offspring colonies but as an unnatural, ungrateful, and unfeeling one. Thus, Oxenbridge Thacher exclaims in *Sentiments of a British American* that "[w]e will not here insist on the parental
tenderness due from Great Britain to us and suggest she must suffer from
sympathy with her children, who have been guilty of no undutiful behavior
towards her . . . . We will suppose her for this moment to have forgot the
bowels of a mother" (495). "Nor," continues Thacher, "will we mention
any possible danger from the alienation of the affections of the colonies
from their mother country" (495) but rather hope "that her colonies now
happily extended may grow in filial affection and dutiful submission to her
their mother; and that she in return may never forget her parental affections" (498). Great Britain is a mother who has forgotten how to be a
mother, who has not only abandoned maternal sympathy but also ne-
glected and betrayed her child in her own pursuit of wealth and empire.
Thacher's curiously constructed sentences, which declare precisely what
they promise not to, strategically imply the threat of a colonial resistance
that would become increasingly explicit in pamphlets throughout the subsequent decade.

The parent-child bond described in Thacher's pamphlet differs in a significant way from the one Jay Fliegelman focuses on in *Prodigals and Pilgrims*
when he discusses the critical function, in American revolutionary rhetoric,
of the contemporary shift in family relations from a hierarchical and patriarchal model to one based on equality and affection. The revolt against patriarchy is indeed evident in the plots of many popular eighteenth-century
texts, which frequently tell stories of children who justifiably abandon tyrannical parents for more affectional bonds. The revolts Fliegelman cites, however, are always against *fathers*. Although an allegorized rebellion against

the patriarch, George III, certainly operates in these texts, they as often reflect the more painful anxiety of separation from a mother and from a mother country. Many of the sentimental novels written in the decade or two following the war allegorize this problematic loss of the mother country and often struggle to reinvent that shattered maternal relation in the same way that the cult of George Washington replaces, in Fliegelman's reading, the loss of King George. The concept of republican motherhood must be understood in the context of this matriarchal relation as much as in that of a patriarchal one.

Not only is Great Britain frequently maternalized, but the colonies too are as often represented as a daughter as they are a son. In fact, the structural opposition—between power and freedom or between corruption and virtue—that this rhetoric consistently reproduced was often most sensationally effective when the colonies were compared to a young woman. Bernard Bailyn describes the imagined Whig sphere of power as "brutal, ceaselessly active, and heedless," while the sphere of liberty "was delicate, passive and sensitive." Only in a footnote does Bailyn acknowledge "[t]he implicitly sexual character of the imagery" in much of this language. There he cites an example in which "'the interest of freedom is a virgin, that everyone seeks to deflower'; if it is not properly protected '(so great is the lust of mankind after dominion) there follows a rape upon the first opportunity.'"[6] Bailyn might also have turned to Thomas Paine for an example of this analogy, for in *Common Sense,* Paine argues for the absolute necessity of colonial rebellion on the basis of certain "injuries which nature cannot forgive; she would cease to be nature if she did. As well can the lover forgive the ravisher of his mistress, as the continent forgive the murders of Britain" (29). One of the rhetorical versions, then, of the Whig opposition between power and freedom or between British corruption and American colonial virtue was the image of a virgin threatened by rape.

Implicit in Thomas Paine's figure of the virtuous but powerless virgin, however, is the assumption that her virtue is passive and must be actively defended or revenged not by herself but by her male lover. However, this notion of a passive virtue is curiously inconsistent with the prevalent eighteenth-century understanding of virtue as a condition of active autonomy that avoided the passive dependence of a state of corruption. Paine's image, then, articulates two versions of virtue: an active civic virtue that is gendered male and a passive sexual virtue that is gendered female.[7] But Paine's metaphor implies a further critical distinction: if the figure of the captive virgin is passive, it is because she represents the colonies' negative relation to power, while Paine's unforgiving lover carries out an active rebellion in order to recover a freedom that is positive. This distinction is generally consistent with American revolutionary rhetoric; it is through such male figures as the oppressed slave and the disenfranchised son that the colonies justify the necessity of a rebellion to preserve their *freedom,* whereas it is through the figure of the captive woman that those colonies most often articulate their changing relation to *power.*

Captive virgins increasingly appear in captivity narratives and sentimental novels of captivity such as *Miss McCrea* and *Charlotte Temple.* Along with pamphlets like Paine's, these texts allegorically represented the relation of the people to the authority of the British state. Such texts successfully mobilized public consensus for a war against Britain by appealing to the sympathies as well as the reason of colonial readers. But these texts reveal a shift in the portrayal of the captive female during the late eighteenth century that is commensurate with the shift in the colonies' relation to power and independence during this period. That change is predominantly from negativity and passive powerlessness to a new conception of power that had to be defined in distinction to the kind of power that Britain and its monarch embodied, since British power represented the antithesis rather than the enactment of freedom. If virtue was imagined in passive terms, how could the citizenry of the American nation claim for itself both virtuousness and the political agency that freed itself from British rule? Colonial narratives of female captivity, as we have seen, were filled with figures who at once represented endangered virtue and aggressively defended it, legitimizing violence through sentimental discourse and its mode of ambivalent identification. The new imagination of national power in postrevolutionary America was articulated through a federalist redefinition of virtue that repeated the ambivalent and sentimental workings of captivity literature.

In fact, the Whig dichotomy between colonial American virtue and British corruption always had a far more legitimate rhetorical existence than a historical one. The complicity of the struggle for freedom with the practice of power was always implicit, as evidenced in the fact that freedom itself was often described as a certain kind of power, whereas virtue seemed inevitably to entail corruption in the very effort to maintain and reproduce itself. But even the rhetorical opposition between these forces became more and more difficult to maintain as the war for independence neared its end. It is at this historical moment that the powerless captive daughter of the revolutionary era is replaced by the republican mother of the new American nation, who practices a form of virtue and of power that is no longer defined as active but as passive, potential, and mediating. This construction of power is far less inconsistent with the form of power articulated by the representational government of the new American republic than most scholars have supposed. The postwar cult of republican motherhood therefore functions, I suggest, as at once a resolution to the crisis of an absent imperial mother and the source of a new conception of American national power that had to

evade the classical association of power with corruption. The captive heroine of the sentimental novel is one of the figures through which that crisis
and the reformulation of power that succeeds it get negotiated.

Captivity and Colonial Virtue

Since the first seventeenth-century colonial American captivity narratives,
female captives, whether authentic or fictional, were predominantly mothers who endured physical and psychological hardship but who also consistently defended their captors against accusations of seduction or rape. Not
until the Revolutionary War do fictionalized narratives begin to portray the
captivity of young virgins who are tortured and threatened with rape. One
of these narratives, titled *The Affecting History of the Dreadful Distresses of
Frederic Manheim's Family,* is set shortly after the colonial army's 1779 defeat
of the Tory-Indian forces in western New York. Two Indians abduct the
twin daughters of Frederic Manheim from their home during the absence
of both parents. The narrative, apparently reported by the father (who was
subsequently taken captive as well), offers a lengthy description of the Indians' torture of the girls, who were stripped naked by their captors and tied
to a tree. The Indians then set on fire hundreds of five-inch splinters that
had been soaked in turpentine and inserted into the daughters' skin "from
their knees to their shoulders" (205). This symbolic gang rape is utterly alien
to the world of earlier captivity narratives, but such sensationalized scenes
are increasingly common in narratives set during the Revolutionary War.
An illustration from the frontispiece of the 1800 edition of this narrative
emphasizes the passivity and immobility of the captive women, as well as
the military and sexual threat of the weapon-wielding Indians who dance
about them (fig. 5).

Through images much like Thomas Paine's, these texts allegorize the
threat of British corruption to colonial virtue while simultaneously demonizing Britain and her Indian allies. But as much Indian-hating as these sensationalized stories indulge in and produce, they contain an even more
forcible anti-British element, since the Indians were typically seen less as autonomous agents of violence than as pawns of the corrupt British military.
Increasingly in captivity narratives of the revolutionary era, the Indians and
the British are conflated as enemies to the colonies, since the British reportedly recruited Indian allies and paid them for each American scalp they
brought back to camp. The colonists largely blamed this practice not on the
Indians, who were said to have been seduced into such behavior by British
money and alcohol, but on the British and particularly on General Burgoyne.[8] A 1778 poem by the Rev. Wheeler Case, for example, has Burgoyne

FIG 5.   Frontispiece, *Affecting History of the Dreadful Distresses of Frederic
Manheim's Family* (Philadelphia, 1800). Photo courtesy of Edward E.
Ayer Collection, The Newberry Library.

proclaim: "Thousands of *Indians* I've supplied with knives, / To scalp your dearest children and your wives; / If I but nod the savage army flies, / And naught is heard but shrieks and female cries" (Dodd 22).

The popular story of Jane McCrea epitomizes this conflation of the British and the Indians, as it also reveals the political efficacy of the figure of the raped virgin in mobilizing colonial consensus for armed rebellion. There are competing versions of the tale, one of which identifies Jane McCrea as an orphan who, while living with her rebel brother, runs off to meet her loyalist lover and is scalped and killed by British-allied Indians along the way.[9] Another version locates Jane McCrea, engaged to a Tory soldier, at home with her mother awaiting his arrival when their home is raided by Indians who shoot the two women and scalp Jane in order to receive a bounty from the British general. Whatever the actual details were, this event quickly achieved an almost mythological status when it occurred in 1777 and was instantly repeated and frequently revised. Its effect on public consensus for the war was immediate, for it reportedly motivated the largest enlistment of patriot soldiers during the entire Revolutionary War. For Jay Fliegelman, this incident is evidence of the close conceptual link between the justification for revolution and the argument for consensual rather than parentally coerced marriage. In his reading, the Indians, acting as the ministers of the severe parent King George, violently deny his loyal daughter her right to marry whom she chooses (*Prodigals* 139). But the Jane McCrea story also justified American rebellion as a necessary revenge for rape, both literal and—as Thomas Paine's call for rebellion in *Common Sense* exemplifies—figurative. As Mary Beth Norton notes, the fear of rape among colonial women was widespread, especially after a 1776 incident in New York and New Jersey in which sixteen girls were held captive for days and raped by soldiers (202–3). Although this particular context for the 1777 McCrea incident is not examined in Fliegelman's analysis, it clearly operates in several versions of the story. The Frenchman René Michel Hilliard d'Auberteuil, who was traveling through the colonies during the early phase of the war, recorded a version of this event in his memoirs, where he claims that the Indians "seized this young victim, carried her into the woods, and stripped her of her garments; and after having performed on her all that their fury and brutality could suggest, they scalped her."[10]

Jane McCrea's violent demise illustrated in perfect Whig terms the potential fate of American liberty—raped and destroyed by the aggressive power of Britain—and presented the necessity of defending that liberty through the active performance of virtue. The story's material effect on military enlistment is evidence that it served as remarkably effective propaganda, particularly during the early years of the war. But the image of an utterly passive and victimized American liberty that Jane McCrea represented did not survive the war. Indeed, it hardly could, for Britain began to look less and less like an agent of unremitting tyrannical power as it sustained increasing military losses. At the same time, American freedom and the military struggle for it began to be more and more difficult to distinguish from power. This shift necessitated the construction of a new notion of power distinct from the purely aggressive and corrupt will associated with Britain. This new power, which was identified with women, was defined as virtue. Thus, while captive females continue to allegorize in postwar literature the status of colonial or republican America, those figures begin to be portrayed not simply as the victims but as the potential agents of power.

Initial changes in the conception of power and virtue are already evident in the differences between the earlier versions of the Jane McCrea incident—Hilliard's journal entry among them—and later ones like the 1784 novel written by Hilliard about the same event. *Miss McCrea: A Novel of the American Revolution* tells a story not of Indian rape but of British seduction. In this sentimental novel the American daughter's demise is attributable less to her disobedience to her parent than to her allurement by British wealth and gallantry. And if in Fliegelman's reading of the McCrea affair, Jane's tragedy is linked to the severity of the father-monarch, in Hilliard's novel it is associated with an absent mother. Unlike earlier versions of the event, this novel begins neither with an Indian attack nor with an already engaged Jane McCrea but with the entrance of the Tory soldier Belton into the Mc-Crea home during a British attack on New York City. Jane, who had earlier been praying for colonial victory, almost immediately succumbs to his charm, for he "was a man of intelligence, he had traveled, and he possessed to an eminent degree that false good breeding and dexterity of language which, lending itself to the concerns of others, only too often conceals a hard and deceitful heart" (28–29). Later that night, while her patriotic American father lies awake thinking of liberty and praying to "the God of mercy who had delivered the Hebrews from the Egyptian captivity" (29), Jane lies awake imagining, in a scarcely veiled sexual fantasy, the captivity of the colonies by the military prowess of Belton. When, in the morning, they both awake to see the results of corrupt British power in the scene of "young girls tearing their hair and running, without knowing where, to hide their shame and their misery," Mr. McCrea rages at the British destruction while his daughter is "immediately charmed by the splendor of the arms, the vivid and varied colors" of the British regiment and by the "nobility and grace" (31) of Belton.[11]

This text clearly employs elements of both a sentimental novel like *Clarissa* and a captivity narrative, patterns that meld in Jane's captivation by Belton, a captivity/seduction that mirrors that of colonial America by the power of the British forces. Belton at one point proclaims to Jane that he has come "under the banners of General Burgoyne to conquer your country and you" (50), explicitly conflating the young woman with America. The threat of that possession and power become clear once Belton, disguised as an Indian, meets Jane at a private rendezvous and attempts to rape her. Although Jane escapes that attack, she is swiftly reseduced by the vision "of the splendor that prevailed at the Court of England . . . and the differences that separate the rich from the poor" and remains as a result "eager to have Belton as a husband, to become a woman of society" (49). Even when the unfortunate Emilia Fairlove, disguised as a soldier in a failed effort to reunite with her lover, Belton, tells Jane her own story of seduction and abandonment by this "son of a baronet" (55), Jane insists on leaving her patriotic father to marry her Tory lover.

Much of Jane's misguidance is attributable to her Irish servant Betsy, an exiled criminal "who had lived for a time among the Indians" (44) and who encourages and assists Belton's enterprise in order to acquire material goods from him. As a result of the self-interested advice she receives from this bad replacement mother, Jane is taken captive, killed, and scalped by Indians on her way to Burgoyne's camp, despite the efforts of the Indian chief Kiashuta to protect and defend her life. When Belton, informed of Jane's death, refuses to commit suicide for her, Kiashuta does. In the 1784 novel it is British nobility more than Indian perfidy that threatens American freedom, and it is the Indian rather than the Royalist who dies in noble protest over the loss of that freedom.

In the same way that the almost ubiquitous mother of earlier captivity narratives is curiously absent from the Manheim one, Jane McCrea's is eliminated from this version of the story. In earlier versions, Mrs. McCrea is either abducted with her daughter while they discussed her wedding plans or dead long before these events occur. In Hilliard's novel, there is absolutely no mention of a mother. Wheeler Case's poem about the incident likewise represents a father grieving for "my *Jenny* roll'd in blood I see / Whom I caress'd and dandled on my knee!" (Dodd 38) but makes no reference to a mother. That absent mother is, in fact, a significant feature in postrevolutionary American novels of sentiment and captivity, and that absence might be taken as a mark of America's attempt to negotiate its national autonomy in the wake of the loss of its "mother country." In fact, the only times the word *mother* appears in *Miss McCrea* are in the phrase "mother country," used for the first time in the father's plea to Jane "to renounce the mother country forever" by refusing to "marry anyone who desires to live as a subject of the king" (40–41). Jane's uncontrollable longing for the mother country that Belton represents might well be a function of the absence of her own mother from this novel, and that longing seems symptomatic of a suddenly and newly independent America only officially separated from Britain the year before this novel was published.

By this date the power relation between America and its mother country, exemplified by the fate of Jane McCrea, has altered significantly since Jane's death was first reported in 1777, and under those circumstances it is hardly surprising that a 1784 novel alters the details of the story. Americans no longer needed to be incited to arms in defense of their threatened freedom, but they did perhaps need to be warned against mourning for the loss of British wealth and protection. In other words, the object of consensus in the public sphere was no longer rebellion against Britain but the construction of a stable national community and a coherent national identity. Jane McCrea's death in this novel is less an event that demands the public's justifiable revenge, as it did in 1777, than an example that should inspire the public's virtuous reformation.[12] Stories of female captivity served a crucial role in constructing a sentimental narrative of American national identity that retained the conviction of national power within the assertion of national virtue.

The difficulties attendant on American independence are, significantly, articulated in *Miss McCrea* through the problem of female independence. In the absence of a mother the colonial daughter must be capable, in effect, of governing herself. Indeed, what has perhaps changed most in this later version of the story is the female captive's implied capacity for active resistance to captivity through the practice of self-government. By suggesting that Jane McCrea, by refusing to heed the rational advice of others, is at least in part responsible for her seduction, Hilliard's novel constructs her as alternately the passive victim and the guilty agent of her own misfortunes. This characterization marks a shift from earlier versions of this story, which stressed the heroine's absolute powerlessness and thus her absolute unaccountability. Revisions in the understanding of human agency by contemporary Americans were characterized by precisely such a dialectic between passivity and activity, between behavior that was necessitated by external events out of an individual's control and behavior that was autonomous or self-determined. Jay Fliegelman's fascinating reading of Jefferson places his Declaration of Independence in the context of this crisis, which claimed the unfettered freedom of individual will at the same time that a belief in external determinism provided individuals with an escape route from the accountability such a free will inevitably saddled them with. *Miss McCrea* does contain a conservative critique of female independence and expresses male fears of women's potential resistance to American republicanism, as June Namias has argued (141). But the novel also suggests that female autonomy be independently regulated through the practice of appropriate forms of conduct. Active self-government and passive patriarchal obedience alternately vie as effective correctives to the example of Jane McCrea.

Sentimental novels reproduced the dilemma of agency and responsibility, not only in their heroines' trials of virtue but in their readers' responses of sympathy. Such novels were equally concerned with how to practice female virtue and with how to inspire their readers to practice such virtue. *Miss McCrea* offers itself as a cautionary tale "for innocent young girls who fear the consequences of" (27) love and claims to transmit that warning through a sympathetic emotional identification between the reader and the heroine. The original publisher's preface insists that this novel "offers the reader a description of emotions that he himself has felt" (19) and like all novels therefore necessitates that "[w]e think and act with characters who are often imaginary" and who experience "sentiments similar to our own" (19). This novel's lesson of virtue is imparted through the operation of sympathy, but this method of education would seem to be as potentially ambivalent as its content, for the publisher claims that in the experience of reading a novel "[w]e hurry to the end without being able to interrupt ourselves, like a lover who does not prolong his bliss by slackening the signs of his ardor but hastens to consummate it" (19). In this description the reader reproduces the behavior of the imperial British villain rather than avoiding the behavior of his colonial American victim. Clearly, the lesson one learns from this novel depends on which character's sentiments one identifies with, for the response of sympathy is as capable as Jane McCrea's virtue was of going astray.

Representation and Renewable Virtue

Published several years after Hilliard's novel but set during the years of the Revolutionary War, Susanna Rowson's *Charlotte Temple* tells the story of a heroine whose virtue is tempted in England and surrendered in the process of crossing the Atlantic ocean. But what separates this novel from other tales of seduction and abandonment is that its heroine, once in the American colonies, recovers her virtue or, rather, reveals that despite her seduction her virtue was never lost. This revision is central to the novel's feminist project, a project similar to the one Mary Wollstonecraft would engage in her *Vindication of the Rights of Women:* the attempt to shift the conception of female virtue away from its equation with sexual purity and, by doing so, to empower women with a form of self-government. Both of these texts traveled westward across the Atlantic much as Rowson's heroine did; they were published in America shortly after appearing in England.[13] But the redefinition of virtue that both Rowson and Wollstonecraft pursue might be placed in the more dialectical context of transatlantic exchanges, which included the transmission eastward of the reformulation of virtue imagined by the newly self-governing American republic. In fact, if *Charlotte Temple* experienced such extraordinary popularity in America, to the extent that it is now consistently classified and taught as an American novel, it may well be because its notions of virtue resonated with those underlying the Constitution of the United States.

Cathy N. Davidson has suggested that Rowson's novel reflects the problematic aftermath of the revolution and the attendant anxieties of independence, to the extent that "the pathos of Charlotte's fall could easily be read as an allegory of changing political and social conditions in early America" (Introduction xi).[14] Davidson does not consider the further possibility, however, that this novel not only reflects the tensions that divided the new republic but articulates an emergent identity for the new nation based on a reconception of virtue. In the process of embodying and transmitting this new form of republican virtue, Rowson's captive and sentimental heroine also constructs a new notion of female power whose practice and limitations suggest those adopted by the government of the American republic.

Like *Miss McCrea*, *Charlotte Temple* offers itself as a cautionary tale whose truth is only necessarily veiled by fiction. Charlotte, like Jane McCrea, is seduced by a glamorous British soldier with "beauty of person, elegance of manner, and an easy method of paying compliments" (28)—the very qualities Wollstonecraft would repeatedly warn her female readers against. Montraville's abduction of Charlotte to America when he leaves to fight in the Revolutionary War is the culmination of a plot largely masterminded—as Jane McCrea's was by her servant Betsy—by Mademoiselle La Rue, the morally questionable assistant at Charlotte's school. La Rue serves, too, as a kind of poor replacement mother to Charlotte, especially once they both leave England for America.[15] Charlotte's mother may not be absent, as Jane's was, but Mrs. Temple's role in the novel is structurally subordinate to those of both Mr. Temple and La Rue. Despite her shadowy presence, however, it is separation from and guilt toward her mother that causes Charlotte the greatest anxiety in America: "[C]ould I but once more see my dear, blessed mother, hear her pronounce my pardon, and bless me before I died; but alas! I shall never see her more; she has blotted the ungrateful Charlotte from her remembrance" (78). To the very end, Charlotte remains this distraught daughter; even after she has given birth to her own illegitimate daughter, she continues in her illness and delusion to be tormented by the image of her mother: "Oh could you see the horrid sight which I now behold—there—there stands my dear mother, her poor bosom bleeding at every vein, her gentle, affectionate heart torn in a thousand pieces, and all for the loss of a ruined, ungrateful child. Save me—save me—from her frown" (111).

Here the allegorical parallel Davidson points to is strikingly clear: the daughter, like the colony, is confronted with the acute anxiety of maternal separation and the terror of radical independence. It is as though the daughter's traumatic guilt even prevents her from recognizing her own parenthood, for "she was not conscious of being a mother, nor took the least notice of her child except to ask whose it was, and why it was not carried to its parents" (111). Only at the very end of the novel, just before Mr. Temple arrives to be sentimentally reunited with his daughter moments before her death, does Charlotte acknowledge her own motherhood. The errors that lead to Charlotte's tragic death are ones her readers are instructed to avoid through the development of a more empowering form of independence.

Susanna Rowson addresses her novel to the figuratively motherless "many daughters of Misfortune who, deprived of natural friends, or spoilt by a mistaken education, are thrown on an unfeeling world without the least power to defend themselves from the snares not only of the other sex, but from the more dangerous arts of the profligate of their own" (5). Like Wollstonecraft's *Vindication,* Rowson's novel proposes to offer such daughters a form of power that would allow them to defend or rule themselves and thus to avoid the fate of Charlotte Temple. But this education is also necessary and important because women represent "that sex whose morals and conduct have so powerful an influence on mankind in general" (6). Virtue is the defining term of that education and of the power it imparts, but virtue in *Charlotte Temple* is not simply the female chastity threatened by the British rapist and defended or revenged by the colonies, as it is in the Jane McCrea narrative. Cathy N. Davidson has suggested elsewhere that *Charlotte Temple* reveals a postrevolutionary sense of betrayal "by the liberal and republican ideal that posited a correlation beween merit (in a woman, read 'virtue') and reward" ("Ideology" 314).

And yet out of such a sentimental imbalance between merit and reward or between Charlotte's essential goodness and her unhappy fate emerges a critical redefinition of virtue—one that this novel shares not only with Wollstonecraft's contemporary feminist text but with the contemporary American theory of political representation. Charlotte Temple, a traditionally unvirtuous heroine who has been seduced by a soldier and abandoned by him in a state of poverty and illegitimate pregnancy, emerges as an examplar of virtue. Her virtue is not Thomas Paine's irrecoverable sexual purity but a virtue to which "many an unfortunate female, who has once strayed into the thorny paths of vice, would gladly *return*" (74; emphasis added). Wollstonecraft similarly argues against that "grand source of female depravity" that insists on "the impossibility of regaining respectability by a *return* to virtue" (242; emphasis added). Charlotte Temple's virtue is, in fact, republican virtue—not in its classical form but as it was reconceived by postrevolutionary American federalists. Central to this reconception is the assumption that political virtue, like Charlotte's sexual virtue, is renewable; it cannot be lost because one might always recover it. Moreover, the modes of power associated with such virtue are not active so much as they are potential, transferable, and mediate. These revisions imagined virtue in significantly different ways from its classical formulation.

J. G. A. Pocock explains that classical virtue "consisted in a particular being's regard for the common good, and was contingent upon his association with other particular beings who regarded the same good through different eyes." Such virtue is practiced in the active relations between individuals who markedly differ from one another in status or character. If, as Gordon Wood has argued, the end of the Revolutionary War provoked a crisis in the practice of virtue and the location of power in the new republic, it was because America had no such "theory of qualitative and moral differentiation between individuals"; it not only lacked a hereditary aristocracy but had failed to produce a natural one (Pocock, *Machiavellian Moment* 520). As a result, there was no way to ensure virtue or to resist corruption within the classical paradigm. That paradigm—whose antithesis between corruption and virtue, as explained above, functioned in the rhetoric of the revolution—was replaced after the war with one of multiple representation.

As Ruth Bloch notes, political representatives were seen to practice a far more self-interested notion of virtue than the selfless virtue of classical republicanism. Meanwhile, the virtue practiced by citizens became aligned with social institutions outside the realm of the state, such as the church, the school, and the family. However, the public's practice of political virtue also crossed the border designated by the public sphere between the state and civil society, although when it did, it was reformulated in ways that contradicted its once defining characteristics of activity and independence. In fact, the political model of representation appeared to promote dependence and to exclude autonomous action, since "[t]he choice of a representative was a surrender, a transfer to another of one's plenitude of power and one's *persona* if not one's individuality" (Pocock, *Machiavellian Moment* 518). Therefore, the people's virtue and the power that virtue wielded were conceived of less in active than in passive or potential terms, just as the power exercised by their representatives was not an autonomous agency but one that operated only by mediation and transfer. The threat to virtue that this surrender of direct action posed was abated in part by the institutionalization of periodic elections, which aimed to prevent or dispose of corruption by allowing virtue to be *renewed*. In the event that virtue were abandoned, it could always be recovered.

Critiques of republican motherhood that insist on the irreconcilability of its passive articulation of female power with the republican ideal of active virtue overlook this significant shift, during the Federalist period, in how that ideal was practiced and regulated. For that reason such critiques miss the theoretical compatibility that republican motherhood shares with the power relations imagined under a representative government. Opportunities for the practice of power by male citizens still remained, of course, inconsistent with those available to wives or mothers, just as the spheres in which such power operated were decisively separate and distinctly gendered. But if, as Linda Kerber suggests, "[m]otherhood was discussed almost as if it were a fourth branch of government" (*Women* 200), then to some extent it followed the same model of representation that the other three branches employed. Mothers practiced an indirect and mediated form of power that was more often called "influence," since they subtly transferred values and ideas to their children and husbands through the medium of education or suggestion. Children were, in this sense, the representatives of their mothers—far more than they were representatives of their fathers—because conduct and manners were transmitted through mothers. The future of virtue in the republic was believed, for this reason, to lie in the hands of its mothers, just as it was presumed also to lie in the hands of its voters. One might even go so far as to say that the political invisibility women suffered from under the condition of coverture—which among other things assumed them to be publicly represented by their husbands—resembles the state of passive dependence in which the republic left its constituents. The only recourse available to unhappy wives was divorce, which allowed them the rather ambiguous freedom to choose, as it were, another representative, even if it never went so far as to allow them to represent themselves.

The renewal of virtue through recurrent elections was not, however, the only corrective to the instability of virtue in the republic. If the active quality of virtue was abandoned, then its devotion to a common good was also replaced by a self-interest that was linked to the rise of commerce and that brought with it inevitable corruption. In the model Pocock outlines, the stability and autonomy that guaranteed virtue were associated with landed property, but that stability became endangered by the unpredictability and dependence fostered by commercial relations of exchange. During the eighteenth century, property increasingly shifted from the fixed form of land to the more imaginary and unstable ones of money and credit, a transformation that was reflected as well in social relations. Pocock explains that, as a result,

> the foundations of personality themselves appeared imaginary or at best consensual: the individual could exist, even in his own sight, only at the fluctuating value imposed upon him by his fellows, and these evaluations, though constant and public, were too irrationally performed to be seen as acts of political decision or virtue. (*Machiavellian Moment* 464)

These problems of a fluctuating and deceptive virtue are central to Rowson's *Charlotte Temple*. It is precisely the problem of how to recognize authentic virtue in a world of unpredictability and interdependence, where deception could so easily mask corruption as virtue, that leads its heroine into such difficulties. Fliegelman, following Ann Douglas, suggests that Rowson's novel ultimately demands the "public legibility" of individuals so that their interior selves are absolutely visible and readable in their faces (*Declaring Independence* 129–30).[16] But Rowson faults those characters who misrepresent themselves publicly no more strenuously than she faults those characters who fail to recognize such misrepresentation for what it is. Colonel Crayton, for example, who marries the deceptive La Rue, "became a dupe to the artifice of others" because he "was easy and unsuspicious himself" (58). The novel's corrective to this dilemma is not just a call for self-evidence but an insistence that individuals practice an educated discernment, that they become, in a sense, better readers. Rowson repeatedly assesses this skill in her characters and constantly monitors it in her audience.

In *Charlotte Temple* a good reader is one who, like Mrs. Beauchamp—the novel's exemplary figure of benevolence—is willing to counteract public opinion when it does not accord with her own feelings. She therefore braves "the fear of derision" and "the scoffs of the world" (74) by offering sympathy and kindness to the shunned Charlotte. Beauchamp's gesture reveals "that the heart that is truly virtuous is ever inclined to pity and forgive the errors of its fellow-creatures" (75), and her exemplary behavior is a model for her readers to follow. Rowson monitors the reader's response to the narrative by continually interrupting the progress of the plot to address the reader. The effect of these frequent imaginary dialogues is to identify virtue in the reader through sentimental response and to ensure that the reader's heart, like Mrs. Beauchamp's, is "inclined to pity and forgive the errors" of the unfortunate Charlotte Temple. Therefore, Rowson claims, if the reader's "heart is rendered impenetrable by unbounded prosperity, or a continuance in vice, I expect not my tale to please, nay, I even expect it will be thrown by with disgust." Rowson virtually gives her readers instructions, for she promises that by the end of the novel "the tear of compassion shall fall for the fate of Charlotte, while the name of La Rue shall be detested and despised. For Charlotte, the soul melts with sympathy; for La Rue, it feels nothing but horror and contempt" (99). The aim of such constant monitoring is precisely the education of her readers, whatever their gender; the reader is to become the benevolent and virtuous Mrs. Beauchamp and to avoid becoming the unfeeling Mademoiselle La Rue.

Rowson attempts to manufacture consent among her readers for a revised opinion of female virtue through the manipulation of sympathy, much as Revere's engraving of the Boston Massacre relied on emotional response to generate consensus for the war. While sympathy has the effect, in the case of Mrs. Beauchamp, of sacrificing one's own self-interest for the benefit of another, it paradoxically proceeds out of self-interest, for Rowson warns her readers that

> when we reflect how many errors we are ourselves subject to, how many secret faults lie hid in the recesses of our hearts, which we should blush to have brought into open day (and yet those faults require the lenity and pity of a benevolent judge, or awful would be our prospect of futurity) I say, my dear Madam, when we consider this, we surely may pity the faults of others. (67–68)

Commercial exchange was intimately linked during the late eighteenth century with interdependent relations of sympathy (Pocock, *Virtue* 49, 147). By the same logic Rowson uses with her readers, however, the corrupting force of commerce could be transformed into virtue not by suppressing but by exploiting self-interest. Thus, James Madison argues in *The Federalist* (no. 51) that the possibility of abuse of power by any one of the branches of government was regulated by "giving to those who administer each department the necessary constitutional means and personal motives to resist encroachments of the others. . . . Ambition must be made to counteract ambition. The interest of the man must be connected with the constitutional rights of the place" (321–22). As Adam Smith likewise had argued, the danger of self-interest would be, paradoxically, controlled by self-interest.

The form of virtue ideally transmitted through the process of reading this novel is one that reputedly gives to women the "power to defend themselves" that Rowson's preface claims they so often lack. It is in this crucial sense that the portrayal of the captive and captivated heroine of the sentimental novel has, by 1791, altered—from the powerless negativity of the threatened American virgin exemplified by Jane McCrea to the embodiment of a positive power that is exercised through a reformulated republican virtue and evidenced in sympathy. This shift, I have argued, is intimately linked with the American republic's effort to reconstruct its own relation to and practice of power in the aftermath of a revolutionary rhetoric that had characterized power as the antithesis of American liberty. The developing cultural emphasis on the republican mother at the end of the eighteenth century stems not simply from the clichéd association of women with virtue, as Mary Beth Norton has suggested (243) but from the rhetorical association of women—particularly of *captive* women—with national power, throughout and beyond the revolutionary era. Female virtue may have been redefined in potentially emancipating ways in conjunction with new forms of republican government, but whatever power such virtue allowed women nevertheless remained confined, held captive, within the maternal role and the sphere of the home. Circulating beyond that sphere results in tragedy for the misguided Charlotte Temple, and the enlightened republican woman of Mary Wollstonecraft's *Vindication* is described, at the end, as a mother.

Coverture and Covert Agency

In his study of the ideology of the American Revolution, Bernard Bailyn locates in the revolutionary trope of colonial enslavement a potent source for the later discourse of abolitionism. An internal critique of American emancipatory ideology is spawned, in this sense, by what amounts to a kind of rhetorical excess in its language that escapes efforts at containment. Critics generally argue virtually the opposite, however, for the future of feminist critique after the American Revolution; they suggest that any rhetorical surplus that might have spoken to the interests of feminism was quickly recuperated after the war and contained by the mythology of the republican mother. Linda Kerber, for example, claims that the republican mother was simply a vicarious and limited way for women to engage in politics through the sphere of the home ("Republican Mother" 219), and Betsy Erkkila has only slightly more optimistically argued that postrevolutionary women could quietly and subversively manipulate republican ideals into potentially critical tools. The public sphere of rioting female mobs and political societies of women, these critics note, disappears for good after the revolution into the private sphere of domesticity and the legal condition of coverture.

I have suggested that the formulation of a mediating and passive female power within the theory of republican motherhood was, in fact, not as inconsistent with the republican ideals of the Federalist period as these critics claim. There exists a certain conceptual compatibility between the transferential and mediate operation of "female influence" and the limitations that a multirepresentational government placed on the practice of power by both citizens and public officeholders. This is neither to elide the fact that both citizenship and political representation were unavailable to women nor to deny the decidedly ambiguous effects of republican motherhood on women's material lives. But if the trope of enslavement returned in a new emancipatory form in the antislavery movement, then the trope of female captivity generated as well a potentially resistant surplus that might propel a feminist critique of republican motherhood. Despite the contemporary emphasis on motherhood, the republican rhetoric of female virtue was not always confined to the domestic sphere, and in some cases this very rhetoric elaborated a fantasy of female escape from the private sphere that held women captive.

The Female Review, a novel written and published in 1797 by Herman

Mann, reveals this latent feminist potential in the ambiguous republican concept of virtue, and it does so by returning to the years of the revolution itself. Mann's novel tells the story of Deborah Sampson, a young woman who, disguised as a man, fought as a soldier in the Revolutionary War. Like both *Miss McCrea* and *Charlotte Temple, The Female Review* claims to simply expand and render more entertaining a true story. That story aims "to extol *virtue*" (41) both within its plot and, vicariously, in its readers, since it is one of the functions of novels, Mann claims, to "irresistibly gain our assent to virtue" (42). Deborah Sampson is this novel's eminent example of American virtue and liberty, and Mann urges his readers to applaud her heroism and to promote those heroic principles as a display to the rest of the world of America's growing national importance and power. The extent to which the concept of female virtue had strayed from its association with sexual purity and toward an explicit association with national power is markedly evident in *The Female Review*. Despite Herman Mann's insistence that the kind of virtuous power his Revolutionary War soldier-heroine exhibits is no longer necessary and should be transferred into the domestic sphere, Sampson's own story and example contain a transgressive excess that utterly evades any such containment.

Like so many of her contemporary novelistic heroines, Deborah Sampson is virtually, though not literally, motherless. Because her mother was no longer able to support the family after her father's death, Deborah is bound in service at an early age to the Thomas family, on whose farm she lives and works. The place of the absent mother in this novel is filled not by the usual immoral and seductive surrogate but by the American nation itself. Sampson is first introduced with the claim that "Columbia has given her birth" (37) and that it is Columbia who is "her common parent" (38). The separation anxiety—either from a mother or from the mother country—that is so evident in other postrevolutionary heroines is missing here; instead it is Deborah's mother who, later in the novel, feels remorse at her daughter's unexplained disappearance. The contrite mother almost resembles the one Oxenbridge Thacher optimistically imagined in his prerevolutionary pamphlet, except that nowhere in this novel is the maternal linked to Great Britain as it was for Thacher; instead, America itself is that mother. Deborah's own mother, who had once desired that her daughter marry a man she did not find appealing, never appears in the novel, and the only time Sampson contacts her mother is by a letter in which she strategically disguises her military actions as domestic chores.

The extraordinary and unprecedented emphasis on motherhood in America that began during this period and increased to a cult by the early nineteenth century must be seen as more than just an effort to constrain the politicization of women after the war and more than simply a traditional association between virtue, however defined, and women. The plots of these popular American novels reveal that the cultural construction of nationhood in early America was deeply linked with this representation of the maternal. Therefore, the contemporary importance of female education was precisely that it was through women, particularly mothers, that this American national identity was transmitted. But it was also transmitted through novels that offered examples of national virtue at the same time that they served as alternative modes of female education. Although Deborah's domestic duties on the Thomas farm necessitated that she end her own official education prematurely, her later actions are offered as a new kind of education that can serve as "a singular paradigm for many" who seek "improvement in knowledge and virtue" (58). In fact, Deborah Sampson explains that "her design . . . was the acquisition of knowledge without the loss of reputation" (115).

Just after her education comes to an unfortunate close, Sampson learns that the British troops have arrived and "that it was the Acts of the British Parliament to raise a revenue, without her consent, that gave rise to these cruel and unjust measures" (76). This pronoun slippage that makes America's consent sound like Deborah Sampson's consent is simply the first mark in this novel of the sustained intertwining of American liberty with female liberty. In the letter Sampson writes to her mother, for example, she apologizes for this "transgression" of concealing her whereabouts but claims that "[t]he motive is truly important" and insists that no events have led to the "prostitution of that *virtue,* which I have always been taught to preserve and revere" (163). That motive, of course, is to render America an "*independent* nation" (164), but that independence is closely tied to Deborah Sampson's own. Shortly after hearing of the British soldiers' rape of colonial women, Sampson has a vision of a bloody serpent emerging from the ocean and approaching her bed "before I had time to dress . . . and [which] seemed to swallow me whole" (82). In response, she bludgeons this seductive symbol of British violence to death and subsequently decides to join the Revolutionary army as a soldier. Her act of physical violence, even if it is simply an imagined one, is nevertheless a far cry from the murdered and powerless Jane McCrea or the virtuous but pathetic Charlotte Temple. Virtue in *The Female Review* is not only moral and intellectual power but a decisively physical form of agency.

It is never entirely clear, however, what Sampson's real motive is for becoming a soldier, despite her patriotic concern over the potential "abolition of our *Independence* . . . by which, we not only mean to be *free,* but to gain us the possession of *Liberty* in its truest sense and greatest magnitude." For the author insists that her patriotic concern "and her propensities for an acquaintance with the geography of her country, were, alternately, severe in her mind" (109). These two overlapping motives inextricably bind female with American independence in this novel. Deborah's wanderlust and desire to see the American country clearly exceed the limits of "the female sphere of action, [which she considered] in many respects, too contracted" (110). Her disgruntlement with this involuntary female captivity, which is like "a prison" or a "too cloistered situation" (112), leads her to critique "the general *standard* of female education" (110), which is dictated by custom rather than reason. Deborah therefore determines to exercise that "*liberty* [which] gives us such ascendancy over old *habit*" (111), after asking herself a series of questions in which her own liberty and that of her country are clearly combined:

> Must I forever counteract inclination and stay within the compass of the smoke of my own chimney? Never tread on different soils; nor form an acquaintance with a greater circle of the human race? Stifle that spirit of *heroic patriotism*, which . . . may terminate in the greatest good to myself, and, in some degree, promote the CAUSE of my COUNTRY? (111–12)

Deborah Sampson participates in the revolution of her country by way of a "revolution of her sex" (224); cross-dressing not only allows her to take part in warfare against Britain but to indulge in a variety of transgressive acts that exceed, to say the least, the traditional female sphere. Sampson's story is virtually a catalog of fantastic male adventures: she resists the affections of a beautiful woman; goes on an expedition to Ohio, where she explores a cave; lives temporarily with the Indians; and kills an Indian in self-defense after he jealously attacks her for being a superior hunter. Later, still keeping her male disguise, she runs a farm and flirts with the neighborhood women. The act of freeing herself from captivity to an irrational custom and that of freeing her country from captivity to a British tyrant are simultaneous. Even after she is honorably discharged from the army as a result of wounds suggestively received in the head and the groin, Deborah Sampson retains her revolutionary disguise until 1784, when the war is finally over; whereupon she puts on female clothes, marries, and subsequently has children. One is tempted to suspect that the obscure publisher and author of this novel is practicing a similar disguise, since the name *Her/man Mann* contains its own subtle gender revolutions.[17]

While the degree of female transgression in Mann's *Female Review* is hardly typical of turn-of-the-century American novels, it does emphasize the fact that the postwar representation of American national virtue could overlap in critical ways with the representation of female power. Deborah Sampson's own story seriously complicates its author's final efforts to reconfine that power in the private sphere of the home, for her story is precisely one of escape from domestic captivity into an independence from gender and class restrictions and into the possibility of free circulation in a public sphere. What allows Sampson's transgressions to take place at all, however, is her male disguise. The possibility that she might be discovered, or uncovered, poses a continual threat to her political autonomy and physical agency. Although few women went so far as Sampson did to take part in the Revolutionary War, those who did actively participate politically in either the patriot or loyalist cause tended to do so in similarly covert roles. Women were often suspected of smuggling, of espionage, and of harboring Tory soldiers or sympathizers in their homes. In 1780, for example, thirty-two women were accused of being spies for or sympathizers with the British (Kerber, *Woman* 49–54). But precisely because the law of coverture declared a woman to have no independent will or political identity other than that represented by her husband, it could also have the effect of shielding women from suspicion of or legal censure for such acts (9). Because the *feme covert* was, as Kerber notes, "covered" by her husband, rendered invisible behind his civic and legal identity, she tended only to be tried for the most overt political crime of treason (121).[18] It was therefore possible that, under the cover of coverture itself, a woman might perform political acts and maintain a political identity of her own.

Court battles in the years after the war over the status of property rights and the payment of debts reflect these implicit contradictions between coverture and female independence. A South Carolina woman was ordered by the court to pay her creditors because her husband was unable to, thereby giving her the independent financial power as well as the legal status of a *feme sole*. The winning argument against her attempt to escape responsibility for her husband's debts contained an implicit critique of coverture by successfully claiming that she attempted "to screen herself from responsibility, under the plea of coverture" (149).[19] In Massachusetts, four years later, however, the court denied Anna Gordon Martin the right to retain a portion of her loyalist husband's confiscated property because, as *feme covert,* she was considered incapable of making a political decision incompatible with that of her spouse. The prosecuting attorney for Anna Martin made the radical argument for the wife's independent political identity outside coverture, although that argument ultimately failed to convince the court.[20]

Coverture essentially rendered women captive; therefore, any attempts women made to escape such captivity by practicing an autonomous political agency had to remain covert. Republican motherhood, with its passive and confined construction of female agency, was in this sense a compensatory solution that added some measure of female power to the republican quotient without disrupting the factor of coverture. But this equation sometimes refused to balance, producing fantastic and popular heroines like Deborah Sampson and Hannah Snell, another female soldier, whose images resembled that of Mary Rowlandson firing a gun in order to resist a different kind of captivity. Even the domesticated and privatized conception of virtue, as Ruth Bloch observes, "contained residues of [aggressive and active] *virtù*, which for a long time helped to legitimate women's activities in American public life" (58). What sanctions that transgressive behavior in *The Female Review* is the vehicle of an ambivalent national virtue. Mann attempts to translate the example of Sampson into the register of republican motherhood through the concept of virtue: "We have now seen the distinction of one *female*," he writes. "May it stimulate others to shine—in the way, that VIRTUE prescribes" (251). If this translation fails, it is because Sampson is able to practice virtue only by escaping from her confinement in the home.

This chapter has traced the discursive exchanges between gender and nation in the late eighteenth century, when the literary representation of the captive female shifted from a helpless figure of threatened sexual virtue to a powerful figure of national virtue, articulating a narrative of colonial dependence, separation from the mother country, and emergent American autonomy. The rhetorical figure of the captive female that at first served to produce consensus for the Revolutionary War continued to function as one of the sites in and through which the new republic articulated its own conception of national power. The dialectic between corruption and virtue and the effort to protect freedom from the force of power are evident not only in the prescriptions of the Constitution and in the debates about it but in sentimental novels of the early republican era, which often worry about this problem through the figure of a captive heroine. Like contemporary political rhetoric, these novels, both in their content and in their reception, consistently reveal the collapse between virtue and corruption even as they insistently assert an absolute distinction between them. They necessarily expose their readers to sometimes appealing examples of female power and agency in the very attempt to warn them against such behavior. Efforts by novelists like Susanna Rowson and Herman Mann to monitor and control readers' responses reveal anxieties about how their narratives of female virtue will be read and translated into action. But it is precisely in the transgressive surplus left over by the inevitable inequivalence of this readerly exchange that the escape from captivity and alternatives to republican motherhood could be imagined. In the subsequent decades national attention shifted from transcontinental colonial relations with Britain to internal colonial relations with Native Americans. As it did, the ambivalent trope of captivity, which provided a rhetoric in which sentimental nationalism cloaked the practice of imperialist aggression, continued to be a site through which U.S. national identity and power were figured.

Chapter 4

THE IMPERIALIST
AUDIENCE: NATIONALISM
AND SYMPATHY IN THE
FRONTIER ROMANCE

EAR THE END OF Ann Eliza Bleecker's 1793 *History of Maria Kittle,* three Englishwomen, all rendered homeless and husbandless after hostile encounters with the Indians, share their sentimental stories with a group of Frenchwomen in Montreal. The three women tell stories that would have been familiar ones to captivity narrative readers, and their stories produce the profusion of tears that increasingly characterized such narratives. Bleecker's text takes the form of a letter written by one of Kittle's female relations, which recounts the heroine's blissful domestic life, her husband's reluctant departure from their home just before it is subjected to an Indian raid, the conflagration of her home, the death of her children and relatives in the attack, and her subsequent grueling journey through the wilderness with her captors. After her redemption, Kittle repeats this tale to her companions in Montreal, who respond by indulging "some time spent in tears, and pleasing melancholy" (52). A Mrs. Bratt follows with a mournful account of her own captivity and the death of her beloved son at the hands of the Indians, an event that causes her violently to "execrate their whole race, and call for eternal vengeance to crush them to

atoms" (55). Moved by Bratt's story, the Frenchwoman Madame de R——
requests yet another narrative from Mrs. Willis since, as one Frenchwoman
claims, "my heart is now sweetly turned to melancholy. I love to indulge
these divine sensibilities, which your affecting histories are so capable of inspiring" (73). Mrs. Willis relates to her now captive audience her escape from
captivity by concealing herself and her children inside a hollow tree and her
subsequent pilgrimage across Canada to locate her husband, only to find
that he died in a Montreal jail before her arrival.

Stories such as Mrs. Willis's observe a sentimental temporality that resembles what Franco Moretti has labeled a "rhetoric of the too late," in which
the continual deferral of reunion, confession, or agnition produces a "moving" effect (160). Moretti offers as an example of this narrative strategy a
scene in which a young son and his father realize at last their mutual affection but only at the father's deathbed. What provokes tears at a scene such
as this is not just the moment of agnition but the fact that such agnition arrives too late, in the same way that Mrs. Willis arrives too late to be reunited
with her spouse. Maria Kittle's narrative, however, eventually recuperates
what is lost from the "too late" by finding resolution in what might be
called the more optimistic but equally moving rhetoric of "just in time."
For after the conclusion of these three "affecting histories," the narrative advances to the sudden arrival of Kittle's husband, who only moments before
had been informed that the wife he believed dead was in fact residing in a
nearby home, to be reunited with his wife. During this melodramatic moment "the spectators found themselves wonderfully affected—the tender
contagion ran from bosom to bosom—they wept aloud" (65).

This unexpected reunion, in which feeling circulates between French
and English subjects alike, recalls the passionate expression of political and
national sympathies encouraged by the women's accounts. Each of these
three narratives maligns the Indians in direct proportion to its praise of the
French for their recognizably European hospitality and benevolence. As
grief for the captive Englishwomen converts into anti-Indian rage, the
weeping audience becomes an incensed one. Madame de R—— marks this
transition and defines these national bonds when she fervently wishes "that
the brutal nations were extinct, for never—never can the united humanity
of *France* and *Britain* compensate for the horrid cruelties of their savage allies" (63). The military alliance of the French and Indians against the British
is redefined here as an opposition between European "humanity" and Indian "brutality." It is the impossibility of balancing this new national equation that leads the audience to fantasize Indian extinction. But the passive
construction and subjunctive tense of her (death) sentence—"that the brutal nations were extinct"—grammatically refuse to attribute any agency to
that accomplishment.

Bleecker's *History,* written in 1779 and published posthumously in 1793, is one of many late-eighteenth-century captivity narratives that emphasize less the detailed experience of captivity among the Indians than the dramatic sensations that the telling of that experience produces. The multiplication of feeling within these successive final scenes suggests what attracted readers to Bleecker's text and others like it: as Madame de R—— insists, spectatorial melancholy is an indulgence, a form of pleasure. Julie Ellison suggests in her analysis of Bleecker's poetry that these "affecting histories" are doubled histories, histories at once of the family and of the French and Indian wars. Ellison argues further that because the discourse of sensibility forges associations between emotion and historical events, eighteenth-century women writers turned to that discourse as a way of moving between the realm of feeling and that of history.[1] I would add that such writers turned more specifically to sentimental narratives of Indian captivity, which offered an ideal entry point into the discourse of history and into the project of nation-building.

The melancholy pleasure that Kittle's Montreal audience and, by the same token, Bleecker's American readers experience from these captivity histories serves as an affective model of what I shall call the imperialist audience, a model that takes on new proportions in the early nineteenth century, when attitudes toward the Indians emerged that would eventually find voice in Andrew Jackson's later rhetoric of Manifest Destiny and his policy of Indian removal. The Jeffersonian project of assimilation that had dominated national Indian policy began to falter in the early 1820s, when southern calls for active removal reached Congress (Horsman 194–95) and the hopeful tone of philanthropists began to shift toward doubt (Sheehan 145). Central to this Jacksonian-era model of the imperialist audience is the subtraction of agency from the historical stage, so that causal aggression looks like inevitability. In his analysis of imperialist fiction, Abdul R. JanMohamed points toward such a formulation when he suggests that "those who have fashioned the colonial world are themselves reduced to the role of passive spectators in a mystery not of their own making" (87). In other words, the imperialist nation imagines itself as an unaccountable audience, affected by a tragic disappearing act that no perceptible agent has effected. The convenient elision of agency allows mourning to be free of responsibility. But it is the accompanying sensation of pleasure that points toward the violence otherwise obscured by tears. Thus, Bleecker's sentimental prose and her narrative's tearful closure in marital reunion are strategies crucially intertwined with her text's imperialist and nationalist politics. In sentimental frontier romances of the later Jacksonian era, the narrative of Amerindian nations always observes the melancholic rhetoric of "too late," while the narrative of the American nation always claims the pleasurable rhetoric of "just in time."

The Frontier Romance and the Captivation of History

More than a century before the publication of Bleecker's *History of Maria Kittle,* captivity narratives maintained and relied on the interpenetration of family history and national history. Mary Rowlandson, for example, inscribes an often detailed record of the battles, conditions, and progress of King Philip's War as she records her personal history of maternal loss, spiritual trial, and domestic return. Furthermore, Rowlandson simultaneously tells these twinned histories and foretells, through the predictive logic of Puritan typology, a redemptive history of the Anglo-American project in New England. Likewise, many colonial American histories, including such massive tomes as Cotton Mather's *Magnalia Christi Americana* and pamphlet-size accounts of the Indian wars, integrate events of Indian captivity into their narratives. Repeatedly, the scene or event of Indian captivity metonymically links, with chains of feeling, the micropolitical realm of the family to the macropolitical representation of America's current state and future condition. From their outset, captivity narratives were intimately involved in the construction as well as the prediction of a "moving" history whose typical narrative logic of inevitability positioned their readers as an imperialist audience.

By the later eighteenth century and the publication of texts like Bleecker's *History,* when captivity narratives and sentimental novels were increasingly indistinguishable from one another, the historical and nationalist components of these texts remain central to their narrative design as well as to their continuingly popular cultural appeal. If the remarkable elasticity of the sentimental trope of captivity operated so effectively—and affectively—during the revolutionary era, it continued strategically to serve the construction of a deliberately national history in early-nineteenth-century novels. Louise Barnett significantly situates Bleecker's *History,* along with Susanna Rowson's 1798 *Reuben and Rachel,* at the beginning of the frontier romance genre so often identified with the later James Fenimore Cooper, his southern counterparts Robert Montgomery Bird and William Gilmore Simms, and their reputed European forebear, Sir Walter Scott. Although Barnett finally echoes a host of critics by dismissing these early women's texts, her chronology nonetheless suggests the possibility of an alternative—and surprisingly matriarchal—genealogy for the American frontier romance, which the effacement of such texts suppresses.[2] While Bleecker's and Rowson's texts owe their own significant debts to the captivity narrative tradition, they also crucially transform the captivity narrative, as Carroll Smith-Rosenberg argues, into a love story ("Subject Female" 500). That love story, however, is as much a national romance as it is a family one.

Two events of Indian captivity are contained in the elaborate family and national history that unfolds in Rowson's novel. Her central characters are the descendants of Columbia, the great-granddaughter of Christopher Columbus and the granddaughter of Orrabella, a Peruvian princess.[3] Four generations later in this genealogy, William Dudley marries Oberea, the daughter of a Narragansett Indian chief who captured him from his childhood home. Dudley, who counts among his paternal ancestors Lady Jane Grey, becomes the chief sachem of the tribe upon the death of his captor-turned-father-in-law. Not until Dudley's son marries into the Quaker Penn family and produces twin children do the Reuben and Rachel of Rowson's title appear. This complex and fantastic genealogy, which begins with the matriarchs Columbia and Orabella, takes up the entirety of the novel's first volume and weaves together into a single heritage European conquerors, Algonquin Indians, British royalty, Peruvian royalty, Protestants, and Quakers. It furthermore weds family history to American history through a series of romantic marriages.

Rowson's second volume traces the attempts of Reuben and Rachel on the one hand to reclaim their rightful inheritance of land on the Pennsylvania frontier and on the other each to marry and settle into domestic respectability. While Reuben's romance is deferred by his captivity among Amerindians, Rachel's is nearly destroyed by her captivity within European perceptions of proper womanhood. Separated by the Atlantic, the twins attempt parallel escapes: the pregnant Rachel circulates around the English countryside in an effort to escape social censure and poverty, while her disinherited brother awaits an opportunity to escape from his Indian captors. Like earlier captivity narratives and novels such as Richardson's *Pamela, Reuben and Rachel* positions the unity and reproduction of both family and nation after the escape from captivity.

Published four years after the American printing of *Charlotte Temple, Reuben and Rachel; or Tales of Old Times* marks Rowson's self-conscious adoption of a specifically American audience, as well as an explicit focus on the discipline of American history. In her preface, Rowson claims that she wrote this novel to interest and to educate young women not only in "history in general; but more especially the history of their native country" (iii). It may have been this early textbook-novel as much as Cooper's 1823 *Pioneers* that inspired a next generation of women novelists to write frontier romances, which combine a romantic marriage plot with events in the nation's historical past.[4] The majority of such novels, which flourished in America between the War of 1812 and the Civil War (Barnett 42), typically begin with familial disruption by historical events of conflict with native Amerindians and end with familial reunion. Two frontier romances of the 1820s, Harriet V. Cheney's *A Peep at the Pilgrims in Sixteen Hundred Thirty-Six. A Tale of Olden Times* (1824) and Catharine Maria Sedgwick's *Hope Leslie; Or, Early Times in the Massachusetts* (1827), echo not only the subtitle of Rowson's earlier work but also its complex dynamics of romance and history, of the family and the nation. In both novels, a romance narrative of deferred marital union coincides with an imperialist narrative of Amerindian dispossession. The narrative movement of erotic deferral seduces the reader into a sympathy that obscures the violence of racial displacement.[5] The attendant sensations of pleasure and melancholy are repeatedly organized and resolved around the scene of Indian captivity.

Surprisingly little attention has been paid to Cheney's book, despite the fact that Sedgwick's novel, which has received a great deal of critical attention in the past decade, depends, to some extent, on Cheney's earlier novel.[6] In fact, *Hope Leslie* offers a critical response to and revision of the historical constructions and evasions of *A Peep at the Pilgrims,* whose author Sedgwick obliquely acknowledges in her book. The sentimental event of captivity is, in both texts, the site of historical construction and revision, as well as the scene that produces an imperialist audience who watch, with pleasurable melancholy, a violent spectacle that both is and is not of their own making.

The Historical Gaze in *A Peep at the Pilgrims*

Harriet Cheney's *A Peep at the Pilgrims* begins in 1636 with the arrival in Plymouth of the Englishman Edward Atherton, an Anglican who has left a distinguished military career behind after the death of his Anglican father and his Puritan mother. If his parents did not share the same religious identity, however, we learn that they did share similar histories of family disinheritance as well as a sense of "forbearance and liberality" that their only son inherits. In fact, it is the "unprejudiced" (1: 20) Atherton's refusal to meet Puritans on the battlefield that leads him to resign his military commission. He subsequently departs on a ship for the New World, watching "with his eyes fixed" (1: 26) the receding shores of the Old World. As soon as he lands on the shores of Plymouth, he hears and is immediately captivated by the disembodied voice of Miriam Grey, emerging from the open window of her home. Atherton attempts to get a look at the source of this voice, but because the inhabitants of the home are "screened from observation by a curtain" (1: 11), he fails. However, Atherton easily locates her at church service the next day, where—although her face is then hidden beneath a scarf and hood—he "scanned" with "diligence every article of her dress and every motion of her person" (1: 33). The intensity and fixity of Atherton's vision is matched only by its persistent failure to catch direct sight of its object, and this inaccessibility generates a longing that fuels the novel's romance plot.

But this initial romance is quickly thwarted by Miriam's orthodox Puritan father, who, quite in contrast to Atherton's own parental examples, will not tolerate his daughter's union with a non-Puritan. In an effort to dispel his romantic disappointment and recover from his thwarted hopes, Atherton leaves Plymouth for Boston. On his approach to the city, in a scene that echoes his departure from England, he gazes from a hilltop on the receding "seat of Indian empire" from which, he notes, the Indians "were still retreating before the advance of civilization, and resigning their territories to the white people" (2: 9). Atherton embarks on a new path of American empire when he joins John Underhill's Boston army in its excursion to defend the Connecticut settlements from attacks by the Pequot Indians. But what might seem at Atherton's departure from Plymouth the novel's abandonment of the romance plot for a historical one becomes instead a collision between them. Located at the site of that collision is the scene of captivity, a scene that, like Miriam's obscured face or the receding terrain of empire, seductively attracts as it retreats from the spectatorial gaze.

When Atherton departs and while her father is absent on a journey to England, the lovelorn but duty-bound Miriam decides to accompany her newly married cousin to her home on an outlying Connecticut farm. There, along with a young girl, Miriam is taken captive by the Pequots.[7] The collision of history with romance at the moment of captivity in Cheney's novel immediately becomes a collusion of interests as well, for the English military desire to defeat the Pequots becomes inseparable from Atherton's desire to protect Miriam and to rescue her from captivity in the wigwam of the Pequot chief Mononotto. Thus, Atherton ostensibly joins the Boston militia less to further unseat Indian empire than to gain empire over Miriam Grey. The romance narrative, here as elsewhere in the novel, displaces history precisely at the moment of agency, of political accountability. On the one hand, the romance narrative and its movement toward domestic union depends on the unfolding of historical events, for it is only by virtue of the Pequot War and Miriam's captivity that the distance between the separated lovers begins to close. At the same time, however, the romance plot is forever eclipsing the historical narrative, distracting the imperialist audience away from the scene of violence. Romance alternately depends on and obscures history as both narratives move toward a teleological end of marital/national union. Captivity serves here not only as the structural and affective link between these two narratives but as the visual and narrative aperture for Cheney's descent into national history.

The captive Miriam, confined in the wigwam of the Pequot sachem Mononotto, is supervised by the sachem's wife Mioma and their daughter, who remains unnamed in the novel. Cheney characterizes the relationship between captive and captor in affectionate, almost maternal terms, for we learn that it was only Mioma's wild grief and pleading to her husband for the lives of the two girls that has kept them alive thus far. Though it is not typical, such affection between Anglo captives and their Indian mistresses is not uncommon in many captivity narratives.[8] In nearly every other respect, however, the portrayal of this captivity departs significantly from the experience documented in earlier narratives. In comparison to long, arduous journeys through the wilderness, Miriam's captivity is a stationary, domestic one. Her greatest trial is not the destruction of her home and family, not the violent deaths of family and friends, not even the rigorous test of physical endurance in a trek through the forest. Rather, Miriam's greatest trial is one of boredom, a boredom generated by her immobile confinement within the wigwam among the Indian women.

Significantly, she does not escape from captivity but is rescued from it. Such rescue is typically legitimated in revolutionary-era narratives by the Indian and British threat of rape, but that threat is often subsumed in the frontier romance by the desire for marital, and American, union. If earlier captivity narratives like Rowlandson's or Bleecker's generally end with the promise of a reunited family, frontier romances end with the prospect of a future family. This shift coincides with a historical shift in national sensibility. What once were seen as external threats to the colonies, such as the Indians, are now seen as internal threats to the unity of the American republic. National stability in the 1820s appeared to depend on eliminating domestic regional, class, and racial factions.[9] This shift must also be seen, however, in the context of the nineteenth-century cult of domesticity, that "empire of the mother," for Miriam's captivity is virtually an Indian version of frontier domesticity. Cheney's strategy of immobilizing the experience of captivity effectively holds Miriam captive in a home not her own and at the site of racial and historical conflict. Although her fondness for her captors would seem to suggest the possibility of transcultural sympathy, her captivity and rescue in fact work to displace sympathy away from the Pequot Indians and the violent scene of their massacre.

Atherton's rescue of Miriam and her young co-captive is thwarted at the last minute, when his ship—captained by a "cowardly Dutchman" (2: 192) —pulls away from the shore and the Indians recapture the group on the shoreline. Mononotto later returns Miriam to the ship, to be exchanged for several Pequots held captive there; but when Miriam reaches the site where Atherton was captured and separated from her, she "covered her face to exclude every object from her view—for every object was associated with the most painful recollections" (2: 222). Miriam averts her gaze here in an attempt to repress memory, a gesture in contrast to earlier descriptions of Atherton's aggressive gaze. Together, however, these scenes point toward a tropology of the gaze that operates throughout the novel. One of the characteristics of Miriam's behavior—and much of her appeal to her several suitors—is her refusal either to bestow or receive gazes. After first hearing her voice through the window in Plymouth, Atherton spends much of the first part of the novel attempting to get a "peep" at Miriam. When he later rescues her from a boating accident, she thanks him full-faced only briefly, until she realizes her error and looks away. When she is brought onto the ship by Mononotto, she and the other redeemed female captive are sent below deck to a cabin, for "they were embarrassed by the gaze of curiosity" (2: 221). Even when Miriam is restored to the house of John Winthrop's son, she does not appear at dinner "from a natural aversion to encounter the gaze of strangers" (2: 234).

By contrast, one sign of Atherton's masculine bravery is his ability to withstand any gaze. While the two females are returned and exchanged, Atherton is retained as a captive by the Pequots, filling the space left void by Miriam's rescue. The violence of the captivity experience as it was represented in captivity narratives emerges only when Atherton takes Miriam's place. It is Atherton, not Miriam, who is bound to a stake, circled by a "horrid war-dance" (2: 224), subjected to torture, and "condemned to pass the night surrounded by his vindictive enemies, whose disfigured countenances glared upon him like demons" (2: 222). Yet unlike Miriam, Atherton is fully able to withstand and return these glares, just as he "sustained the haughty gaze of Mononotto with dignified composure" (2: 223).

This succession of gazes might be taken as instances that exemplify the novel's project as a whole. Cheney's title presents the text as a "peep" at Pilgrim life, suggesting a secretive and forbidden gaze into America's past, backward to an event that retroactively becomes an early monument to national history. Indeed, the audience's peep back nearly a century to "olden times" is, no less than the lovers' romantic gazes, characterized by the dynamics of captivation and foreclosure. If the audience's historical peep is the text's most overarching gaze, however, that gaze is conspicuously and deliberately averted from the novel's central historical event, the Pequot massacre. Cheney describes the English army's preparation for battle and their trying journey through the wilderness to the Pequot fortresses in careful detail, almost as though the physical mobility and suffering absent from Miriam's captivity are sympathetically transferred to the army. All the stereotypical trials of a captive's trek—physical weariness, hunger or an utter distaste for Indian food, passage over difficult terrain and through a hostile climate, laden with infants or provisions—are experienced by the troops: "The English endured excessive fatigue and suffering throughout the day; the weather was oppressively warm; they were almost destitute of suitable provisions, and obliged to travel through a pathless wilderness, encumbered with heavy arms and ammunition" (2: 246). The infant has been replaced by artillery, but this moving story of resistant mobility works as effectively for the English army as it did for English captives.

By the time the narrative reaches the battle itself, the romantic and historical narratives move inseparably toward their progressive ends. The event of captivity has made the reunion of Miriam and Atherton contingent on the English defeat of the Pequots; historical events have been seductively co-opted and justified by romantic desire. And yet when the narrative does reach the battle, it abruptly draws back, refusing to represent the scene by pleading—quite suddenly and rather illogically, given the novel's otherwise unhesitant depiction of historical events and figures—a refusal to tread into the discourse of history: "it is not our intention to invade the province of the historian, by entering into the details of this sanguinary conflict, from which the feelings of humanity recoil with horror. Suffice it to say, a complete victory was achieved by the conduct and intrepidity of the English" (2: 250). The horror that leads Cheney herself to shield her eyes here is reminiscent of Miriam's "covered . . . face" at the site of "the most painful recollections." This novel's effort to construct retroactively a historical memory for the American nation relies on an act of deliberate forgetting that is inscribed in its very center.[10] The imperialist audience is both attracted to and repelled by this unsightly yet significant symptom on the body of national history.

Despite Cheney's horrified refusal to gaze on what we might identify as the face of this historical scene of genocidal violence, she does go on to explain, in an agentless past tense, that

> the laurels of the conqueror were unhappily stained with the blood of the innocent and defenceless. In little more than an hour, a flourishing village of seventy wigwams was reduced to ashes, and upwards of six hundred Indians,—the aged, and the feeble infant, the warrior in his strength, and the mother with her helpless children, were destroyed by the sword, or perished in flames.
> The English had only two killed . . . . (2: 250–51)

The only grammatical agents of anti-Indian violence here are swords and flames, not English subjects, and even then such agency is further displaced into the passive voice. This unwatchable event is ambivalently presented as both a horror and as cause for national celebration. Cheney notes that "considering the weakness of the colonies . . . their success appears almost miraculous; and under the smiles of Heaven can only be attributed to the prompt and cheerful exercise of th[eir] intrepid valour" (2: 256). The tentative return to a providential Puritan mode of historiography here strategically invokes the agentless grammar of divine intervention. Mention of the subsequent swamp battle, in which most of the Pequots who survived the fire were either killed or taken captive, is concluded with the satisfied claim that "[t]his second victory was complete, and the brave and powerful tribe of Pequods was totally exterminated" (2: 256). This sentence literally pauses midway between "victory" and "extermination," not to link the two events but to shift from the register of pleasure to that of melancholy. The sentence, like Cheney's narrative, would seem to pose a contradiction between "the theoretical justification of exploitation and the barbarity of its actual practice" (JanMohamed 103). JanMohamed argues that imperialist fiction relies on a manichean opposition that subordinates before it disposes of the colonized other. Cheney's novel, however, relies equally on a sentimental discourse that does not justify barbarity by subordinating the other so much as it screens the very problems of justification and barbarity beneath the irresistible forces of passive inevitability. If Cheney and her audience can indulge in pleasurable melancholy, it is because the grammar as well as the gaze of her narrative effaces agents.

The contradictions and evasions that mark the representation of Anglo-Indian contact and conflict persist to the end of the novel, when Atherton exhibits a sudden and surprising sympathy toward the captured Indians—now described as "children of the forest"—who "are to be sent to Bermuda as slaves" (2: 267). Given his vehement role in their genocidal defeat only pages earlier, Atherton's response is unexpected even if it is supported by the sympathetic logic of his own captivity. Such contradictions call to mind narratives like Rowlandson's, but the tension between her typological representation of the Indians as agents of Satan and her "realistic" representation of humane Indians remains unresolved in a way that Cheney's contradictions do not. Cheney's text, which indulges both in racial stereotype and transracial sympathy, relies on the sentimental affect of imperialist spectatorship, which not only accommodates but in fact requires both Atherton's violence and his pity. His passive response of "being moved" by Indian removal effaces active aggression, just as romantic desire effaces historical violence. It is this structure of imperialist affect that allows Cheney to appropriate the historical event of the Pequot massacre for nationalist purposes while remaining critical of its excesses; her novel struggles to build a national memory on an event whose details she would rather forget. Just as it had during the postrevolutionary era, the distracting mechanism of captivity launches a progressive and sentimental narrative of the American nation precisely by obscuring its violent and colonialist origins.

Pequots, Seminoles, and National Unity

To the 1824 readers of Cheney's novel, the fate of the Pequot Indians may well have resonated as a potential future for the American nation itself. An example of a failed and fragmented nation, the Pequots and their vanished empire function as a kind of negative model and critical warning to the troubled American union. The Pequot War, in fact, would no doubt have recalled Andrew Jackson's Seminole War, resolved just years before amid much dispute over the legislative as well as the moral legitimacy of his actions. And Jackson's political discourse, no less than frontier romance novels, linked nation and family through affective rhetoric. If Atherton's role in the Pequot massacre is emotionally justified by his desire to protect Miriam, Jackson's rationale for the Seminole War was likewise a defense of American women and children from Indian violence, a logic that, according to Michael Paul Rogin, "freed Jackson to urge American attacks on Indian women and children" (196) and to burn Seminole villages. Only once the war ended, Rogin notes, did Jackson begin to refer to the Indians as his children, a discursive and sentimental shift reminiscent of the victorious Atherton's sudden reference to the Pequots as "children of the forest." Jackson's Indian Removal Act of 1830 simply brought together into policy proremoval attitudes that had been circulating for decades in the South and West and conceptions of Indian extinction and European expansion that were gaining ground with proponents of scientific racialism.[11] When agents of Indian removal used Atherton's phrase "children of the forest," they were repeating the sentimental strategies as well as the language of frontier romances.

The elision and displacement of racial violence in *A Peep at the Pilgrims* also resemble the political strategies of Jackson's presidential campaigns in 1824 and again in 1828, in which he distracted public attention away from his reputation for aggressive violence by promoting the platform of national defense and focusing on affectively unifying the nation "around its past" (Rogin 255). Jackson's later presidency consistently screened the brutality of Indian removal beneath a romance narrative of national progress in which events like the Seminole wars became deliberately historicized. Jacksonian speeches literally are frontier romances that, no less than Bleecker's or Cheney's texts, sentimentally construct the American public as an imperialist audience. In 1830, for example, Jackson reflected to Congress on the "happy consummation" of his Indian policies before he went on mournfully to claim that "[t]o follow to the tomb the last of his race and to tread on the graves of extinct nations excite melancholy reflections" (qtd. in Dimock 35). The latter sentence strategically chooses an immobile infinitive over an active subject, a grammar that marks contemporary frontier romances as well as captivity narratives.

A later congressional speech on Indian removal delivered by President Jackson is inserted into an enlarged 1836 edition of Massy Harbison's captivity narrative, and that speech is followed by the editor's self-justifying conclusion that "[h]appy will it be for [the Indians], if by these means, they are saved from destruction" (Winter 71). Only by so effacing grammatical and historical agency is Jackson, like Cheney, able to watch retroactively without also taking part in the simultaneous dramas of Indian "disappearance" and U.S. expansion. The logic of causality requires an agent, but the grammar of empire escapes the dictates of causality by transforming actors into their own audience. In the bizarre theater of empire, the stage is a kind of mirror in which the audience, moved to delightful tears, watches a blurred reflection of its own passivity.

At the moment that both Jackson's and Atherton's Indians are infantilized, the wars that eliminated them begin curiously to age, to recede into a distant historical past. The Seminole wars take on, in the Jacksonian rhetoric of the too late, an aura of "pastness" that at once removes them from present accountability and gives them the value of antiquity. In a similar maneuver, Cheney looks back from a sudden distance at the Pequot War as a historical instance of great "native" importance that, because it "strikingly exhibits the firmness and courage of the early settlers of New England" (2: 256), is able to counter the felt superiority of European conquests. What Cheney sees as the excessive and inappropriate violence of the Pequot massacre is displaced by the event of captivity, and the subsequent injustice of selling Indians as slaves is attributed not to the marauding soldiers but to the intolerance of the Puritan leader, Henry Vane, and his administration. Captain Miles Standish, Atherton's cousin, claims at the end of the novel that "[t]he rulers alone, have the responsibility . . . and they have been so long exercised in the school of persecution, that it would seem they have grown enamored of its discipline" (2: 268). While it is unclear who specifically Standish means by "the rulers," it is quite clear that it includes neither Underhill and his army nor John Winthrop, who at that time was dispossessed of direct political power.

This critique of an antiquated Puritan intolerance is typical of American historical romances, whose plots generally end with a victory over intolerance in an example of progressive history. Thus, Mr. Grey's resistance to Atherton's Anglicanism and his refusal of the young man's request for Miriam's hand in marriage are of course recanted and exchanged for consent in the novel's conclusion, as a direct result of Atherton's rescue of Miriam from Indian captivity. The promise of this marriage, moreover, crystalizes Atherton's decision to remain in America, where we learn that he eventually becomes "a sincere, but liberal Puritan" (2: 275). Atherton is the figure in the book who, from the beginning, has stood between one history—his own genealogical roots in the long past of England—and another, the promise of a progressive future in America, whose subsequent empire he helps set into motion. It is not only Atherton's prospective marriage to Miriam that leads him to remain in America, since they could conceivably return to England; it is as much the fact that, by taking part in this first distinctly "native" victory, in which the name of the Pequots "became extinct, and their country alienated to the English" (2: 256), Edward Atherton's romance has become America's history. Atherton decides to forsake England and his genealogical past in order to move forward into American history.

Contemporary captivity narratives like Harbison's deploy a similar sentiment when they insist that captives endured "the scalping-knife and tomahawk, that they might turn the barren land into a fruitful field" (iv). In an early-nineteenth-century America increasingly defined by Jacksonian aggression toward Indians, Native American opposition to Anglo-American hegemony disrupts and destroys Indian unity but produces American unity along the way. Cheney asserts that Atherton would go on, in his future liberalism, to correct the errors of the persecuting Puritan rulers. Yet the event that facilitated such correction, the Pequot War, paradoxically generates its own errors, errors that bear an uncanny resemblance to those Cheney's progressive history aims to correct. Her novel's historical gaze, distracted as it may be by the erotics of captivity, nevertheless cannot help but partially expose the extraordinary violence of Indian war and removal. Although Cheney suppresses any overt critique in the interest of constructing a national romance based on this historical event, a critical and resistant surplus to that history is inscribed within her text. That surplus becomes accessible by a reentry into history through the events of Indian captivity.

Historical Revisionism in *Hope Leslie*

By complicating Cheney's representation of the Pequot War and of Anglo-Indian race relations, Catharine Maria Sedgwick's *Hope Leslie* problematizes the founding of Jacksonian national romance on events of anti-Indian violence. *Hope Leslie* was published three years after *A Peep at the Pilgrims,* and Sedgwick acknowledges the earlier novel when she marks the absence of particular historical events in her own text with a reference to Cheney's. In the chapter that offers a recollection of the 1636 Pequot massacre, Sedgwick notes that "the anecdote of the two English girls, who were captured at Wethersfield, and protected and restored to their friends by the wife of Mononotto, has already been illustrated by a sister labourer" (56).[12] The "sister labourer" is, of course, Cheney, the center of whose novel is the unseen scene of that massacre. The narrative of *Hope Leslie* begins after the Pequot War has ended, and Sedgwick's acknowledgment of Cheney's novel suggests that she deliberately begins where Cheney leaves off in an effort to add to, rather than repeat, the historical narrative begun by her "sister labourer." But the project of *Hope Leslie* is historical restitution as much as it is historical continuation, for Sedgwick repeatedly turns her narrative gaze toward those scenes from which Cheney's gaze was averted. Whenever Sedgwick's novel works to restore agents to the stage of empire, it places her audience in an affective quandary.

Hope Leslie begins not with the sole arrival of an English son to the colonial settlements but with several arrival narratives. Years earlier, we learn, the orphaned Puritan William Fletcher left England, where he was forbidden to marry his Anglican cousin and true love, Alice Fletcher. When the narrative begins, Alice's two daughters, Hope and Faith Leslie, arrive from England after the death of their parents to become the wards of Fletcher's New World family. This transatlantic arrival is paired, however, with the arrival of Mononotto's daughter, who was captured during the Pequot War, at the Fletchers' frontier home. If orphaned English subjects repeatedly arrive in the colonies to found family and national histories, the Indian subject arrives at this site severed from her family and her now fragmented tribe in order to work as a servant for the Fletchers. At the end of *A Peep at the Pilgrims,* when the captured Indians are exiled into slavery, John Winthrop assures Atherton that Mononotto's daughter, who assisted in the attempt to rescue Miriam, would remain in safety. Sedgwick not only adopts Cheney's character at this moment of narrative abandonment, but she furthermore names the daughter of Mononotto and Mioma (or Monoca, as Sedgwick calls her) Magawisca. This initial substitution signals Sedgwick's recognition of the successive acts of oblivion that make Cheney's construction of a national memory possible, even if it is only to replace oblivion with another fiction. By giving Magawisca a central and heroic role as well as a historical memory and voice, *Hope Leslie* counters even as it repeats the romantic history constructed in *A Peep at the Pilgrims.*

Sedgwick, like Cheney, employs events of captivity as a point of entry into the realm of history, and it is through the affective manipulation of such events that she embarks on the task of historical revision. There are a multitude of successive captivities in *Hope Leslie,* beginning with the captivity of Alice Fletcher by her Anglican and royalist father in order to prevent her from marrying her Puritan cousin and emigrating with him to the colonies. This early error and failed romance will ultimately be remedied by the prospective marriage of Fletcher's son Everell and his adopted daughter Hope Leslie. As Alice's early captivity suggests, this novel does not always situate the scene of captivity at the site of racial conflict and cross-cultural contact.[13] My focus here, however, is on those specifically transcultural captivities through which Sedgwick constructs a counter-memory to Cheney's national narrative, captivities that work to reopen the text of history in order to expose the details from which Cheney's peep is averted.

Magawisca's arrival as a servant in a Puritan home is an example of the kind of English philanthropy and protection promised by Winthrop at the end of *A Peep at the Pilgrims*. But Sedgwick's portrayal of Magawisca's condition reverses the operation of sympathy by insisting that her audience watch not their own benevolent reflection on the historical stage but Indian actors. When Magawisca is invited into the Fletcher cabin, she appears as an alien cultural curiosity, bare-armed, with feathers and "rings of polished bone" in her hair, dressed in garments painted "with rude hieroglyphics" and wearing beaded moccasins (23). Mrs. Fletcher responds with domestic displeasure at receiving an "Indian girl for household labor," and the hostile maid Jennet refers to her as "Tawney" and "savage." These subordinating gestures are undercut, however, by the displeasure and hostility of Magawisca, whose "eyes had turned on Jennet, flashing like a sun-bean through an opening cloud," and by Everell's sympathy toward the Indian's "natural feeling," which "touched the heart like a strain of sad music" (24–25). This first scene of contact moves toward a reversal of the positions of cultural dominance and subordinance that it initially seems to reproduce.

When Magawisca finally speaks in her own language, to an Indian messenger who arrives with the scalp of the Pequot chief Sassacus, she overturns her employers' benevolent claim that she has been fortunately rescued from "the midst of a savage people" to be "set in a christian family" (24). Far from being rescued, Magawisca asserts that she has been taken captive. This exchange is conducted in her own language, thereby alienating her captors, who "could not understand" and who look on "with some anxiety and displeasure" (26). Magawisca gives the Indian messenger her bracelet with instructions to take it to her father, Mononotto, and to "[t]ell him his children are servants in the house of his enemies" (26). In a racial reversal of the captivity narrative scenario, the Indian Magawisca is the figure enslaved by her military antagonists, the English. In fact, Magawisca's message and token is much like the one sent by Miriam and delivered by Mioma's daughter in *A Peep at the Pilgrims*. Atherton learns that Miriam is held captive only after Mononotto's daughter offers him a note scratched into bark. Just as this handwriting sample, a token of Miriam's identity, encourages Atherton to rescue her, so does Magawisca's bracelet result in Mononotto's attack on the Fletcher home to rescue his captive children and to avenge the family and tribal deaths suffered in the Pequot War. But here the Indian is a direct agent of her own escape rather than an indirect agent for the rescue of an

English captive. Just as Miriam wants both to escape and to ensure that her former captors be treated kindly, Magawisca is torn between loyalty to her father and tribe and a desire to protect her Puritan captors from harm.

The chapter in which Sedgwick expressly refers to Cheney contains two accounts of the Pequot War that figures so centrally, if only by its descriptive absence, in *A Peep at the Pilgrims*. The first is given to Everell Fletcher by the servant Digby, whose participation in that war authorizes his claim that "these Pequods were famed above all the Indian tribes for their cunning" (43). Though Digby's narrative is reputedly engrossing as well as authentic, Sedgwick does not directly represent it in her text. She notes only that

> [t]he subject of the Pequod war once started, Digby and Everell were in no danger of sleeping at their post. Digby loved, as well as another man, and particularly those who have had brief military experience, to fight his battles over again; and Everell was at an age to listen with delight to tales of adventure and danger. They thus wore away the time. (43)

What might seem simply a vague repetition of Cheney's averted gaze, however, becomes supplanted by a second narrative of that same event, offered to Everell this time by Magawisca.

While secretly awaiting the appearance of Mononotto outside the Fletcher home, Magawisca informs Everell that "[i]t was such a night as this—so bright and still, when your English came upon our quiet homes" (46). Her subsequent narrative of the English attack on the Pequot village, presented in a direct discourse and detail lacking in Digby's account, forces a crisis in the political and national sympathies generated by texts like Cheney's or Ann Eliza Bleecker's. In Magawisca's account the beleaguered army is an Indian one, and the helpless captives are a family of Indians. Sedgwick argues in her preface for a revision in the representation of "[t]he Indians of North America," whose "own historians and poets, if they had such, would as naturally, and with more justice, have extolled their high-souled courage and patriotism" (6). Magawisca serves as Sedgwick's imagined Indian historian, who exposes what is obscured in Cheney's representation of the Pequot War. Her Indian history employs the affective logic of Cheney's text to reassess Cheney's historical narrative. In Magawisca's version emotion links not family to the American nation but Indian family to American family. This alternative history, furthermore, turns Jacksonian rhetoric against Jacksonian policies by paralyzing nationalist sympathies at a crucial moment, just before the expected arrival of Mononotto "determined on the rescue of his children" (57). Magawisca's vivid memory reconstructs the violent destruction "in our own homes, [of] hundreds of our tribe" and her vision of "[t]he bodies of our people . . . strewn about the smouldering ruin" (49). Because this image precedes the subsequent Indian attack on the Fletcher homestead, the reader's response of sentiment is prevented from converting into anti-Indian rage. Such rage instead belongs to the defeated Pequots.

The friendship that Cheney proclaims was bred between the English and the Indians following the Pequot War is contested by Sedgwick's portrayal of the shamed and enraged Mononotto, intent on "the infliction of some signal deed of vengeance, by which he hoped to revive the spirit of the natives, and reinstate himself as head of his broken and dispersed people" (57). The outcome of this violent attack poses the problem of emotional undecidability: Mrs. Fletcher and her infant son are killed, and the child Faith Leslie and Everell are taken captive, while Magawisca and her brother Oneco escape from captivity to be reunited with their father. Mononotto announces his victory when, disposing of his son's English dress, he claims that "[t]hus perish every mark of the captivity of my children" (65). Affect extends here in two irreconcilable directions; the sensations of pleasure and melancholy are not wedded but divorced, not reconciled but disturbingly at odds. This conflict of feeling remains unresolved because it is unaccompanied by the imperialist temporality of the inevitable; here Indian disappearance is replaced by Indian resistance. The Amerindian narrative briefly adopts the rhetoric of "just in time," while the Anglo-American one succumbs, momentarily, to the grief of the "too late." Only at the end of her novel— when, in the wake of Magawisca's departure, Everell and Hope plan their wedding—will Sedgwick reverse these rhetorics.

Despite her ultimate escape from physical captivity, however, Magawisca remains in another sense captive within the discursive constraints of Sedgwick's Anglo-American textuality. Indeed, despite "her Indian garb" (22), Magawisca appears in many ways as a Europeanized and thus familiarized Indian woman. Like Mary Jemison, held captive in her own enormously popular captivity narrative (published, significantly, the same year as Cheney's novel), Magawisca is a sentimental heroine who speaks English and feels sympathy for her white captors. But for its racial reversal, her narrative of Indian "courage and patriotism" otherwise resembles Cheney's account of English "intrepidity." Magawisca's history, too, is a seductive romance that disrupts the discourse that contains her only by employing that discourse against itself. In other words, Magawisca's sentimental history of the Pequot War repeats Cheney's but with a critical difference. This strategic repetition resembles the mimicry that Homi Bhabha associates with the colonized and that articulates cultural difference from a site located "between the lines and as such both against the rules and within them" (*Location* 89). When these scenes from *Hope Leslie* are read against Harriet Cheney's earlier novel, the particular effects of such mimicry on historical representation become evident. Sedgwick's text does not replace American with Pequot history so much as it radically questions the construction of authoritative history altogether.

Everell responds to Magawisca's counter-memory of the Pequot War by realizing that he had previously only heard its details "in the language of the enemies and conquerors of the Pequods; and from Magawisca's lips they took a new form and hue" (53). "This new version of an old story" seems to Everell not simply a different version but the right one, for it "remind[s] him of the man and the lion in the fable. But here it was not merely changing sculptors to give the advantage to one or the other of the artist's subjects; but it was putting the chisel into the hands of truth, and giving it to whom it belonged" (53). When sculptor and sculpture, author and text, exchange roles, historical representation is exposed as a fiction, as an undecidable romance. This undecidability mirrors the affective conflict inspired in Sedgwick's audience. Sympathy can no longer translate into justifiable rage, and the temporality of history abruptly stalls. Everell's national sympathies —formed by official accounts of Indian wars by William Bradford and William Hubbard—suddenly shift their identification, for his "imagination, touched by the wand of feeling, presented a very different picture of these defenceless families, pent in the recesses of their native forests, and there exterminated, not by superior natural forces, but by the adventitious circumstances of arms, skill, and knowledge" (54). Everell restores causality to the agentless grammar of Jacksonian manifest destiny. When, on the following page, Sedgwick quotes descriptions of the Pequots and of their massacre from Bradford's *Of Plymouth Plantation* and Hubbard's *A Narrative of the Indian Wars in New England,* she invites a critical rereading of these texts by exposing the textuality and thus the undecidability of any narrative of American history.[14]

The discursive constraints on Sedgwick's project of historical restoration are perhaps most evident in her portrayal of the novel's central captivity episode. Like the unseen Pequot battle at the center of *A Peep at the Pilgrims,* Faith Leslie's captivity remains unwitnessed. This aperture into Amerindian history and culture simply will not open, much like the historical captivity on which it is based—the 1704 capture of Eunice Williams, daughter of the Puritan minister John Williams and a distant relation to Sedgwick herself.[15] Hope Leslie's desperate and continuing attempt to meet with her sister—who, seven years after her capture, has abandoned any English identity, married Magawisca's brother Oneco, converted to Catholicism, and speaks only in tribal dialect—recalls the attempts of Eunice Williams's family to encourage her to leave the Indians and return to her biological family and culture. On first sight of her "lost sister," at a meeting reluctantly arranged by Magawisca,

> Hope uttered a scream of joy; but when, at a second glance, she saw her in
> her savage attire, fondly leaning on Oneco's shoulder, her heart died within
> her . . . and instead of obeying the first impulse, and springing forward to
> clasp her in her arms, she retreated . . . , averted her eyes, and pressed her
> hands on her heart, as if she would have bound down her rebel feelings. (227)

Hope's averted eyes here mirror Sedgwick's narrative gaze and recall Cheney's repetition in *A Peep at the Pilgrims* of Miriam's refusal to look. Sedgwick attempts to represent neither Faith's "captivity" nor her life among the
Indians. But whereas Cheney and Miriam refuse to look, Sedgwick and
Hope finally look, only to see nothing.

After refusing to discard her Indian clothes for English ones, Faith speaks
to her sister through Magawisca, who translates her responses into English.
When Hope asks, in the language of captivity narratives, whether her sister
"remembers the day when the wild Indians sprung upon the family at
Bethel, like wolves upon a fold of lambs? . . . when Mrs. Fletcher and her innocent little ones were murdered, and she stolen away?" Magawisca translates Faith's reply that "she remembers it well, for then it was Oneco saved
her life" (229). Repeatedly, Hope's sentimental appeals to family history fail
to reach her sister; although they translate linguistically, they fail to translate affectively. What to Hope seems Faith's inability to remember is for her
Indianized sister simply the memory of a different family history, like Magawisca's alternative memory of national history. Faith Leslie remains unrep-
resented because unrepresentable, her history a silent void that escapes both
her sister's pleas and Sedgwick's Anglo-American discourse.

Debt, Loss, and Magawisca's Missing Limb

Faith Leslie, as a subject and a body reinscribed by cultural exchange, is rendered unreadable. Her captivity is a border crossing without return, and
this transgression inverts the cultural logic of escape and revenge. When the
national enemy appears as a family, in Magawisca's moving Pequot War
narrative as in Faith's refusal to leave home, imperialist affect stumbles over
its own contradiction. Pleasure and melancholy will not be reconciled. Everell's captivity, unlike Faith's, ends with his return. But he returns to family
and nation with a surplus, a cross-cultural debt that crucially alters the affective economy of captivity. In her earlier narrative to Everell, Magawisca recounts her eldest brother Samoset's heroic defense of the Pequot fort before
being taken prisoner by the English. When Samoset refused to exchange
military information for his life, his captors "with one sabre-stroke . . . severed his head from his body" (51). This familial and national loss through

FIG 6.   *The HORRORS of WAR a VISION Or a Scene in the Tragedy of K: Rich[ar]d: 3,*
December 1, 1782. Courtesy of the Library of Congress.

death operates emotionally, as it does in Bleecker's *History of Maria Kittle,*
to justify revenge. Thus, Mononotto, obeying the "natural justice" (92) of
the Indians, determines to sacrifice Everell Fletcher in exchange for the
death of his son Samoset.

Magawisca's appeals to her father and her attempts to facilitate Everell's
escape all fail to alter the course of this justice. In a final attempt to save the
life of her friend, who was taken captive in the effort to allow her own escape from captivity, Magawisca actively intervenes to repay her debt. When
Mononotto raises his hatchet over Everell's head in the act of retributive
violence, "Magawisca, springing from the precipitous side of the rock,
screamed—'Forbear!' and interposed her arm. It was too late. The blow
was levelled—force and direction given—the stroke aimed at Everell's neck,
severed his defender's arm, and left him unharmed. The lopped quivering
member dropped over the precipice" (93). Magawisca's action settles her
account, but the weight of her severed arm falling over the cliff measures the
debt incurred by the escaped Everell. Loss can only be mourned or revenged,
possibilities combined in the response of melancholy pleasure. Debt, on the

FIG 7.   "JOIN or DIE," *Boston Gazette,* May 21, 1754. Courtesy of the Massachusetts Historical Society.

other hand, can only be repaid or forgiven and inspires the responses of anxiety and accountability. When the white captive's escape is accomplished by the sacrificial agency of an Indian woman rather than the agency of a male Anglo-American patriot, the Jacksonian imperialist equation between Anglo-Americans and Amerindians is radically reconfigured.

The image of Magawisca's severed body, quite literally "rent by a divided duty" (80), recalls popular revolutionary-era iconography representing Britain and America. The colonies were frequently portrayed as an Indian woman, and one 1782 print represents her with a knife thrust into her bloody and "mangled breast," prevented by British imperial violence from feeding her children (fig. 6). The colonies also frequently appeared as a snake hewn into pieces, and this image's imperative caption, "Join or Die," called for the national healing of this amputated body (fig. 7). Another revolutionary image of imperial Britain, circulated in prints by Benjamin Franklin and others, is that of a woman whose colonial limbs have been severed from her body (figs. 8 and 9).[16] The image of Magawisca's amputated arm fuses and revises these earlier images to suggest the threat of Anglo-American imperialism to the coherence of the Amerindian body.

But this iconography of divided bodies also illustrates the effect of imperial violence on the fluid movement of commerce. This corporeal imagery of national or communal integrity appears as early as 1630, in John Win-

FIG 8.   *BRITTANNIA MUTILATED or the Horrid (but true) Picture of Great Britain. when Depriv'd of her Limbs. BY HER ENEMIES,* November 29, 1774. Courtesy of The Library Company of Philadelphia.

throp's corporate metaphor of the body. In "A Model of Christian Charity," Winthrop portrays the successful Company of Massachusetts Bay in New England as a body whose various parts are in a relation characterized by "the sweete Sympathie of affeccions" (290) and are held together by "the sinewes and other ligaments" (292) of Christian love. This sympathetic relation, however, is also an economic one, for this body is further kept intact by the divinely sanctioned (im)balance between rich and poor. Debt, Winthrop insists, must be repaid according to the laws of commerce and can be forgiven only when the debtor has "noething to pay thee"; "[e]very seaventh yeare," he suggests, "the Creditor was to quitt that which hee lent to his brother *if* hee were poore" (286; emphasis added). Debt becomes loss by the rule of mercy but only after the rules of commerce and repayment fail. By insisting that both affection and wealth circulate together to keep the communal corpus whole, Winthrop's metaphor underwrites the colony's stability with an economic sentimentalism that precludes the possibility of perpetual debt.

The narrative of *Hope Leslie* resumes precisely seven years after Magaw-

FIG 9.   Benjamin Franklin, *MAGNA Britannia: her Colonies REDUC'D*, circa 1766. Courtesy of The Library Company of Philadelphia.

isca sacrifices her arm to save Everell's head. Everell returns from an education in England with a sensibility of this debt, for when Digby suggests that he once believed Everell "as good as mated with Magawisca," the youth replies that "you do me honour, by implying that I rightly estimated that noble creature; and before she had done the heroic deed, to which I *owe* my life" (214; emphasis added). When, during Hope Leslie's later meeting with her sister Faith, Magawisca is unexpectedly taken captive and—suspected of mobilizing Indian retaliation against the English—imprisoned in the Boston jail, the opportunity for repayment is staged. Magawisca pleads at her trial for release from an indefinite imprisonment by arguing, through the use of the rhetoric of the captivity narrative, that such a fate is a "death more slow and terrible than your most suffering captive ever endured from Indian fires and knives." In a final appeal, Magawisca discards her mantle to expose "[h]er mutilated person" before recalling Governor Winthrop's own debt to her family: "to my dying mother, thou didst promise, kindness to her children" (293).

Torn between the anti-Indian sentiments of national defense on the one hand and transnational sympathy on the other, Magawisca's audience encounters an emotional undecidability similar to the one generated by Mononotto's attack/rescue at the Fletcher home. By unveiling what cannot be seen, the unrestorable missing limb, Magawisca produces "in the breasts of a great majority of the audience, a strange contrariety of opinion and feelings" (294). Once again, this conflicted response will not resolve into the imperialist sensation of a pleasurable melancholy. The audience does not gaze passively on an obscured scene of cultural loss, on the inevitability of Indian disappearance; instead, they are paralyzed by their unobscured vision of cultural debt, of an unrepayable Indian dispossession.

Andrew Jackson built his early legal career on a complete dismissal of John Winthrop's rule of mercy, on the refusal to convert debt to loss regardless of the debtor's poverty or the duration of the debt. As a lawyer, Jackson represented creditors in suits against those refusing to pay their debts. He spent years repaying debts of his own, an experience that, according to Rogin, fostered Jackson's lifelong hostility to debt evaders. Rogin suggests that only Jackson's obsession with debt equaled his obsession with Indian removal. The two were, of course, inseparable, since Indian lands were repeatedly possessed in exchange for unrepaid tribal debts. The laws of the market, which were characterized by that same passive inevitability ascribed to Indian "extinction," both justified Indian dispossession and, by eliminating agency, erased the guilt of accountability. By so displacing aggression by inevitability, Rogin notes, Jackson became a "passive spectator of a policy he had actively advocated" (213).[17] If Indian monetary debts to the whites were paid by land, forcing Indian removal, the white moral debt for the Indian deaths caused by removal was sometimes repaid with money. But more often, Indian deaths were represented not as a debt but as a spectacle of loss, which the imperial nation could only watch and mourn. The discourse of manifest destiny allowed the imperialist audience to paradoxically forgive their own debt.

Hope Leslie reflects the anxiety of debt current in Jacksonian America but radically counters Jacksonian absolution by refusing to balance and therefore to close this cultural account. Before Magawisca's trial, Hope Leslie reminds Governor Winthrop of "the many obligations of the English to the family of Mononotto—a debt, that has been but ill paid." When Winthrop replies, "That debt, I think was cancelled by the dreadful massacre at Bethel," Hope invokes Magawisca's absent arm when she recalls "another debt that never has been—that scarce can be cancelled" (274). Everell's attempts at both "open intercession" and "clandestine effort" on his creditor's behalf fail miserably. When he attempts to remove the bars to Magawisca's cell, early detection causes him to flee. When he tries to persuade Esther Downing, to whom he is engaged, to assist him, her "religious duty" prevents her from interfering without "scripture warrant" (278). It is finally through the agency of Hope Leslie that Magawisca is rescued and Everell redeemed from his own botched rescue attempts. In fact, as Carol J. Singley notes, it is always "through the wits and magnanimity of the female characters" that the errors of patriarchal leaders are corrected in this novel (116). It is as though Sedgwick takes advantage of Jackson's own imperialist refusal of historical agency to deed agency to Anglo-American and Amerindian women.

Hope Leslie ends with Magawisca's departure in a canoe to the uncertain future of her family and tribe. After she "disappeared for ever from their sight" (334), Hope and Everell finally confess their love and move toward the union that corrects the intolerance of their parents' generation. In the end, this novel repeats the national romance that it elsewhere complicates and resists. But *Hope Leslie* finally closes not with the promise of this future marriage but with Esther Downing's spirited defense of her refusal to marry. Her example, writes Sedgwick, "illustrated a truth, which, if more generally received by her sex, might save a vast deal of misery: that marriage is not *essential* to the contentment, the dignity, or the happiness of woman" (349–50). This ending refuses the romance of marital union and, by implication, national union. In the frontier romance tradition these paired resolutions enable a national narrative to progress by suturing events of imperialist violence. Esther's resistance therefore upsets the affective logic on which the historical romance relies, and by doing so it recalls the empty scene of Faith Leslie's refusal to return and the void of Magawisca's unrepayable debt. Sedgwick ultimately leaves her audience captive in the affective predicament on whose resolution imperialist and nationalist sentiment relies.

Chapter 5

SYMPATHETIC AGENCY
AND COLONIZATION
IN *UNCLE TOM'S CABIN*

JAMES BALDWIN BEGINS "Autobiographical Notes," a piece specifically written to introduce the essays collected in *Notes of a Native Son*, with a description that moves from his early production of novel plots to his mother's constant production of children. "In those days," he writes, "my mother was given to the exasperating and mysterious habit of having babies. As they were born, I took them over with one hand and held a book with the other. . . . in this way I read *Uncle Tom's Cabin* and *A Tale of Two Cities* over and over and over again" (3). The image of Baldwin as a youthful and reluctant proxy mother voraciously consuming sentimental Victorian fiction takes on a confessional quality against the book's first essay, "Everybody's Protest Novel." Here Baldwin lodges an impassioned critique of *Uncle Tom's Cabin*, the presumably formative book that he once read "over and over and over again." He claims that the "virtuous rage" of its antislavery stance is based largely on the fear "of being hurled into the flames, of being caught in traffic with the devil" (17), and dependent on the rather self-satisfied argument that such practices are "perfectly horrible" (13). Furthermore, he notes, the novel opposes black as "the color of evil" to the goodness and whiteness of Christianity. When Baldwin dismisses *Uncle Tom's Cabin* as "a very bad novel" and rejects its "self-righteous, virtuous sentimentality" (14), his judgments are both aesthetic and political. His list of the novel's problems—its vigorous but utterly ineffective polemic against slavery, its portrayal of black forbearance and docility, its "medieval" Christian vision, and its manichean and colonialist binary logic—are precisely those he associates with sentimentality, which, for Baldwin, operates essentially as a pleasing mask that conceals violence, inhumanity, and fear.

Over forty years after "Everybody's Protest Novel," *Uncle Tom's Cabin* continues, perhaps more than ever before and perhaps more than any other novel, to be equated both aesthetically and politically with sentimentality; its literary and historical value seems increasingly to hinge on the political efficacy deeded to sympathy.[1] The final pages of the novel contain one of the touchstone passages for this debate, for Stowe's "Concluding Remarks" offer the "Christian men and women of the North" surprisingly passive and private strategies to combat the public evil of slavery: they can "feel right" and they can "pray" (624–25).[2] This solution to the national problem of slavery has led some critics to condemn, as Baldwin did, the failure of Stowe's sentimentality to translate into social change. Others have argued for the novel's political power by linking Stowe's proposal for reforms motivated by sympathetic Christian mothers with the goals and practices of nineteenth-century religious and feminist programs. At stake in this current debate has been not only the literary value but the feminist potential of domestic sentimental fiction, an issue that does not factor into James Baldwin's earlier discussion.

Yet the problem Baldwin directs our attention to—the representation of race within Stowe's sentimental discourse—has tended to recede from this more recent discussion.[3] Indeed, when Stowe's feminist defenders and detractors do converge, they generally agree on one point: that the novel's ambivalent *racial* politics, its simultaneous abolitionism and racism, can be accounted for by its ambivalent *sentimental* politics, by the limitations of antebellum domestic and religious ideology. Too often, however, this formulation serves to subordinate discussion of Stowe's representation of race, if not to excuse the demeaning depictions of Blacks to which Baldwin draws our attention. These depictions, of course, were already an issue for debate in nineteenth-century abolitionist circles, as Ann Douglas acknowledges when she notes that "Victorian abolitionists, white and black, sometimes hesitated to praise a book that urged a procolonization policy and apparently emphasized black docility" (Introduction 11). But Douglas, who has elsewhere argued that the sentimentalism of novels like *Uncle Tom's Cabin* reinforces and supports a consumer culture that impedes effective political change, goes on to claim here that "Stowe's religion protects her from racism," since her characterizations of passive and infantilized Blacks were consistent with antebellum Christian postures.[4]

Using Stowe's own Christianity as a shield, Douglas defends her against charges of racism but never addresses the related issue of colonization. In doing so, Douglas repeats Stowe's similar evasions. In a letter to Frederick Douglass, Stowe sought to address his criticism of her novel's appeal to the church and to African colonization. But while she defended the former at great length, she never got around to addressing the latter (Stepto 141). Jane Tompkins addresses neither race nor colonization in her vehement defense, in *Sensational Designs,* of the efficacy of Stowe's sentimental strategies. Directly challenging Ann Douglas's earlier critique, Tompkins argues that *Uncle Tom's Cabin* "functions both as a means of describing the social world and as a means of changing it. It not only . . . recommends a strategy for dealing with cultural conflict, but is itself an agent of that strategy, putting into practice the measures it prescribes" (135). By insisting that the novel works politically because its readers believed it would work, Tompkins, too, returns to Stowe's own sentimentalism to rescue her text. Tompkins cites Stowe's political conservatism only to argue that this "very conservatism—her reliance on established patterns of living and traditional beliefs—is precisely what gives her novel its revolutionary potential" (145). Although Tompkins's reference here is to conservative forms of domestic economy rather than to representations of race, her argument might apply and has been applied to the novel's other political agendas.

Gillian Brown, who extends and modifies Tompkins's feminist thesis, suggests that Stowe's procolonization stance is the logically necessary outcome of her proposed mode of domestic reform. Slavery in *Uncle Tom's Cabin,* Brown argues, disrupts the sentimental economy of the household by bringing the vagaries of the marketplace into the kitchen. Because Stowe associates blackness with the chaotic disorder of exchange, she must exile her free black characters at the novel's end to ensure the stability of the home (55–60). These feminist analyses all emphasize the Christian and domestic sentimentalism of *Uncle Tom's Cabin;* when they do address the novel's racialist and colonizationist elements, they inevitably account for them through the lenses of domestic ideology and sentimental discourse.

Its profoundly affective antislavery message and its immense popularity have raised *Uncle Tom's Cabin* to the status of *the* American abolitionist novel, despite the complicating exodus of the extended Harris family and Topsy to the colony of Liberia at the conclusion of the book. This ending, however, cannot be easily reconciled with abolitionism. By the 1850s the dominant abolitionist movement in America had, for two decades, been defining itself in opposition to the African colonization of freed slaves. William Lloyd Garrison, together with James Forten, took on the American Colonization Society (ACS) in Garrison's 1832 *Thoughts on African Colonization,* charging its supporters with racial prejudice, pecuniary self-interest, fear of insurrection, and the delay of immediate emancipation (10–15).[5] The novel's conclusion therefore compromises what would otherwise be its committed abolitionist message, and this compromise disturbed committed nineteenth-century abolitionists like Garrison and Douglass. Rather than treat its resolution as aberrant, as the unfortunate conclusion to an otherwise abolitionist novel, as generations of critics have, I propose to consider its colonizing gesture as central to *Uncle Tom's Cabin* and, moreover, a gesture compatible with its politics of sympathy.

The novel relies throughout on a profoundly colonizationist sensibility that is consistent with its representation of race and with Stowe's formulation of a political agency allied with maternal influence. To emphasize colonization in *Uncle Tom's Cabin* is not to deny, however, that the book urges emancipation as the only possible solution to slavery both as an immoral institution and as a national crisis. Indeed, for Stowe, the immorality of slavery is experienced nationally, as a sin whose commission is—and whose retribution will be—shared by the American nation as a whole. But while the novel argues for emancipation (a cause that, of course, was always part of the procolonization position as well), it also stumbles over the problem of incorporating the bodies of Blacks into the national body once liberation is effected. Its solution is not local incorporation but incorporation by annexation, by the voluntary exile of Blacks to Liberia, a site proposed to be at once a separate nation for Americans of African descent and a transatlantic extension of an American empire. Moreover, this solution looks and works very much like sympathy itself does, and both strategies involve a model of agency that presupposes and perpetuates a definitive and corporeally marked boundary between races. By resituating *Uncle Tom's Cabin* in this way, I aim to emphasize its participation in what Laura Wexler calls "the expansive, imperial project of sentimentalism" (15), a project flagged in James Baldwin's essay but overlooked by recent feminist debates on the novel.[6] This revision suggests as well that the novel's participation in nineteenth-century racial imperialism may determine the political limitations of its sentimentalism, as much as its sentimentalism might account for its problematic representation of race.

African colonization might have been a consistently Jacksonian solution to the problem of slavery, a version of Indian removal applied to African descendants in America. Both Indian removal and the colonization of ex-slaves were once proposals developed by Thomas Jefferson, who claims in *Notes on the State of Virginia* that after emancipation all former slaves should "be brought up, at the public expence, to tillage, arts or sciences, according to their geniusses, till the females should be eighteen, and the males twenty-one years of age, when they should be colonized to such place as the circumstances of the time should render most proper" (137–38). Had Andrew Jackson not been such a vociferous proslavery advocate and slaveowner,[7] he very well might have adopted the latter as well as the former of Jefferson's solutions to the problem of racial conflict in America. Jackson's ceaseless effort to expand American empire under the guise of manifest destiny remained continental, however, and the subjugation of Indians was a practice of what Michael Paul Rogin calls *"internal* imperialism" (167; emphasis added).

Many early advocates of the ACS argued that the transportation of freed slaves to Africa would enable the commercial expansion of a vaster, transatlantic American empire. American colonizationists, P. J. Staudenraus notes, applauded the ACS's policy of expansion in Liberia as "the first step in building an American empire" (157). Liberia's first colonial agent, Jehudi Ashmun, wrote to the secretary of the ACS, reminding him that "[y]ou have, Sir, founded an empire" (159). *Uncle Tom's Cabin* represents African colonization as an opportunity to export an infinitely more valuable American possession than grain or cotton; Stowe constructs Liberia as a prosthetic extension of a specifically Christian and maternal American empire, a child of sorts to the mother country.[8] The transportation of former slaves to Liberia positioned them as agents of such American values, much as the New York merchant Arthur Tappan planned to train and export young black men from America "to become *Commercial Agents*" in Africa (163). To this extent, when Abraham Lincoln later reputedly ascribed to Stowe an alarming and amusing degree of agency in initiating the Civil War, he was flagrantly misreading her best-known novel. The divisive violence and national upheaval of the Civil War was precisely what *Uncle Tom's Cabin* wanted most to avoid. It discouraged active resistance within the continental body of the nation by building and populating the Liberian imperial limb, which would at once separate Blacks from and tie them to America. Furthermore, autonomous human agency was a concept that apparently caused Stowe a great deal of personal discomfort and that she frankly disavowed when she claimed that God had written her novel. But it is the autonomous agency of Blacks that her novel works most deliberately to contain through its scheme of African colonization.

Captivity and Slavery

When Stowe published *A Key to Uncle Tom's Cabin* in 1853, she sought to support the authenticity of her depictions of slavery by offering factual examples "selected out of a mountain of materials" (*Key* v). Both the novel and its supporting documentation derive their affective power from a strategy Stowe claimed to borrow from the eighteenth-century's foremost man of feeling, Laurence Sterne. Sterne, she noted, "says that when he would realize the miseries of captivity, he had to turn his mind from the idea of hundreds of thousands languishing in dungeons, and bring before himself the picture of one poor, solitary captive pining in his cell" (*Key* 152).[9] In order to mobilize such emotional realization in her readers, Stowe encouraged them to sympathize with particular stories of oppressed and fugitive slaves. Critics generally acknowledge that, both in the *Cabin* and in the *Key,* she gathered some of this material from a growing body of slave narratives. It is also likely, however, that she turned to the earlier genre of the Indian captivity narrative as a source for her moving depictions of the abuses of slavery and for the affective logic of her antislavery argument.

Henry Bibb's slave narrative, for example, which Stowe is often suspected of borrowing from in her novel, includes an account of his enslavement among the Cherokee Indians.[10] Her character George Harris invokes the genre of the captivity narrative when he responds to a white acquaintance's suggestion that he submit to slavery rather than escape from it:

> I wonder, Mr. Wilson, if the Indians should come and take you a prisoner away from your wife and children, and want to keep you all your life hoeing corn for them, if you'd think it your duty to abide in the condition in which you were called. I rather think that you'd think the first stray horse you could find an indication of Providence—shouldn't you? (184)

George appeals here to Mr. Wilson's sympathy by comparing slavery to white captivity and by mobilizing the affective strategies of this earlier genre. Sentimental captivity narratives, like slave narratives, generate sympathy for their captive figures by emphasizing the disruption of the family, the destruction of maternal ties, the helplessness of physical torture, and the sometimes murderous violence of the captors.

But Indian captives were almost always white Euro-Americans, whose narratives legitimized not only their own active escapes but an active cultural retaliation against the demonized Indian tribes. The sympathetic identification of readers with captives, underwritten by national as well as racial likeness, motivated at the same time that it masked the retributive violence of Indian wars and Indian removal. Captivity narratives, as I have argued, consistently obscured even as they documented transcultural exchange. By emphasizing the impassibility of such borders and the necessity of maintaining and policing them, such narratives also sentimentally concealed the agency of white captives who transgressed that cultural boundary. If slavery was a form of captivity, it was one in which the racial roles of captive and captor were significantly reversed, and this reversal necessitated a reorientation of the relations and effects of sympathy.

One interesting example of this phenomenon occurs in the 1836 captivity narrative of Mary Godfrey, who hides with her four daughters in a swamp when she hears that the Seminoles and their allies, who are violently resisting the treaties that followed Jackson's victory against them, are approaching her home. While hiding, one of the "800 captured or runaway negroes from the South" (*Authentic Narrative* 4) who had joined the Seminole cause discovers them and "approached them with an uplifted axe, apparently intent on their destruction." But when Mary Godfrey points to her infant, "the negro dropped his axe, . . . appeared much affected, and broke silence by assuring Mrs. G. that she had nothing to fear." The escaped slave proceeds to feed, warn, and protect the concealed Godfreys during the remainder of the battle, for the knowledge "that he had two children who were held in bondage by the whites" and who might suffer "a similar fate by the hands of the white men in whose power they were!" (*Authentic Narrative* 10) leads him to sympathy rather than violence. Because antislavery novels were generally addressed to an explicitly white audience, they had to establish a similar form of sympathetic identification across, rather than within, racial boundaries. However, such literature resolutely resurrected this boundary at the moment when the affective force of sympathy might convert, as it did in captivity narratives, into aggressive rage and a legitimized vengeance. In *Uncle Tom's Cabin* that boundary is reinscribed in the space between the American and African continents.

Stowe's novel revises the strategies of most captivity narratives when it invites its audience to cross sympathetically a specifically corporeal border — the bodily border of racial difference — and thereby to take action on behalf of African American slaves, to act as white agents for black bodies. Debates about the efficacy of this sympathetic transference have centered around the agency of white readers and have therefore missed its other function: strategically to defuse the threat of black agency, which, for Stowe as for many of her white contemporaries, was virtually indissociable from the possibility of slave insurgency and rebellion.[11] Despite the notable docility with which Stowe invests the black bodies in her novel, those bodies continue to pose this capacity for independent agency, a threat that is removed only once they are exiled and transformed into agents for the values of a white American nation. *Uncle Tom's Cabin* therefore turns to colonization as a scheme that obviates violence by redefining domestic racial borders as imperial umbilical cords. The geography of African colonization ultimately mirrors the mapping of sympathy in the novel: as white readers maternally watch black bodies through a distancing veil of tears, white America peers across the watery expanse of the Atlantic from the mother country to an African outpost of black Americans.

Of the three best-selling captivity narratives in the history of the genre, one was an account of the captivity of an African American man among the Cherokees.[12] *A Narrative of the Lord's wonderful Dealings with John Marrant* was first published by the Rev. Mr. Aldridge in London in 1785. Although it was reprinted four times that year and appeared in numerous editions throughout the British colonies, it was not published in America until 1820.[13] The culture of anti-Indian sentiment in the early years of the American republic accounts, in part, for this delay. The audiences who welcomed Ann Eliza Bleecker's *History of Maria Kittle* and similar narratives of marital reunion amid anti-Indian rage may not have responded to Marrant's account of the Cherokee tribe's turn to benevolence after their captive successfully converts them to Christianity. Marrant's narrative never demonizes the Indians; in fact, the Cherokees' conversion unites them with their captive-turned-minister in a Christian community where violence becomes unthinkable and utterly obviates even the imagination of escape. When, after living for nearly two years among the southern tribes, Marrant experiences "an invincible desire of returning home," the Cherokee "king" escorts him "60 miles with 140 men" toward Charleston, South Carolina (Aldridge 194). After his return home, Marrant is pressed into the British navy and subsequently emigrates, first to England and finally to Nova Scotia, where he went to preach among the black loyalists who had fled America after the Revolutionary War.

Although the ACS proposals were certainly the primary source for pro-colonization arguments during the nineteenth century, Stowe's resolution to *Uncle Tom's Cabin* bears some interesting parallels to this earlier and unusual captivity narrative. In fact, the American publication of Marrant's text coincides with the period of the most intense activity within the ACS. John Marrant's narrative not only promotes religious sentiments similar to Stowe's, but it significantly ends with the departure of the freed black captive from the American continent to a community of black colonists in Nova Scotia, a departure emphasized in the title of his text, *A Narrative of the Lord's wonderful Dealings with John Marrant, a Black, (Now gone to Preach the Gospel in Nova-Scotia)*. This narrative may well be one potentially significant but overlooked source for Stowe's novel, since the two texts have in common a central figure much like Uncle Tom, a deathbed scene like Little Eva's, a typological narrative structure that consistently ascribes agency to divine providence, a hyperemotionalism rooted in Christian feeling, and the willing self-exile of African American Christians to distant colonies. Although it has often been misread as one, Marrant's text is not a slave narrative, and Marrant himself, a free man who was born in New York, was never a slave. No mention is made of Marrant in the *Key,* but this absence is not wholly surprising. The planned section on "the characteristics and developments of the colored race in various countries and circumstances," which presumably would have included documentary examples of free Blacks such as Marrant, was eventually omitted by Stowe when the material on slavery turned out to be so vast (*Key* v). But whether or not Marrant's text was a direct source for the material and organizing logic of *Uncle Tom's Cabin*, reading the two texts together serves to illuminate the particularly racial character of Stowe's sentimental imperialism.

Conversion, Typology, Agency

Like many captivity narratives, John Marrant's resembles spiritual autobiography, since it narrates his own path to conversion before recording his subsequent successes in converting others. But in every other respect, Marrant's story bears little resemblance to contemporary narratives of Indian captivity. As a youth in Charleston, Marrant studied the violin and French horn so successfully that he soon found himself, at the age of thirteen, a performer at local "balls and assemblies" and "supplied with as much money as I had occasion for" (Aldridge 181). On the way to one performance he passed a crowded Methodist assembly where the itinerant preacher George Whitefield was delivering a sermon. Marrant, prepared to disrupt the meeting by blowing his French horn among them, suddenly felt instead "[t]he Lord accompany the word with such power, that I was struck to the ground, and lay both speechless and senseless near half an hour" (182). His former life of pleasurable indulgence, of "drinking in iniquity like water" (181), abruptly ends when he wakes to find "a woman throwing water in my face" (182). He abandons his musical career and, subject to frequent outburts of tears, returns to his family. Gradually convinced that he has become insane, his family increasingly persecutes him, until he flees, with only a Bible and hymn book in hand, "over the fence, about half a mile from our house, which divided the inhabited and cultivated parts of the country from the wilderness" (185).

Seeking religious freedom, Marrant crosses the boundary to a new world, which he gradually colonizes through the deployment of evangelical Christianity. After living for two weeks off of grass and muddy water, he meets an Indian with whom he travels and hunts deer for over two months. When the two arrive at the Cherokee village, Marrant is instantly ordered to be executed and is confined to a "dungeon [which] became my chapel" (189). His death is miraculously averted, however, for when Marrant begins to pray in the Cherokee tongue, which he learned while traveling with the Indian hunter, "the executioner was savingly converted to God" (190). The Cherokee king, still determined to sacrifice Marrant, is likewise converted by his captive's preaching, and as soon as "the king himself was awakened," the prisoner was "set at liberty" (193). The condition of captivity and hence the necessity of or desire for escape ceases with the captors' religious conversion, after which "the poor condemned prisoner had perfect liberty, and was treated like a prince. Now the Lord made all my enemies to become my great friends" (193).

The Cherokees' religious conversion accomplishes two crucial revisions in the captivity scenario: it erases the desire for vengeance typically produced by the asymmetrical power relations of captivity, and it subordinates the national difference between captive and captor to a common Christianity that colonizes the Cherokee nation within English imperial interests. In fact, the mark of authentic conversion in Marrant's narrative is the disappearance of hostility with the recognition, through Christianity, of the captive's national superiority. The Cherokee king, Marrant notes, eventually comes to feel "the same strong bias toward my country, after we had asked Divine direction" (194). Evidence of Marrant's unsuccessful attempts to convert the nearby Creek, Choctaw, and Chickasaw tribes is that these tribes "have often united, and murdered all the white people in the back settlements" (193–94). This violence leads him to conclude that none "of these three nations were savingly wrought upon" (194). When Marrant later meets the Cherokee king at the Revolutionary War battle at Charleston, both are aligned with the British forces against the rebel colonists. The king, whose daughter also was converted by Marrant, tells his friend that "he was glad to see me; that his daughter was happy, and sometimes longed to get out of the body" (199). Christian conversion emancipates the captive and colonizes the captors, and it accomplishes both without violence.

Uncle Tom's Cabin likewise nominates conversion over conflict as the route to both emancipation and national unity. A self-appointed Methodist preacher like the captive Marrant, Uncle Tom refuses the options of violent retaliation and active escape by devoutly adhering to Christian precepts and feeling. Tom passively submits to the sale of his body, to separation from his family, and to Legree's abuse by conferring his fate to God's will. But if Christianity cannot emancipate Tom's body as it could Marrant's, it is because Tom's body is inescapably racialized and therefore bereft of agency, in a way that Marrant's is not. The sentimentality of *Uncle Tom's Cabin* is supported throughout—as James Baldwin astutely noted—by a compelling fear of vengeance, a threat that is located in the novel's black bodies. Augustine St. Clare is the figure who most consistently voices this threat in his references to the revolutionary uprisings in France and St. Domingo (391), and in his pronouncement that "[o]ne thing is certain,—that there is a mustering among the masses, the world over; and there is a *dies irae* coming on, sooner or later" (344). For Stowe, as for St. Clare, there is no distinction between an incipient slave rebellion in which "the masses are to rise, and the under class become the upper one" (392) and the coming Christian millennium that St. Clare's mother warned him of as a child. The one is the earthly sign and fulfillment of the other. In her concluding chapter, Stowe literally repeats St. Clare's earlier question—"But who may abide the day of his appearing?" (344, 629)—when she cites the recent revolutions "in all nations and languages" as evidence for the coming "kingdom of Christ" (629).

According to P. J. Staudenraus, the ACS, influenced by nineteenth-century Calvinist evangelism, subscribed to the belief that "a ruling Providence guided nations to ruin or salvation" and that nations, unlike individuals, "received their punishments and rewards on earth" (vii–viii). Stowe tells her readers at the novel's end that "[t]his is an age of the world when nations are trembling and convulsed." She quotes from Scripture a warning of violence—"he shall break in pieces the oppressor"—and reminds Christians "that prophecy associates, in dread fellowship, the *day of vengeance* with the year of his redeemed" (629). Here Stowe articulates the evangelical position from which feeling right and praying are admissible solutions to slavery, insofar as these practices ideally invite the conversion experience that will eliminate vengeance, as it does in Marrant's captivity narrative, by bringing on emancipation. Yet if such preaching and praying preserve the captive John Marrant within a Christian community that expands to include his captors, such tactics woefully fail to free, much less preserve, Uncle Tom. The destruction of Tom's body finally works only to facilitate the escape of the lighter-skinned slaves Cassy and Emmeline.

Stowe's politics of conversion relies on a typological framework in which agency operates ambiguously at best, but agency is problematized in the novel as much by the representation of race as by the reliance on typology. As Benilde Montgomery notes, Marrant's text resembles Rowlandson's seventeenth-century captivity narrative more than contemporary ones because it observes a typological mode of narrative construction. By identifying himself with a series of biblical figures, Marrant's captivity experience retells salvation history in George Whitefield's evangelical mode (Montgomery 106–7). But while Marrant, like Uncle Tom, is most consistently linked with the biblical figure of Christ, his identity slips along an axis that is cultural as well as typological. When he returns home from his sojourn among the Cherokees, Marrant claims that "none knew me" (Aldridge 195), for he was dressed "purely in the Indian stile; the skins of wild beasts composed my garments; my head was set out in the savage manner, with a long pendant down my back, a sash round my middle, without breeches, and a tomahawk by my side" (194). His own family fails to recognize him, not only because of his Indian dress but because they believe he had been "torn in pieces by the wild beasts." He learns that, after his disappearance, his family "went three days into the woods in search of him, and found his carcase torn, and brought it home, and buried it, and they are now in mourning for him" (195). "Thus," he claims, "the dead was brought to life again; thus the lost was found" (196). Marrant's return to the scene of his own mourning marks his rebirth, as his captivity narrative typologically fulfills the redemptive history of Christ; at the same time, however, he is significantly reborn in the guise of a Cherokee Indian.

Stowe explicitly associates Uncle Tom with Christ's conversional power when she aligns him with "One whose suffering changed an instrument of torture, degradation and shame, into a symbol of glory, honor, and immortal life" (583). Uncle Tom, like John Marrant, might well claim that "[t]he more they persecuted me, the stronger I grew in grace" (Aldridge 184). But if Tom reenacts the martyrdom of Christ, he is a Christ who is neither emancipated nor returns, whose rebirth is figured only in the promise of his ascension to a home in heaven. Tom's death is portrayed as a willing and necessary sacrifice, for "[l]ike his Master, he knew that, if he saved others, himself he could not save" (584). Uncle Tom and John Marrant are both types for Christlike biblical figures, but Tom does not survive his bodily disintegration as Marrant does because he lacks the latter's transcultural mobility. Marrant's powers of conversion depend in part on his ability, including the ability of his body, to move between cultural categories. Tom, on the other hand, is burdened by a body that is confined within the static racial category of blackness, and when he converts others, it is from this immobile position. George Shelby decides to emancipate his slaves, for example, at the sentimental moment when it becomes too late to save Uncle Tom, an action that is something of a conversion as well as an act of benevolence that compensates for Legree's violent excess. George's behavior here is offered as an example of proper Christian rectitude and feeling, but what motivates his action and what the text highlights is the physical image of Uncle Tom's mutilated passive body.

Jane Tompkins has illustrated that *Uncle Tom's Cabin* employs a typological framework for both its narrative structure and its political efficacy (134). By positioning secular history as a version of biblical history, whose prearranged outcome is dependent only on the faithful reliance of the Christian subject on God's will, typology exiles human agency from the progressive narrative of history. Typology displaces agency into the register of the divine: fortuitous events are ascribed not to human actions but to providential intervention. Therefore, like the Puritan Mary Rowlandson, who prefers to "wait God's time" rather than attempt an escape from captivity, Tom rejects Cassy's offer of escape from Legree with the conviction that he will be freed "in God's time" (560). Marrant, too, observes the continual providences of God in guiding and preserving him through his unusual pilgrimage and later adventures on a British naval ship. Such providential occurrences as being directed to water while dying of thirst, being preserved from wolves, or being saved from drowning position the subject as the passive recipient of divine direction. Such events, however, must be set against the conversion experience of Marrant's captors, where the captive himself serves as a mediator for a divine agency that operates through him and that operates successfully in part because of his experience of cultural exchange. As Montgomery notes, Marrant's increasingly "transethnic" character positions him as a cultural mediator, a liminal trickster figure (111). It is his ability to speak the Cherokee language, learned while hunting in the forest with an Indian, that saves Marrant from the executioner's hatchet and that enables him through ceaseless efforts at prayer and preaching to convert the Cherokee king.

If typology diminishes by obliterating the self within the confines of a type, it simultaneously magnifies the self by endowing it with the value and power of that type. The Methodist George Whitefield's evangelical conversions likewise participated in this concurrent emphasis on and away from the self (Ruttenberg 431). The moments of conversion in Marrant's narrative illustrate such slippage between self-effacement and self-enlargement, but they also betray the slippage of agency between the registers of the divine and the human. Furthermore, that slippage occurs along a transcultural axis that is erected once the captive speaks the language and wears the garments of his captors. Christian feeling becomes the vehicle for eliminating national distinctions as well as the screen for concealing cultural exchanges between the African American captive and his Cherokee Indian captors. The racial difference between Marrant and his captors does not factor into this process; indeed, his own racial identity is never mentioned in the text itself.

Marrant's facility as cultural mediator, his bodily capacity to inhabit both Christian and Amerindian cultures, enables his freedom from captivity. In *Uncle Tom's Cabin,* on the other hand, emancipation occurs not through a single mediating body but only by substituting one (white) body for another (black) body. With Uncle Tom's death, the capacity for agency is transferred from the black slave to the sympathetic white slaveowner. While Tom disavows the use of physical violence, George Shelby, "blazing with wrath and defiance," "with one indignant blow, knocked Legree flat upon his face" (592). The activities of passive martyrdom and of active emancipation are divided here along racial lines, when George Shelby, who is designated "our hero" (587) once he frees the slaves he has inherited from his father, takes up the heroic role associated with Tom at the moment of "indignant" physical violence.[14] Because black characters in *Uncle Tom's Cabin* either flee America or die enslaved in it, political agency is explicitly left to Whites who, ideally, will sympathetically reproduce "Mas'r George's" final gesture of benevolent but somewhat qualified emancipation: "It was on his grave, my friends, that I resolved, before God, that I would never own another slave, while it was possible to free him" (617).

Race never enters Marrant's narrative as a category of difference, and were it not for the words "a Black" in its title, readers would have absolutely no indication of the captive's racial identity. As an operative category of difference in *Uncle Tom's Cabin,* however, racial identity is furthermore represented as inflexible, as a static category indelibly written onto the body. This schema prevents the transracial movement of Uncle Tom and therefore, in his capacity as a typological figure, of the movement of divine providence into the realm of human agency. In a sense, Uncle Tom does not escape from slavery because—unlike Cassy, Emmeline, Eliza, and George—he is too black. Ultimately, the condition for black agency and thus for the escape from slavery in *Uncle Tom's Cabin* is the mimicry of whiteness, the ability to covertly transgress the color line, and that ability resides in the inescapable corporeality of skin color.

Compromise and Corporeality

Uncle Tom dies, of course, because Simon Legree violently beats him to death; but by resigning the fate of his body to "God's will" and by rejecting the use of Legree's own means to save his body, as Cassy would have him do, Uncle Tom dies in another sense because he refuses to strike a compromise between his spiritual and his corporeal life. The two inhabit utterly distinct realms in Tom's final hours, when the more Legree tortures his slave's unresistant body, the less he is able to access Tom's "heart." The deaths of Uncle Tom and Eva St. Clare share this refusal of compromise. Eva dies because she lacks her parents' or Mr. Shelby's ability to accommodate her acute Christian sensibilities to the horrors of slavery. But in Eva's case, corporeal disintegration proceeds through the avenue of the heart; she is literally killed by an excess of sympathy, by the inability to preserve the body from the consuming effects of feeling. Whereas Uncle Tom is afflicted with the augmented burden of corporeality, Eva's corporeality increasingly dissolves, and this dissolution facilitates her capacity to mediate across racial boundaries. The huge scene of Little Eva's death, which marks the sentimental apex of Stowe's novel, recalls a similar scene from John Marrant's captivity narrative.

After Marrant returns to Charleston to be tearfully reunited with his family, he befriends "a child seven and a half years old named Mary Scott," whom he finds one day measuring graves in a cemetery in order to determine "if there were any so small as herself." When Marrant questions her actions, she replies "I shall die, Sir," and "continued to express her desire to depart, and be with Christ, rather than to live till she was grown up" (Aldridge 197). After this event, the child "was observed to be always very solid and thoughtful"; when she and Marrant "read and prayed together . . . she appeared much affected" and "spent her leisure time in reading God's word and prayer" (197–98). Marrant recounts a moving deathbed scene remarkably like Little Eva's:

> I found her lying on the bed, with her eyes fixed up to Heaven; when turning herself and seeing me, she said, "Mr. Marrant, don't you see that pretty town, and those fine people, how they shine like gold?—O how I long to be with my Lord and his redeemed Children in Glory!" and then turning to her parents and two sisters . . . she shook hands with them, and bade them farewell; desiring them not to lament for her when she was dead, for she was going to that fine place where God would wipe away all tears from her eyes, and she should sing Hallelujahs to God and the Lamb for ever and ever, and where she hoped afterwards to meet them; and then turning again to me, she said, "Farewell, and God bless you," and then fell asleep in the arms of Jesus. This afterwards proved the conversion of her mother. (198)

This scene vividly mirrors Eva's penetrating vision of heaven when she describes to Uncle Tom "great gates of pearl; and you can see beyond them—far, far off—it's all gold." Like Mary Scott, Eva assuredly pronounces to Uncle Tom that "I'm going *there*" (382) and tells her father that "I had rather be in heaven" (402). She confidently predicts to Uncle Tom the moment of her own death just as Mary tells Marrant that "she should certainly die before six o'clock that evening" (Aldridge 198). If before her death, "Eva appeared more like her former self than ever she had done since her sickness" (425), Mary appears an hour before her death "to all appearance pretty well recovered" (Aldridge 198). But while the deathbed of Eva is surrounded by the bodies of slaves whose darkness is enhanced by the contrast to Eva's paleness, the factor of race is absent from Mary Scott's scene of death. Even the body of Mary Scott is unmarked in Marrant's narrative by racial identity; she remains defined only by her size.

Eva St. Clare's primary physical attributes are her size and her whiteness. Critics consistently refer to her as "Little Eva," despite the fact that she is never called "Little Eva" in the novel. But like the child Mary Scott, who measures the size of grave plots to find ones as small as she is, it is precisely Eva's diminutive size that endows her with such import and impact. Susan

Stewart has argued that minute objects are commonly endowed with an enlarged sense of interiority; any diminishment in size corresponds to an exaggeration in significance. Miniatures, including the child and the toy, are associated with a theatricality and with an accessibility to otherwise secret worlds, including the world of the dead (38–57). The theatrical deaths of Mary and Eva perform precisely this mediation between worlds and mobilize the conversion of others through such mediation. Like the typological self, the paradoxically expanded subjectivity of the miniature positions it between otherwise noncontiguous worlds. Thus, Eva's liminality, like John Marrant's among the Cherokees, allows her to serve as a conduit for grace; as Uncle Tom insists, "when that ar blessed child goes into the kingdom, they'll open the door so wide, we'll all get a look in at the glory" (425).

Whereas John Marrant's body bears the inscriptions of another, cultural mediation that assists his mediation of the divine, Eva's power of mediation relies on the translucency of her white body. As her illness proceeds to consume her, even the "intense whiteness of her complexion" dissolves until, devoid of any marks or inscriptions, her skin becomes "singularly transparent" (345) and her body as weightless as "a wearied dove" (421). Marrant's and Eva's bodies share different forms of mutability that facilitate their mediation between worlds and thus their ability to inspire conversion experiences. Uncle Tom's large black body, on the other hand, is defined by its lack of any such elasticity. If Uncle Tom must forsake his body in order to save his soul, it is because his body, indelibly inscribed by slavery and race and thus burdened by an extreme physicality, poses a roadblock that obstructs mediation. Unlike the exchanges between Marrant and the Cherokees, Mary Scott and her mother, or Eva and Topsy, spirit will not transmit through Tom to Legree because for the master his slave is only a body, a "blasted black beast" (507), an "old cussed black shell" (508) with an "old black gash" (558) for a mouth. When Legree gives Tom "a heavy blow cross the cheek" (507) and "a violent kick with his heavy boot" (508), the slave's body possesses a weight and an opacity that utterly contrasts to Eva's virtual bodilessness.

In this respect, Stowe's novel resembles much antislavery fiction which, as Karen Sánchez-Eppler notes, urges black emancipation only as it exterminates black bodies (113). Black freedom is therefore positioned as implicitly noncorporeal. In its scenes of death, Stowe's novel aims to fill the nostalgic space vacated by the body with an experience of conversion that is at once religious and political. But the political efficacy of *Uncle Tom's Cabin,* which calls for sympathetic exchange across the boundary of race, is burdened by the opaqueness and untranslatability that it ascribes to the black body. While these bodies can be "Christianized" and "civilized," they can never be made white, and this corporeality continues to impede national conversion as well as national unity. The problem Stowe's novel poses therefore is how to facilitate conversion without sacrificing individual bodies but also, and more pointedly, without destroying the national body.

Stowe claims to have been compelled to write *Uncle Tom's Cabin* after the Compromise of 1850 and the subsequent ratification of its Fugitive Slave Bill. The 1850 Compromise, which followed the American war with Mexico, ushered in the era of a "new imperialism" by incorporating into the Union territories acquired in the peace treaty with Mexico. But it also marked some of those acquired lands as slave territories, while implicating the North in the institution of slavery with the inclusion of what would become the Fugitive Slave Law. The Compromise explicitly aimed at preserving the stability and integrity of the body of the Union. The political rhetoric of Compromise supporters such as Daniel Webster appealed to a sentimental national feeling that would heal sectional divisions within the national body through mutual sacrifice.

Uncle Tom's Cabin protests and refuses the 1850 Compromise by posing it as an impossible compromise between sin and salvation. The novel's final sentence insists that "[n]ot by combining together, to protect injustice and cruelty, and making a common capital of sin, is this Union to be saved" (629). Stowe would erase the territorial markers of slave state and free state, but her "romantic racialism" retains and emphasizes the markers distinguishing black and white bodies.[15] Even once slaves become free, whether by escape or emancipation, they cannot escape the ineffaceable category of race. When Stowe lists former slaves now living and prospering financially in Cincinnati, the first item in her descriptions identifies and quantifies them racially: "K——. Full black; dealer in real estate," "G——. Full black; coal dealer," "W——. Three-fourths black; barber and waiter" (627). These Cincinnati businessmen might be seen as examples indicating an alternative to black emigration and African colonization, but not necessarily. The ACS advocated the education and Christianization of emancipated slaves, like these Ohioans and like Stowe's fictional Harris family, before their exportation. George Harris's letter defending his decision to emigrate furthermore argues that the claim to American national identity is founded on whiteness. George's ability to "pass for an American" and "mingle in the circles of the whites" is dependent on the fact that "my shade of color is so slight, and that of my wife and family scarce perceptible" (608). Americanness and whiteness, national and racial identity, are fused here, and the very need to "pass for an American" implies that George is not an American any more than he is white. *Uncle Tom's Cabin* ultimately imagines a national Union that becomes free of internal division by removing black bodies after having rendered them American in every sense other than color.

Black Agency and the "Freedom That Was Alarming"

For all its insistence on the structural immobility of racial categories, *Uncle Tom's Cabin* contains examples of racial transgression that at once code the act of freedom as "white" and expose the simultaneous pleasure and threat to Whites of such transgression. Stowe's slaveowners frequently take a subversive pleasure in the unruly actions of their slaves; indeed, the more politically paralyzed the slaveowner feels, the greater is his or her fascination by such actions. St. Clare, who is admittedly consumed by his own passivity, delightedly watches the performances of Topsy. When she mispronounces words or twists their meaning, he "took a wicked pleasure in these mistakes, calling Topsy to him whenever he had a mind to amuse himself." Although he reputedly "took the same kind of amusement in the child that a man might in the tricks of a parrot or a pointer," when he describes himself to Miss Ophelia in Topsy's terms of "I's so wicked!" (369), it is clear that he also indulges his own fantasies of subversion vicariously, by watching and enjoying the actions of Topsy.

Although for different reasons, Mrs. Shelby is just as politically paralyzed as St. Clare. The limits of Mrs. Shelby's power become evident when she adamantly insists that she "would as soon have one of my own children sold" as she would permit the sale of Eliza's son Harry, just as her husband is signing a bill of sale that exchanges Harry for cash. After she fails to intercede on her slaves' behalf, Mrs. Shelby "stood like one stricken. . . . rested her face in her hands, and gave a sort of groan" (84). The degree of her passive powerlessness here provides the measure of her extreme delight after she later learns that Eliza has taken action to escape. When "Black Sam" manufactures a series of mishaps that conveniently delay Haley's pursuit of Eliza and Harry, his antics resemble minstrelsy in their reliance on stereotypes of black buffoonery, and they provide considerable entertainment value for his mistress. As Richard Yarborough accurately claims, Sam and Andy contribute to Eliza's safe escape not out of sympathy for her plight but out of a desire to win favor with Mrs. Shelby (47). In their strategic disruptions of a slave trade controlled by white males, they enact a displaced form of agency: Sam and Andy act on behalf of, as agents for, another. Later Mrs. Shelby mildly rebukes Sam for these "errors" (135), but while he is performing them he spots her "up stars at the winder. . . . laughin'" (102).[16] Mrs. Shelby scarcely represses her pleasure in Sam's subversion of Haley's hunt, a subversion that—because she authorizes it—she can indulge in as if it were her own. But as Sam clearly realizes, sanction quickly becomes discipline when his actions are divorced from his mistress's own desire to act.

By enjoying the peculiar pleasure of acting without having to act herself,

Mrs. Shelby serves as a model for the operation of a sympathetic agency on which the politics of Stowe's novel is constructed. Black agency is repeatedly authorized in *Uncle Tom's Cabin* only when it is co-opted by whites, a paradigm mirrored in the project of African colonization. It is therefore in keeping with the novel's disavowal of black agency that the escape of Eliza Harris, who dramatically crosses the Ohio River out of slave territory by leaping from one unstable fragment of ice to another, is shifted into the passive terms of providence. Sam's account of her escape shifts between his own fascination with Eliza's active bravery as she went "clar over t' other side of the current, on the ice, and then on she went, a screeching and a jumpin'" and his explanation—offered largely to impress his mistress with his piety—that "dis yer's a providence" of "De Lord" (134–35). When Eliza describes her river crossing to Senator and Mrs. Bird, she insists several times that "[t]he Lord helped me" (148). These recourses to providence and divine intervention diminish the autonomy and contain the transgressiveness of her actions. The image of Eliza's escape inspired in nineteenth-century America a phenomenal cultural appeal, suggesting that Stowe's audience shared Mrs. Shelby's disavowed indulgence in her slave's agency. Illustrations for the novel and advertisements for dramatic productions of it represented, more than any other scene, Eliza crossing the icy Ohio. Such illustrations are notable not only for their popularity but for their depiction of Eliza as a distinctly white woman (figs. 10 and 11). Like every other slave character who successfully escapes in *Uncle Tom's Cabin,* Eliza is representationally rendered white in her moment of escape.

George Harris escapes by adopting the disguise of a European gentleman who appears "very tall, with a dark, Spanish complexion, fine, expressive black eyes, and close-curling hair, also of a glossy blackness. His well-formed aquiline nose, straight thin lips, and the admirable contour of his finely-formed limbs, impressed the whole company instantly with the idea of something uncommon" (180). In addition to the dyes applied to his skin and hair, it is George's inheritance of "a set of fine European features, and a high, indomitable spirit" from his white father that enables him to pass as an aristocratic gentleman far more cultured than the white men he meets in the tavern. His self-assurance as he "seated himself easily on a chair in the middle of the room" and ordered his servant to "see to the trunks" (181) is in marked contrast to Mr. Wilson, who "looked round the barroom with rather an anxious air," suspiciously stowed his suitcase under his corner chair, "and looked rather apprehensively" around him (177). Like Mrs. Shelby's response to Eliza's flight, Wilson is both fearful of and thrilled by the fugitive's bravery, exclaiming at once that "my very blood runs cold when I think of it—your condition and your risks!" (189–90) and "Well! go ahead, George, go ahead" (188).

FIG 10.   Lithograph, Chez Miné, "Eliza Crossing the Ice" (n.d.). Courtesy of Harriet Beecher Stowe Center, Hartford, CT.

George appeals to Wilson's sympathy by relating accounts of his mother's torture by a cruel master, of the whipping of his sister for refusing her master's sexual advances, and of his own master's attempts to separate him from his wife. Stowe recurrently appeals to the sympathy of her readers through the pathos of family history, much as earlier captivity narratives did. In addition to coding the agency of slaves as white, through the paired mechanisms of racial appropriation and pleasurable indulgence, Stowe sanctions each escape by recourse to family feeling. By invoking his female relations and the threats to their maternalized and sexualized bodies, George assures his protection by Mr. Wilson. Likewise, Eliza's departure from the Shelby plantation is inspired purely by her maternal desire to save her son, whom she clutches in her arms as she valiantly leaps from ice floe to ice floe and who appears as white as she in the illustrations of this scene. Like the subtle transgression of Mary Rowlandson into Algonquin culture or the more radical one of Hannah Dustan's escape out of it, the transgression of slaves

FIG 11.   "Eliza Crossing the Ice" (n.d.). Courtesy of Harriet Beecher Stowe Center, Hartford, CT.

over the border into the free states is both justified and minimized by the invocation of sentimental motherhood.

Cassy represents the novel's most dramatic example of a radical black agency tamed and disciplined by the power of the maternal. Cassy's history of violence includes the attempted murder of her former master with a bowie knife, the murder of her infant son by laudanum, and a plot to murder Legree in his sleep with an ax. She holds a stilleto blade to Emmeline's neck during their later escape, promising to kill her if she faints. When Cassy fantasizes "a day of judgment," her claim of "won't there be vengeance, then!" (522) harbors the danger of an antiwhite violence that both St. Clare and Stowe dread. By urging Tom to help her kill the drunken Legree, Cassy aims to mobilize, by the hands of slaves, that judgmental vengeance. Tom's refusal to comply with her request appeals to a more providential history. When he tells Cassy that "[t]he Lord hasn't called us to wrath. We must suffer, and wait his time" (561), he attempts to remove the act of redemption from the realm of human agency, where it invariably suggests an insurgent black violence.

But it is the presence of Emmeline, more than Tom's Christianity, that finally subdues Cassy into organizing a strategic escape that does not destroy bodies. Emmeline casts the reluctant Cassy in the role of a mother by insisting on behaving "like a daughter" (580) to her. In order to fulfill her maternal relation to Emmeline and to remove her from the power of their master, Cassy takes on the haunting form of Legree's dead mother. In doing so, she invests that figure—whose influence was, like Mrs. Shelby's, so pathetically ineffectual in her own life—with a suddenly remarkable power over her son. In Legree's increasingly tormented mind, the images of his once-forgiving mother and his angry female slave work in unison to afflict him with a fear of gothic dimensions.[17] Like Harriet Jacobs, whose story Stowe was familiar with well before its publication in 1861, the two women return to inhabit the garret of their master's house, where they exercise a power over the man who had formerly oppressed them and survey the effects of that power from the vantage point of a "loop-hole in the garret" (597). Cassy, promenading as a ghost—a being defined by its lack of corporeality—invariably appears as "something *white,* gliding in!" (596; emphasis added), as "a stern, *white,* inexorable figure." When she and Emmeline leave the house, it is reported that "some of the negroes had seen two *white* figures gliding down the avenue towards the high-road" (597; emphases added). The female slave's power over her master, which is enhanced by this apparent loss of body and of her body's blackness, utterly contrasts to Tom's lack of influence over Legree. Cassy's subsequent passage out of slave territory requires that she adopt the appearance and demeanor of a wealthy and cultured "Creole lady," an impersonation facilitated by her former life "in connection with the highest society" (597) as well as by her quadroon racial status. Here as elsewhere in the novel, black slaves are rendered white at their moments of active agency. Cassy's aggressive violence is tamed by resurgent maternal sentiments, and her flight, like Eliza Harris's, is affectively justified by her maternal protection of Emmeline.

Cassy's disguise as the white ghost of a white mother allows her to practice, Stowe writes, "a freedom that was alarming" (594). Endowed with a license to roam about the house and plantation undetected and at will, Cassy represents a freedom that is "alarming" in more than one sense. This phrase suggests not only the frightening properties of incorporeal beings like ghosts but also a mobility that is excessive and unauthorized because it is indulged in by a woman, particularly by a slave woman. In response to Philip Fisher's assertion that sentimental fiction was potentially "radical" and "dangerous" in its "extension of full and complete humanity to classes of figures from whom it has been socially withheld," Laura Wexler has asked "dangerous for whom?" Stowe's characterization of Cassy in what amounts to whiteface prompts a corollary question: "alarming to whom?" One might respond here as Wexler does to the former question; like sentimental fiction's extension of subjectivity to social "others," Cassy's freedom is alarming not to Cassy but to Stowe and her intended readers (Wexler 17). Readers' response to Cassy, however, would likely have been as ambivalent as Mrs. Shelby's response to Sam or St. Clare's to Topsy. Cassy represents the novel's only example of female influence that effectively generates self-liberation. By mimicking a white mother, the slave Cassy practices a degree of influence that the novel's free white women lack and that its female readership might have found as pleasurable as it was disconcerting. Those readers might very well have delightedly indulged in this scenario of a woman's influence grown so forceful that it dwarfs the household's violent patriarch into a terrified and almost infantile submission. But because it is enacted by a black woman, who has moreover indulged in murderous violence, such an agency remains "dangerous," a sign of the rebellious potential for vengeance that this novel hopes to prevent.

Wexler notes that if objects of novelistic sentiment (such as slaves) posed a danger to their readers, those readers in turn often became sources of danger to the "objects" they believed they had discovered. The sentimental project of incorporating the socially dispossessed functioned by imposing dominant cultural values on those able to conform to such predetermined standards. Such mechanisms of incorporation, including later-nineteenth-century educational institutions that urged the domestic paradigm onto Native Americans and former slaves, often employed forms of cultural violence that were both deployed and masked by sentimental strategies (Wexler 17). *Uncle Tom's Cabin* offers an early model of this project of sentimental imperialism when it finally scripts Cassy and the rest of the Harris family into an exemplary model of domesticity. The reunion with her daughter Eliza completes the process of domestication begun by Emmeline, and soon "such a change has passed over Cassy, that our readers would scarcely recognize her. The despairing, haggard expression of her face had given way to one of gentle trust. She seemed to sink, at once, into the bosom of the family, and take the little ones into her heart, as something for which it long had waited." A rejuvenated motherhood quickly results in religious conversion as well, for "Cassy yielded at once, and with her whole soul, to every good influence, and became a devout and tender Christian" (607). The Canadian household of the Harrises, presided over by a now "more matronly" (604) Eliza, resembles the ideal Quaker household ruled by the benevolent Rachel Halliday. This scenario retroactively diminishes Cassy's former violence and dissolves the "freedom" that would have appeared so "alarming" to Stowe's readers. Sentimental feeling thus accomplishes in *Uncle Tom's Cabin* what Christian conversion does in John Marrant's captivity narrative: it colonizes those deemed capable of vengeance within the values and interests of the nation, thereby eliminating the potential for violence and creating new agents for the nation. Stowe's former slaves, by conforming to a cultural ideal of Christian domesticity, are robbed of any agency that does not further the interests of that ideal. Indeed, they literally become the sympathetic agents of that ideal once they determine to cross the Atlantic in order to import "the tide of civilization and Christianity" (609) into Africa.

Maternal Empire and Colonization

Sentimental fiction has traditionally been characterized in gendered terms that distinguish it from those practices, institutions, and spheres of power relegated to men. The sentimental novel's opposition to the marketplace, to commerce, and to the masculine public realm has virtually become a critical cliché even while its effectiveness in altering the agendas of that realm remains ambiguous at best. This ambiguity is, in fact, the inevitable result of the overdrawn opposition between a private, feminine, and affective domesticity, on the one hand, and a public, masculine, and rational civil sphere on the other. The question of how and whether feeling right and praying might abolish slavery is, of course, a question of how and whether practices associated with the former sphere can intervene in and alter the policies of the latter. This dichotomous model is perpetuated as much by sentimental fiction itself as by criticism about it. By reproducing and reinforcing the ineffaceable borderline erected by sentimental novels between gendered public and private spheres and by hinging those novels' value on their capacity to move "private" domestic values into the "public" arena, this model inevitably suppresses the extent to which these two realms can share similar agendas.[18]

The imperialist dimensions of Stowe's project suggest, for example, that *Uncle Tom's Cabin* operates less in opposition to than in tandem with such "male" imperialist practices as land acquisition and Indian removal. Nineteenth-century domestic literature frequently referred to the home as "the empire of the mother," an arena imagined as separate from but analogous to the national empire (Ryan 97). Maternal empire was imagined as a terrain ruled and expanded not by aggression or violence but by gentleness and influence. While Andrew Jackson and his successors acquired territory through warfare with Indians and Mexicans, women supposedly acquired greater spheres of influence through the quiet manipulation of husbands and children. As Henry Wright, originator of "the empire of the mother" slogan wrote, "So far as human agency is concerned the mother makes the man."[19] The influence wielded in the domestic empire theoretically produced trained agents who would transport its values out of the home and into national politics. Stowe's novel not only applies the strategies of this maternal empire to further the ends of a national empire but reproduces the same racial hierarchy that characterizes the latter. Therefore, when Elizabeth Ammons claims that *Uncle Tom's Cabin* places motherhood in opposition to "the politics of men," her formulation misses the ways in which the politics of white motherhood could very well be aligned with "the politics of [white] men" (161).

As Wexler emphasizes, the "tender violence" deployed under the auspices of a sentimental and domestic culture did not necessarily challenge so much as it repeated the violence of more explicitly aggressive imperialist policies. This crucial relation is obscured when the maternal and national empires are characterized in opposing terms, for "[a]s long as the arena of the sentimental encounter is imagined mainly as a private, contained, bookish, housebound space . . . the deeper tracings of its terrorism against non-readers and outsiders cannot be conceived" (Wexler 37). By retracing and reifying the boundary between private and public realms and by statically and exclusively locating sentiment in the former, both sentimental fiction and its critics deflect attention away from movements and exchanges across that border. These exchanges come into focus once we allow that the scenario of colonization at the end of *Uncle Tom's Cabin* harbors a sensibility that has a central and constitutive, rather than tangential and mistaken, relation to the novel's logic of sympathy.

Stowe repeats the Jeffersonian model of colonization when she advocates the sentimental education of freed slaves as an imperative precursor to their transportation to Africa:

> To fill up Liberia with an ignorant, inexperienced, half-barbarized race, just escaped from the chains of slavery, would be only to prolong, for ages, the period of struggle and conflict which attends the inception of new enterprises. Let the church of the north receive these poor sufferers in the spirit of Christ; receive them to the educating advantages of Christian republican society and schools, until they have attained to somewhat of a moral and intellectual maturity, and then assist them in their passage to those shores, where they may put in practice the lessons they have learned in America. (626)

This vision supports James Baldwin's charge against the protest novel genre with which he associates *Uncle Tom's Cabin;* the central aim of such fiction, he argues, is "something very closely resembling the zeal of those alabaster missionaries to Africa to cover the nakedness of the native, to hurry them into the pallid arms of Jesus and thence into slavery" (20). Stowe's project for refashioning former slaves is analogous to her transformation of Cassy from an autonomous agent of black resistance to an agent for the cultural values of a white empire. Although George Harris yearns for a separate, "African *nationality*" (608), Stowe's characterization of Liberian colonization envisions an Africa that is nothing less than a black version of America, populated by citizens who resemble Americans in every respect other than color.

When Stowe appeals to the "mothers of America" through the quintessential deathbed scene of maternal powerlessness and loss, she advocates the sympathetic transmission of the mechanisms of a maternal empire to a national scale: "[b]y the sick hour of your child; by those dying eyes, which you can never forget; by those last cries, that wrung your heart when you could neither help nor save; by the desolation of the empty cradle, that silent nursery, pity those mothers that are constantly made childless by the American slave-trade!" (623). Like children, "those who formerly were slaves" have "capabilities" (626) and potential that maternal influence and education can fashion in its own image before being exported out of the home and the school. Maternal influence is a form of agency that operates only by indirection and displacement, by reproducing itself in those whom it colonizes with the tools of sentimental culture. The ACS, which experienced a brief upsurge in support and effectiveness in the early 1850s after a decline two decades long, imagined its own project in precisely these terms. By transporting trained black Americans to Africa, the nation was reproducing itself and extending its own sphere of cultural and commercial influence. Both Stowe and the ACS encouraged a sentimental emphasis on the expanding empire of Christianity and civilization, thus masking the cultural violence as well as the racism that some saw as inherent to the colonization project.

The charge of racism was one of many leveled by those opposed to the ACS and its proposals. In 1849, Frederick Douglass argued that colonization "was geared to divert the attention of free blacks from the political and economic deterioration of slavery, and the growing effects of the antislavery movement" (qtd. in Kinshasa 131). Samuel Cornish, editor of *The Colored American,* co-wrote with Theodore Wright in 1840 a text whose title conveys its sentiments: *The Colonization Scheme Considered, in its Rejection by the Colored People—in its tendency to uphold Caste—in its unfitness for Christianizing and Civilizing of the Aborigines of Africa—and for putting a stop to the African Slave Trade.* While the majority of free Blacks in antebellum America sided with Cornish, attitudes toward African colonization were as fractious among black as among white abolitionists. In the same year that Douglass published his attack on colonization, for example, Henry Highland Garnett published a piece in *The North Star* explaining his conversion to the belief that colonization was the only route to the empowerment and enfranchisement of black Americans.[20]

Stowe's own position within the nineteenth-century debate between colonizationists and abolitionists was remarkably indeterminate. Her novel was adopted by supporters of both groups, each of whom marshaled it as a weapon against opponents. At the same time, as many colonization advocates as abolitionists also criticized the novel. Although her father, Lyman Beecher, was committed to colonization while still professing to be abolitionist, Stowe generally disagreed with his more conservative ideas. She also reportedly argued at length with a friend, Professor Upham, challenging his espousal of colonization (Hedrick 205). Such evidence, while inconclusive, still contradicts the position assumed in the conclusion to *Uncle Tom's Cabin.* Her proclaimed but never fulfilled promise to Frederick Douglass that she would address his opposition to her novel's espousal of colonization indicates as well what seems best characterized as indecision or ambivalence. But precisely as a result of Stowe's political indeterminacy on this issue, the novel almost miraculously served to unify divisions within antislavery circles. Its ambiguity, together with its author's vacillations, rendered it particularly effective in manufacturing widespread consent for the opposition to slavery. Yet it was always on this more general platform of opposing slavery that colonizationists and abolitionists met. The question that divided them was less about slavery than about nationalism, namely, the relationship between national and racial identity. Two scenes of emancipation from the novel's close might serve to illustrate the novel's position on this question.

George Shelby, the novel's only white liberator, performs an act of purely local emancipation, one that is not only limited by the qualifying clause "while it was *possible* to free him" (617; emphasis added) but that is furthermore resisted by the slaves' cry: "We don't want to be no freer than we are" (616). Agency here is in the hands of the repentant slaveholder; he acts on behalf of a group of slaves who virtually reject any agency that might be deeded to them as a result of this gesture. As it is represented in this scene, Stowe's program for political change resembles the model of sympathetic realization she borrows from Laurence Sterne, who could recognize the horrors of confinement only by imagining "one poor solitary captive pining in his cell." This is a politics of the singular, prompted by an affect that only the particular can inspire, and it would seem to be this kind of a politics that is offered to the book's white readership.

But while Stowe provides her white readers with instructions for what "every individual can do" (624) to oppose slavery within America, the escaped slave George Harris defends his decision to emigrate from America on the basis of an inverse politics. "[W]hat can I do for them, here?" he asks. "Can I break their chains? No, not as an individual; but, let me go and form part of a nation, which shall have a voice in the councils of nations, and then we can speak. A nation has a right to argue, remonstrate, implore, and present the cause of its race,—which an individual has not" (610). George Harris insists on the necessity of a collective rather than an individual agency, but one that must function from outside the American nation itself. His argument assumes an alliance between national and racial identity, and it also points toward another agenda behind Stowe's exile of black bodies: those bodies continue to harbor an active and resistant agency even after shedding the white disguises that facilitated their self-liberation. Had this proposal worked as George Harris imagined it would, white America—like Mrs. Shelby's spectatorship of Sam or St. Clare's of Topsy—might have watched with a disavowed but profound pleasure the success of Liberia as if that success were America's own.

When the former Indian captive John Marrant, having been ordained as a Methodist minister at Bath, leaves England for Nova Scotia in response to his brother's request that "some ministers would come and preach to them," he is inspired by both national and Christian sentiments. Marrant claims to have "a feeling concern for the salvation of my countrymen" and to feel "continual sorrow in my heart for my brethren, for my kinsmen, according to the flesh" (Aldridge 200). His oblique references here to what may be family feeling or a sense of national or racial community vaguely resemble George Harris's far more explicit alignment with the "African race" (Stowe, *Uncle Tom's Cabin* 608) of his mother. With a missionary goal like that of the converted Topsy, Marrant travels to Nova Scotia in order "that strangers may hear of and run to Christ; that Indian tribes may stretch out their hands to God; that the black nations may be made white in the blood of the Lamb; that vast multitudes of hard tongues, and of strange speech, may learn the language of Canaan, and sing the song of Moses, and of the Lamb" (Aldridge 200). By imagining the transcendence of national and linguistic difference in a community defined largely by its dedication to Christianity, Marrant aims to reproduce on a larger scale his earlier successful conversion of the Cherokees (although here this conversion is figured also as a metaphoric whiteness).

This conclusion to his popular captivity narrative bears a compelling resemblance to Stowe's conclusion to *Uncle Tom's Cabin*. But Marrant's vision of an essentially transracial Christian society in a Nova Scotia inhabited by substantial populations of Whites, black loyalists, and Indians,[21] contrasts with the American empire in *Uncle Tom's Cabin*, which is unified by Christian sentiment but segregated geographically along racial lines. Joan Hedrick, Stowe's most recent biographer, somewhat weakly ascribes her book's colonizationist conclusion to "a certain lack of attention" prompted by the latent influence of her father (235). This pervasive critical tendency to annex the novel's final chapters, thus repeating its own gesture of exile, and to render Stowe passively unaccountable for their sentiments prohibits a consideration of the profound impact that the politics of racial imperialism have on the sentimental politics of *Uncle Tom's Cabin*. The political categorization of her text has not been resolved by locating biographical evidence for Stowe's opinion on African colonization, and the novel's ending cannot be dismissed simply by citing her adamant antislavery position. The appeal to the African colonization project is finally not a function of the novel's attitude toward slavery but of its representation of race and particularly of the "alarming" possibilities of a black agency not in the service of the Christian and maternal empire of white America.

Chapter 6

LOOPHOLES OF RESISTANCE: STRATEGIES OF MIMICRY IN *INCIDENTS IN THE LIFE OF A SLAVE GIRL*

THE POSSIBILITIES FOR AGENCY that *Uncle Tom's Cabin* imagines for its black characters suggest a modified version of the impossible options that for Frantz Fanon formed the colonizer's demand to the Negro: either *"turn white or disappear"* (100). In Stowe's novel, when African Americans become agents, they momentarily turn white and then leave America altogether. While George Harris clearly fulfills both these options by turning white and then leaving, he also defends his departure by positioning Liberia as a route of escape from a specifically nationalist version of the colonizer's impossible demand, for he suggests that it is only by turning (and staying) white that one can be recognized as an American. His argument assumes that sociopolitical agency can operate only on behalf of a nation, an identity denied him as a black man in America. "Americans" of African descent must therefore forsake America in order to change it and claim a national identity by becoming Africans.

The slave narrative was perhaps the primary genre in antebellum America implicitly to critique and reject the terms of the colonizer's demand to "turn white or leave." A narrative such as Harriet Jacobs's account of her life within and escape from slavery articulates for Blacks a subjectivity and an agency that their exclusion from the category of citizenship seemed to deny them. By remaining black and in America, Harriet Jacobs exposes (by inhabiting) a fissure in the edifice of national identity, much as she eventually does in the system of slavery. If Stowe's novel mobilizes the logic of the colonizer from the position of a specifically maternal nationalism, then Jacobs's 1861 *Incidents in the Life of a Slave Girl* might be said to challenge dominant notions of both the national and the maternal from the position of the colonized. Moreover, her challenge proceeds by miming the very strategies of sympathetic exchange on which Stowe's earlier novel relies.

Jacobs wrote her narrative secretly, at night in the attic of her employer's house—a scenario that repeats the confining conditions of her own escape from slavery, just as it also resembles Stowe's depiction of the escape of Cassy and Emmeline from Legree by hiding in and haunting the attic of his house. Unlike her fictional counterparts, Harriet Jacobs neither "turns white" in her act of escape (if anything, she "turns blacker" by applying charcoal to her face while disguised as a sailor) nor abandons America after her escape. Instead, her narrative unsettles the implicit equivalence between the categories of nation and race, between Americanness and whiteness, that Stowe's character George Harris posits. By inhabiting both physical and rhetorical sites where her readers, like her captors, do not expect to find her, Jacobs performs a catachrestic strategy analogous to what Homi Bhabha characterizes as colonial mimicry, a repetition that produces a difference that is "*almost the same but not quite*" or, in his play on Freud's description of the "mixed race" figure, "*Almost the same but not white*" (*Location* 89).[1] Indeed, Jacobs's text works to institute and negotiate a scenario of sympathetic exchange that advances an abolitionist agenda by suggesting to her readers that she is "almost the same [as they] but not white." From the disjunctive margin of that inequivalent and sentimental "almost" emerge Jacobs's antislavery and antiracist arguments. But this tactic of reducing, without quite eliminating, difference unavoidably suggests also that Harriet Jacobs's readers are just like her, if not quite. A rather different critique—of the promises and rewards of national identity for American subjects—takes form at this anxious site of near resemblance, a site that turns out to be in this narrative a somewhat less than sentimental one. The affective and agential strategies mobilized in *Incidents in the Life of a Slave Girl* circle around the familiar figure of a captive woman, but in this case she is multiply confined, captive several times over.

Located in the exact center of the text is a chapter whose title, "The Loophole of Retreat," refers to the tiny crawlspace above her grandmother's shed, where Jacobs hides for seven years in an effort to escape her master's persecution and the "peculiar institution" of slavery that authorizes that persecution. This chapter's central location, whether the result of accident or design, suggests its structural significance within Jacobs's narrative. Yet its centrality is by no means obvious, for "The Loophole of Retreat" goes just as easily unnoticed in the middle of forty-one unnumbered chapters as it becomes—after careful enumeration—potentially quite prominent, as the hinge that balances twenty chapters on either side. It is almost as though it is hidden in plain sight, much like the body of Harriet Jacobs herself, who finally discovers the safest hiding place to be the most obvious one imaginable: in her own grandmother's house and in the center of her master, Dr. Flint's, domain.

What Jacobs calls her "loophole of retreat" thus provides a strategic site for concealment even as it masks its own location. This spatial loophole becomes for Jacobs a means of escape from slavery, and her manipulation of textual loopholes in dominant discourse allows her narrative to escape, as well, from the constraints necessarily imposed on it by dominant cultural paradigms. This tactical operation of the loophole, elaborated and performed with such remarkable effect in *Incidents,* challenges on the one hand the model of agency advanced in *Uncle Tom's Cabin* and on the other the model of agency associated with the work of Foucault. Jacobs's loophole operation allows for sites and performances of resistance within any discursive structure, including ones that, as some descriptions of Foucauldian theory would have it, effectively exile autonomous agency by producing and then recuperating their own opposition. The critical rebuttals of this paradigm advanced through Lacanian and pragmatist theory, rebuttals I examine later in this chapter, have all solved this dilemma only by ignoring its very basis: Foucault's important critique of the individual subject as she or he is produced by institutional structures. The figure of the loophole permits a reconfiguration of agency that accommodates that critique while rescuing agency from its apparent confinement within determining and thus inescapable structures. It does so by recognizing that agency must be located not within the confines of the individualized subject but in the zone of contact between subject and structure, amid the friction generated when subjects inhabit interstitial sites within institutions and discourses. Because debates about agency have centered on the category of the subject, they have overlooked the fissured architecture of the structure, which might be said to have been hiding in plain sight all along.

Confession and Concealment

Lydia Maria Child introduces Harriet Jacobs's slave narrative with a gesture of unveiling that promises a subsequent revealing. In her editor's introduction, Child confronts the difficulty of offering to the public Jacobs's account of sexual oppression by claiming that "[t]his peculiar phase of Slavery has generally been kept *veiled;* but the public ought to be made acquainted with its monstrous features, and I willingly take the responsibility of presenting them *with the veil withdrawn*" (4; emphasis added). Child's theatrical, almost voyeuristic gesture suggests that what will be revealed is not only the body of the desirable female slave but the truth about that body and about the southern institution of slavery that has inscribed it. A similar language of unveiling proliferates throughout Jacobs's own text, in her recurrent promises "to tell . . . the truth" (53) and to "not try to screen [her]self" from "the painful task of confessing" (54). Jacobs's larger project is to lift the veil of deception that hangs between the North and the South, and it is therefore for her northern listeners—even those whose "ears are too delicate to listen to" (4) the details of her story—that Jacobs constructs the personal history that was denied her in the South. By confessing the history of her concealed body, Jacobs constructs that body as a text for "the women of the North" (1) who, in this sense, function as her confessors. Thus, her narrative appropriately ends with a statement that suggests on the one hand freedom and on the other self-display: "[w]hen I rode home in the cars I was no longer afraid to *unveil* my face and look at people as they passed" (200; emphasis added).

Clearly, however, the recurrence of such verbs as *screening, veiling,* and *hiding* signifies in this text a concern with secrecy as much as with exposure. For all its confessional rhetoric this narrative seems finally far more concerned with that which is hidden, disguised, or kept secret.[2] Slaves are marked by the lack of a last name and quickly learn to keep the name of the father silent. Slavery is characterized as a condition whose "secrets . . . are concealed like those of the Inquisition" (35), and that actively promotes such deception, for Jacobs claims that "[s]o far as my ways have been crooked, I charge them all upon slavery" (165). Slavery enforces secrecy, makes speaking the truth an impossibility, and consigns one's personal history and genealogy to silence. If the North acts as confessor in Harriet Jacobs's narrative, the South plays the role of concealer.

It is perhaps because slavery demands such concealment that slaveowners are so obsessed with what might be kept secret from them. Jacobs first hides from her master when he attempts to visit her during an illness. When he later "demanded to know where I was when he called," Jacobs answers by *confessing the truth:* "I told him I was at home. He flew into a passion, and said he knew better" (61). Because the truth is bound to appear to her inquirer so unlikely, Jacobs is able both to confess and to keep her secret at the same time.[3] Later, when Jacobs's "grandmother was out of the way he searched every room" (81) in a futile effort to find the lover he was convinced that his slave was hiding from him. Such anxiety and obsessive suspicion belong not only to Dr. Flint; the preacher, Mr. Pike, delivers a sermon accusing the slaves of being "hidden away somewhere" "[i]nstead of being engaged in worshipping" (69), and the chapter titled "Fear of Insurrection," which describes the southern slaveholders' response to the Nat Turner Rebellion, reveals a search for conspirators so frantic that one of the few safe places for a slave was to be already confined and concealed in jail.

Jacobs's text is filled with moments such as these that are characterized above all by a palpable sense of panic on the part of the slaveholders, those subjects who, in the colonialist scenario of the antebellum American South, should have had least cause to fear. These instances document what Diana Fuss, following Bhabha, characterizes as "narcissistic authority evolv[ing] into paranoiac fear" (147), a reversal or slippage inherent to the ambivalent relations of power that mark colonialism. If Harriet Jacobs repeatedly logs such "incidents" as these in her account of "the life of a slave girl," it may well be because when such authority betrays itself in this way, "the rents and divisions within colonialist narratives of domination become more visible" (Fuss 147). It is precisely those rents and divisions that Jacobs and her text repeatedly inhabit and exploit.

Incidents represents concealment as that which slavery both demands and fears; concealment produces a reservoir of secrecy that perpetuates slavery but also unsettles it from within. The central act of concealment contained in this confessional text—Jacobs's seven-year confinement in the crawlspace of her grandmother's shed—reveals the potential of that hidden space to facilitate agency. A multitude of smaller but similar acts occur within this text: Jacobs's grandmother "screened herself in the crowd" (21) in order to see her captured son Benjamin without his knowledge, the slaveholder Mr. Litch "was so effectively screened by his great wealth that he was called to no account for his crimes" (46), and Jacobs narrowly escaped detection in the shed only because she "slunk down behind a barrel, which entirely screened [her]" (152). Concealment—whether by crowds, wealth, or barrels—continually marks off in this text a protective space from which one might gaze or act, even if it is only to gaze, like Aunt Marthy, at acts of oppression, or to act, like Mr. Litch, in oppressive ways. It is therefore as imperative to inhabit such spaces as it is to uncover them, generating a process that continually encloses even as it exposes. Such interplay between confession and concealment characterizes, of course, all autobiographies.[4] Harriet Jacobs's text, however, continually demonstrates that these two operations are mutually implicated in each other, that hiding is always accompanied by exposure, that enclosure always performs an escape. It is this complex relation between concealment and confession that ultimately enables a black feminist agency to operate in Jacobs's narrative. That double movement structures both her strategy of a quite literal resistance to the oppressions of slavery and patriarchy, and a literary strategy of narration that resists a dominant abolitionist discourse that, as Karen Sánchez-Eppler has shown, was largely appropriated by white feminists for political purposes considerably more self-serving than black emancipation.

The Loophole and the Law

If "the loophole of retreat" chapter in Jacobs's *Incidents* marks and conceals its own importance, then the phrase that makes up its title amplifies this significance through a series of intertextual references. The phrase "loophole of retreat" originates in William Cowper's 1784 poem *The Task,* where it designates a site from which "[a]t a safe distance" the poet can protectively observe the extent of the world's woes:

> 'Tis pleasant through the loop-holes of retreat
> To peep at such a world . . .
> . . . .
> Thus sitting, and surveying thus at ease
> The globe and its concerns, I seem advanc'd
> To some secure and more than mortal height,
> That lib'rates and exempts me from them all. (184)

Cowper's hidden loophole is a specifically domestic site—his poem begins by singing, with whatever mock heroism, the praises of a sofa—and the strategic location of that loophole grants him not only a liberatory escape from the world's injustices but the power of surveillance over those practices.

Because quotations from Cowper's antislavery poems often served as epigraphs to chapters in slave narratives or abolitionist fiction, it is quite possible that Jacobs intends a direct reference to Cowper in her chapter title. Yet it is also possible, especially if Jacobs's editor, Lydia Maria Child, influenced or undertook the naming of chapters, that it refers to Child's own use of the phrase in the preface to her 1826 novel *Hobomok*. Child anonymously writes there in the persona of a reclusive man who "so seldom peep[s] out from the 'loop-holes of retreat' upon a gay and busy world" (4) that he experiences great insecurity about offering his historical novel to the public. Once the gender of the novel's real author is exposed, as it soon was after *Hobomok*'s publication, the phrase inevitably conveys here, too, a specifically domestic space. Whether Child or Jacobs generated the title, however, the word *loophole* combines a set of definitions that elucidate the larger textual strategy of Jacobs's narrative. According to the *Oxford English Dictio-*

nary, the first definition of loophole is "[a] narrow vertical opening, usually widening inwards, cut in a wall or other defence, to allow of the passage of missiles." In addition to describing the crawlspace Harriet Jacobs eventually inhabits, this definition's battle imagery perfectly describes the saga of Jacobs's defense of her body against strategic attacks on it by Dr. Flint. She occupies a position that, like the loophole described here, is simultaneously defensive and offensive. Although Jacobs inhabits the descriptively "female" space of the loophole, she deploys from that space the kind of "male" power that one would ordinarily associate with "the passage of missiles." For Jacobs, however, those weapons are not missiles, but the letters (missals?)[5] addressed to Dr. Flint that she arranges to have postmarked from New York to convince him of her escape.

Those letters are one means by which the power relation between master and slave is structurally reversed once Jacobs conceals herself in her loophole of retreat. Jean Fagan Yellin's claim that Jacobs "uses her garret cell as a war room from which to spy on her enemy and to wage psychological warfare against him" (xxviii) both contains the sense of loophole as fortification and suggests the extent to which power has been redistributed between them. Jacobs's powerlessness as a slave is exemplified by Flint's belief that she "was made for his use, made to obey his command in *every* thing" (18) and "that she was his property; that [she] must be subject to his will in all things" (27). Whereas Jacobs had formerly been compelled to accept and read the notes with which Dr. Flint persecuted her, from the garret she controls his behavior by compelling him—by way of her letters—to travel north in search of her, repeating or miming the colonizer's authority and returning the inverted terms of that authority to him. Yet this seeming shift in the site of authority toward the slave functions only to the extent that it publicly disavows that shift, since Jacobs's gestures succeed only insofar as she carefully maintains their (and her) invisibility to the master. Her discourse of resistance is therefore located at what Bhabha calls "the crossroads of what is known and permissable and that which though known must be kept concealed; a discourse uttered between the lines and as such both against the rules and within them" (*Location* 89). It is precisely at such a site that I locate Jacobs's agency as well as her discourse, an agency that operates not just from the interstitial time lag where Bhabha would place it but from an interstitial *space* that both is and is not within the domain of slavery.

As a slave, Jacobs was not only utterly subject to the command of her master but was the constant object of his gaze as well: "My master met me at every turn, reminding me that I belonged to him, and swearing by heaven and earth that he would compel me to submit to him. If I went out for a breath of fresh air, after a day of unwearied toil, his footsteps dogged me. If I knelt by my mother's grave, his dark shadow fell on me even there"

(28). Jacobs escapes such surveillance only by going into a captivity that in many ways enacts the conditions of slavery on a hyperbolic scale. The absence of freedom, the physical hardships, the separation from children and family, and the secrecy that all mark the slave's condition are repeated and exacerbated by Jacobs's confinement "in her dungeon." Yet that repetition is one with a signal difference, a difference that is concealed within the enormity of hyperbole, for "[a]lone in my cell . . . no eye but God's could see me" (133).

Not only is Jacobs free from Flint's gaze, but she has appropriated the power of surveillance for herself, since through her "peeping-hole" she is able "to watch the passers by," including Dr. Flint, without being seen and to "hear many conversations not intended to meet my ears" (117). Jacobs becomes an eyewitness to slavery, occupying a position of spectatorial "objectivity" that William L. Andrews has argued is usually filled by the abolitionist editors of slave narratives while the ex-slave authors more commonly serve as the subjective and participatory "I-witness" to their own experience (*To Tell* 65). These two positions clearly conflate in Jacobs's loophole, where she is able to observe the system of slavery at the same time that she inhabits its very center. Thus, like Cowper, Jacobs is able to survey "[a]t a safe distance" the "globe and its concerns," and although her space of confinement is far from conventionally domestic, one of its most important characteristics is that it allows its occupant to survey her children with a protective and disciplinary maternal gaze.

By inhabiting this spatial loophole, Jacobs inadvertently enacts a second definition of the word as "[a]n outlet or means of escape. Often applied to an ambiguity or omission in a statute, etc., which affords opportunity for evading its intention" (*OED*). This sense of the word generally refers to the law, particularly to written law, where a loophole is not produced so much as it is discovered, and even then it is typically discovered only by accident. Although such escape routes, once detected, are often closed down, by logic every law—no matter how carefully phrased—contains a loophole, since every law contains the permanent possibility of a loophole. A loophole uniquely allows one to transgress the law without actually breaking it and thus to elude as well any potential punishment for that transgression. Harriet Jacobs's loophole condition is precisely such a simultaneous inscription and transgression of the law of slavery. She is able to reverse the master-slave power relation and to assume a kind of power associated with men only because that reversal and deployment are concealed and contained within the semblance of black enslavement and female powerlessness. Jacobs's relation to that power shift is neither one of conscious premeditation nor one of unconscious passivity. Her unexpected leverage over her master follows solely from her fortuitous location in the loophole. Her resultant access to agency is a circumstance of which Jacobs, it seems, becomes only gradually aware and that she begins only cautiously to exploit.

Both her physical and textual strategies succeed because they mime — sometimes to the point of hyperbole — those systems or discourses that otherwise oppress her.[6] The ironic force of that mimicry discovers within those structures loopholes that escape detection because they are concealed by what appear to remain dominant hierarchies and power relations. Inhabiting those loopholes can transform them into sites of resistance: it is because Harriet Jacobs inhabits a structural site where the practice of power seems so incredibly unlikely that she is able to get away with her resistance to and manipulation of her master.[7] Thus, by inhabiting a loophole in the first, more spatial sense of the word — as a defensive and enclosed space — Harriet Jacobs enacts the second, more textual definition of loophole as "a means of escape"; she has discovered and retreated into a *loophole* in the patriarchal institution of slavery. Jacobs's loophole of retreat is the most confining space imaginable, but it becomes a space of escape.

Subject and Structure

The operations of concealment and confession that play so critical a role in Harriet Jacobs's narrative of slavery and escape also form the subjects of much of Michel Foucault's work, which has focused on structures such as the clinic, the asylum, and the prison, which hold individuals captive. Texts like *Discipline and Punish,* his study of the birth of the prison system and its normalizing practices of confinement and surveillance, and the first volume of *The History of Sexuality,* which argues that the confession is a truth-producing practice that generates rather than represses (as psychoanalysis would have it) discourse about sexuality, reveal that confession and concealment combine to form a power relation that produces and exposes. The pastoral or criminal confession makes hidden thoughts known, while institutional concealment opens the body and its behavior to the disciplinary gaze. Foucault's confessional economy acknowledges a necessary relation between hiding and revealing, wherein "the obligation to conceal [is] but another aspect of the duty to admit" (*History* 61). But that economy has been repeatedly criticized for too perfectly reproducing (confessing) all that it consumes (conceals).

By the same token, the model of Bentham's panopticon that Foucault uses to define a new disciplinary architecture in which the subject internalizes the power relation that subjugates him or her has been accused of positing a totalizing economy of complete recuperation. Perhaps the most common formulation of the status of agency in Foucault's works on the prison and on sexuality argues that subjects are inescapably determined by their historical and cultural context and therefore inevitably support and repro-duce the dominant power structures they might have set out to resist and subvert. Rather than repeat this debate, however, I aim to shift its terms by focusing instead on the implications and possibilities of Foucault's critique of the individualized subject. Where might one locate the source of that re-cuperative movement assigned to Foucault's confinement of agency? Does the panoptic eye in fact see everything, or does it have a blind spot?

While her subject is specifically Foucault's influence on film theory, Joan Copjec's Lacanian critique of the panoptic model insists on the subject's ca-pacity for keeping secrets and concealing thought and thus locates that blind spot in panoptic theory's disregard of what she calls "the permanent possibility of deception" (65). Faulting Foucault for denying repression and thus a split subject, Copjec argues that "the orthopsychic relation (unlike the panoptic one) assumes that it is just this objective survey [which the subject performs on itself] that allows thought to become (not wholly visible, but) *secret;* it allows thought to remain *hidden,* even under the most intense scrutiny" (63). Copjec's analysis reveals that because the contents of the un-conscious can remain undetectable, the subject can practice deception and thus can always undermine the ideal functioning of the panoptic gaze. There-fore, any confession remains incomplete, its economy imperfect, leaving an inevitable and unrecuperable surplus. Copjec's solution significantly recog-nizes and accommodates the possibility of that concealed surplus, although it does not address the questions of whether and how this excess might translate into a comparable hiding place for the body, nor how it might en-able escape or resistance. In this particular instance, bringing Lacan to the rescue of the Foucauldian panoptic trap springs that trap only to finally re-trap the possibility of agency within the unconscious, where it might be said to suffer a kind of paralysis.

That paralysis resembles the very predicament that the psychoanalytic approach set out to solve, a predicament associated with the new historicist paradigm's seemingly irresolvable opposition between independent agency and historical determinism. Anthony Appiah has called that new historicist problematic "structural determinism" (66) and has further suggested that its grounding opposition is based on the mistaken belief that subject and structure are connected categories and that their terms belong to the same discourse. Appiah argues instead that subject and structure represent "two different discursive economies" (79) whose distinction should be recog-nized and maintained, since "[e]verything that a theory of structure claims to explain belongs to the language, the discourse, of the structure; to insist on autonomous agency within this discourse is, if I may say so, simply to change the subject" (84). His pragmatic solution is accordingly a complete separation of discourses. As Appiah himself acknowledges, however, such a separation would continue to dissolve in practice, where the impassable subject/structure gulf, which he insists exists, is continually crossed. Instead of disconnecting these two terms from each other, I propose to shift attention toward the space signified by the slash that already (dis)connects them. It is in that juncture where subject and structure meet, rather than in an independent discourse of the subject, that I wish to locate agency. The problem is not, as Appiah suggests, that the independent categories of subject and structure have been falsely wedded but that the categories of subject and agency have been so.

Perhaps the most consistent and consistently overlooked aim of Foucault's own work is to critique and oppose processes that individualize the subject. Despite the fact that Foucault has claimed, for example, that "the political, ethical, social, philosophical problem of our days is not to try to liberate the individual from the state, and from the state's institutions, but to liberate us both from the state and from the type of individualization which is linked to the state" ("Subject" 216), the notion of agency in general remains constructed in terms of the (individual) subject. As a result—and as new historicist criticism reminds us—agency necessarily becomes a *form* of subjection even as it struggles *against* subjection. The ongoing critical debate over the problem of agency often spins in the kind of recuperative circle marked out by this last formulation, and it does so, I am suggesting, because it remains unable to think agency other than in terms of an autonomous subject working against, rather than within, the structure.

From this perspective, then, the circularity of the subject/structure debate is as much the point of Foucault's work as it is a problem with it. "To change the subject"—to change the meaning of Appiah's phrase—has always been one of the primary aims of Foucault, who has claimed that "[w]e have to promote new forms of subjectivity through the refusal of th[e] kind of individuality which has been imposed on us for several centuries" ("Subject" 216). Why not refuse, then, the individualization of agency and its entrapment in the discourse of the subject and posit instead an agency that operates within not only the discourse but the very architecture of the structure? Only by shifting the conceptualization of agency away from the subject and toward the structure might one locate sites that, like loopholes, escape detection and thus enable resistant agency. This is to argue that, like every law, every structure contains a loophole (since it always contains the possibility of a loophole) regardless of how carefully it is designed—like, for example, a panopticon or slavery—to eliminate the possibility of subversion or escape.[8] Those seemingly monolithic methods of surveillance that ostensibly make escape from detection impossible may finally enable escape by the very fact that they make it seem so impossible.

Discussions among historians about agency within slavery and black culture reveal a problematic tension between oppression and resistance similar to the one associated with Foucault's work. Slavery was characterized by Stanley Elkins's once influential thesis as an institution with a disciplinary structure so total that resistance to it was ineffective if not impossible. Elkins maintained that North American slavery was a "closed system" that prevented rebellion because slaves had no access to standards of judgment or modes of behavior outside the institution that contained them. Elkins's many critics resisted this monolithic construction by insisting that this closed system in fact contained openings where subversion and sometimes escape could occur. For the most part, these critiques focus on the existence of a distinct culture within the slave community that offered residual or emergent alternatives to the dominant culture.[9] More recently, Clarence E. Walker has accused this "slave community/culturalist paradigm" of "romanticizing" the notion of community and overestimating its force as an autonomous culture. Walker urges "black history to rise above the romantic and celebratory" by acknowledging the tensions within any oppressed community and by recognizing the extent to which marginal groups internalize dominant culture (xviii).[10] Walker's critique does not specifically address the question of agency, but it is nevertheless an important intervention in a debate that has tended to move in cycles that alternate between emphasizing the psychological and physical damage produced by slavery, on the one hand, and the liberating and revisionist potential of black communities within slavery on the other. Walker's project of deromanticization, like Foucault's of deindividualization, explicitly warns against too easily making claims for autonomous resistance and implicitly suggests the need to reformulate conventional constructions of agency.

The example of Jacobs's text opens the possibility of a model for agency that falls between the culturalist paradigm and its critique, a possibility suggested by the fact that her text might be used to support both positions. Walker, for example, uses *Incidents* to illustrate that a slave community often did not devalue dominant taboos like illegitimacy, since the pregnant Jacobs fears the censure of her grandmother as much as that of her readers (xvii). At the same time, her narrative clearly serves as an ideal example for those historians intent on asserting the possibility of resistance within slavery. However, Harriet Jacobs's loophole of retreat does not so easily fit the culturalist model. Although she receives communal support, her hiding place can hardly be considered a cultural realm analogous to the family or religion, and it is certainly not a space that can be readily romanticized. Aunt Marthy's garret does not offer a retreat from the oppressive conditions of slavery—as, one might argue, the communal life in Aunt Marthy's house does—so much as it enacts a repetition of them. Because this loophole so resembles that which it opposes, it evades the conceptual opposition between oppression and resistance, as well as the critical opposition between Elkins's "closed system" and the more optimistic emphasis on black community or culture. Harriet Jacobs escapes reigning discourses and structures only in the very process of affirming them. She disobeys social norms of proper motherhood, for example, precisely in order that she might eventually enact those norms.[11]

The example of agency provided by Harriet Jacobs's slave narrative reveals that when Foucault announces the arrival of "a panopticism in which the vigilance of intersecting gazes was soon to render useless both the eagle and the sun" (*Discipline* 217), he fails to consider that panopticism carries within it the inevitable blind spot associated with its predecessors; the loophole, both as hiding place and as escape route, is that blind spot, and it is that blind spot in which secrets reside and through which bodies may escape. The paralytic circularity of the subject/structure debate can be circumvented by relocating agency in the juncture between the structure and the subject, in sites that elude the gaze not because they are outside the structure (or distinct from its culture) but because they are so clearly and centrally a part of it. Harriet Jacobs inhabits such a fissure in the very architecture of the "'patriarchal institution'" (146)—a structure that she has already ironized by means of framing quotation marks—and that fissure eludes Dr. Flint's searching gaze because it is located directly in front of that gaze. The loophole is in this sense akin to the sites of feminist agency posited by Teresa de Lauretis as "the elsewhere of discourse here and now, the blind spots, or the space-off, of its representations. I think of it as spaces in the margins of hegemonic discourses, social spaces carved in the interstices of institutions and in the chinks and cracks of the power/knowledge apparati" (25): patriarchy's space-off, Dr. Flint's blind spot, the loophole of retreat. The garret of the shed beside Harriet Jacobs's grandmother's house was the least likely place of escape because it was from the beginning the most likely place of concealment: "it was the last place they thought of. Yet there was no place, where slavery existed, that could have afforded me so good a place of concealment" (117).

Sentimentality and Slavery

In her struggle against slavery and patriarchy, one might claim that Harriet Jacobs practices a kind of camouflage, since she hides by miming the confinement and suffering that characterize those very conditions against which she battles.[12] Jacobs's physical strategy of escape and her narrative strategy of protest are finally quite alike in their fortuitous and effective use of camouflage. While Jacobs's body is inscribed by the law of slavery, through the figure of the loophole she simultaneously transgresses, even as she embodies, that law. Jacobs's use of the sentimental discourse prevalent in popular nineteenth-century American novels like *Uncle Tom's Cabin* operates by a similarly double movement. Just as her hyperbolic miming of the condition of slavery marks a rupture that her body can inhabit and from which a feminist agency can operate, her employment of a sentimental discourse aligned especially with the fiction of white feminist-abolitionists opens loopholes within that discourse that allow her to critique it.[13]

Jacobs clearly employs the strategies and structures of sentimental fiction throughout her narrative in an effort to inspire her northern female readers to respond emotionally to her story and to translate that affect into moral behavior. The similarities, for example, between her text and Samuel Richardson's *Pamela* suggest the extent to which Jacobs may have consciously borrowed from that genre.[14] Conscious borrowing, however, was hardly necessary, since in mid-nineteenth-century America both women's writing and abolitionist writing were largely characterized by sentimentality. As it did in captivity narratives and sentimental novels of captivity, that discourse appealed to a reader's sympathy through scenes of often theatrical pathos and plots of familial separation and individual trial—scenes and plots that, as we have seen, frequently turned around the figure of a captive woman.

For all its participation in sentimental conventions, there are, of course, several places where Jacobs's text reveals significant disjunctions between standard sentimental plots and the facts of her own life. Those moments include her decision to take a lover, the birth of her two children out of wedlock, and the impossibility of her story ending in marriage—differences that lead Jacobs to suggest that "the slave woman ought not to be judged by the same standard as others" (56). William L. Andrews has argued that interstitial or liminal narrators like Jacobs were able to fashion new versions of self by virtue of their "betwixt and between" position (*To Tell* 175, 203). Thus it is the disjunction between the cultural ideal embodied in the cult of true womanhood and the impossibility that Jacobs could ever conform to such an ideal that leads her to suggest the need for an alternative standard for the slave woman. The political imperative of this text is located in the sentimental gap between identification and imitation, between Jacobs's acceptance of the gendered standards shared by her targeted audience and her limited ability to enact that standard given the circumstances of her own life.[15]

Such revisions of the conventional sentimental narrative, however, signal less significant moments in Jacobs's text than those in which she stages an outraged condemnation of sentimentality. By far the most bitingly ironic depiction of sentiment is Mrs. Flint's response to the death of Aunt Nancy. Jacobs writes that "Mrs. Flint had rendered her poor foster-sister childless, apparently without compunction; and with cruel selfishness had ruined her health by years of incessant, unrequited toil, and broken rest. But now she became very sentimental." The worst effect of such displays like the grand funeral, at which "the mistress dropped a tear, and returned to her carriage, probably thinking she had performed her duty nobly," is that

> Northern travellers, passing through the place, might have described this tribute of respect to the humble dead as a beautiful feature in the "patriarchal institution;" a touching proof of the attachment between slaveholders and their servants; and tender-hearted Mrs. Flint would have confirmed this impression, with handkerchief at her eyes. (146)

Jacobs's intent in exposing Mrs. Flint's performance is therefore to unveil such sentimentality's deception of the North, to reveal the violence that sentimentality conceals. She manipulates a similar unveiling, with similar irony, when she includes the highly sentimental letter written by Dr. Flint to her in New York. Pretending to write as his own son, Flint tells Jacobs that he "sympathize[s] with you in your unfortunate condition," promises to "receive you with open arms and tears of joy" (171), and describes the death of her aunt as someone who "taught us how to live—and, O, too high the price of knowledge, she taught us how to die! Could you have seen us round her death bed, with her mother, all mingling our tears in one common stream, you would have thought the same heartfelt tie existed between a master and his servant, as between a mother and her child" (172). Despite Jacobs's use of sentimental discourse throughout her narrative, in these two instances Jacobs attacks sentimentality as deceptive, as a discursive technique that hides rather than confesses the truth. Such an offensive against sentimentality from within sentimentality resembles Jacobs's strategy of escape from slavery by miming its conditions.

Indeed, the movement of sentimentality throughout this text is like the movement of the loophole, which inscribes that which it simultaneously transgresses. This double action constitutes a fundamental property of sentimental discourse, which employs the very tactics it attempts to argue against and whose politics therefore seem to be so easily recuperated. The politics of sentimentality have been trapped in a debate that bears some resemblance to the division that marks debates about agency: on the one hand, there are those who see sentimentalism as a legitimately liberating discourse that gives women access to a revisionist economic and political power; and on the other, there are those who see it as a rationalization of dominant orders that deny women power.[16] As a result of this fundamental ambivalence, conservative and progressive claims are frequently made for the same sentimental text. The strategy of mimicry with which Harriet Ja-

cobs responds to a conflict with a master who oppresses her and to a sentimental discourse that marginalizes her reveals in its double movement the
source of that ambivalence. Sentimental discourse, like colonial mimicry,
"can be disruptive and reversionary at once" (Fuss 148), necessarily generating both reactionary and radical effects. It is precisely this contradictory dynamic, however, that (un)covers loopholes, loopholes that, as we have seen,
can serve as sites of agency. Confession conceals as much as it reveals; it constructs veils in the very gesture of unveiling.

That play between concealing and revealing secrets structures the very
functioning of sentimental discourse, which typically claims tears as a mark
of its success. Those tears are not, as one might imagine and as sentimental
texts themselves suggest, a sign of the catharsis of complete confession but a
sign rather of confession's inevitable incompleteness; it is as though the
tears that are secreted (in the sense of produced) substitute for and serve as a
sign of that which remains secreted (in its other sense as hidden). Perhaps
the moment of greatest pathos in her narrative, for example, is when Jacobs's son runs, covered with blood from being attacked by a dog, past her
hiding place while she remains unable to comfort or even speak to him.[17]
The sentimental moment occurs when Jacobs's desire to confess—to reveal
the secret of her location in the loophole of retreat—is repressed and she is
forced instead, like the reader, to endure the suffering of passive spectatorship. That pathos is generated in the disjunction between what is confessed
and what is concealed or—to recall Mary Rowlandson's first outburst of
tears in the first text studied in this book—between what should happen
and what does happen. Harriet Jacobs's narrative insists that the cultural
and discursive interstices generated by such disjunctions are sites that enable agency.

Jacobs's immediate political goal of encouraging her readers to resist the
Fugitive Slave Law points out a loophole in that law that also enables agency.
Since northerners were expected to report runaway slaves so that they might
be returned to their southern owners, this law required rather than forbade
action in order to be obeyed. As a result, by simply remaining passive and
silent, it was possible to transgress and resist the Fugitive Slave Law without actually breaking it. One might claim that such passivity mimics northern abolitionists' failure actively to oppose slavery, particularly considering
that the capture and execution of the radical antislavery activist John Brown
occurred not long before the publication of *Incidents*. Given the camouflage
effect of mimicry, detection of such passive resistance would be virtually impossible. The absence of Harriet Jacobs's final chapter on the John Brown
incident from her published narrative suggests that even Lydia Maria Child's
opening promise of confession and unveiling practices its own concealment. Child, in fact, advised Jacobs to excise that last chapter and to add in-

stead an internal chapter on the southern response to the Nat Turner Rebellion.[18] Though Child's advice may have been artistic or financial (encouraging greater aesthetic cohesion or better sales) rather than political, its effect is nevertheless to end *Incidents in the Life of a Slave Girl,* as Jean Fagan Yellin has pointed out, on a personal and sentimental rather than a public and political note (xxii). This text's ending might therefore conceal another one, and the chapter added in its stead suggestively portrays the paranoiac anxiety among southern Whites about what might be concealed from them. In that added chapter, marauders search through Jacobs's grandmother's house for secrets. All they uncover, however, are letters that, Jacobs explains to them, "'are from white people. Some request me to burn them after they are read, and some I destroy without reading'" (66). Lydia Maria Child and Harriet Jacobs present this narrative to the North as a true and complete confession from an escaped female slave. Yet that supplementary chapter and its unread letters stand as one sign, perhaps, of the North's resistance to a different kind of historical and political consciousness, one that presses at the sentimental seams of this text, where confession and concealment overlap.

National Subjects and National Agents

If sentimental fiction aimed to inspire sympathetic identification in its readers, that response, especially in the case of abolitionist literature, ideally translated into political action. The dynamics of identification's oscillation between similarity and difference—a process elaborated in chapter 2 as a movement between an imaginary identification with a likable image one wants to resemble and a symbolic identification with the often unappealing position from which that image is rendered likable—operate in Jacobs's slave narrative as they did in earlier narratives of Indian captivity. While her readers, like Jacobs herself, identify with the ideal of passive white womanhood the heroine strives to resemble, they necessarily identify also with the aggressive position of her captor/master, Dr. Flint, from which that ideal is seen as attractive. Just as in Cotton Mather's account of Hannah Dustan's captivity or in Richardson's *Pamela,* Jacobs's account of captivity acquires its sentimental affect, its "moving" quality, from the movement of identification between these two incompatible registers. Likewise, Jacobs's active agency, which mimes the tactical manipulations of the slaveholder Flint, is blurred by the moving representation of Jacobs as a slave mother, immobilized, separated from her children, and enduring extraordinary suffering in the confining garret of her grandmother's shed—an image of maternalism and passivity.

Colonial American captivity narratives at once encouraged and disavowed readers' identification with the captive heroine's active agency, as a way both to legitimate and to mobilize aggressive violence against her captors. The mother whose body, figured as an engine of national reproduction, was reputedly being defended by such violence is repeated in *Incidents in the Life of a Slave Girl* with a difference so profoundly startling as to invert the sentimental nationalism of captivity narratives into an outraged national critique. Rather than inspire the attendant sensations of sympathy and rage that, in captivity novels like *Miss McCrea,* could lead readers to be willing to die for their country, *Incidents* turns those sensations against the abstract entity of the nation itself. This is not to say that maternal affect does not play a role in Jacobs's text; in fact, it is perhaps the central relation Jacobs invokes to legitimate her escape from slavery and from Flint, much as the heroines in captivity narratives did. But for this heroine the sensations of motherhood are split from within by the devastating knowledge that she is reproducing the institution of slavery by producing children whom the laws of her nation consider commodities. Few descriptions of her children are not accompanied by this reminder. Her master greets the news of the birth of her son with a claim to ownership when he informs her that "my child was an addition to his stock of slaves" (61), and the birth of her daughter serves as a reminder of the sexual violence allowed by the "patriarchal institution" against the bodies of slaves: "Slavery is terrible for men," she notes, "but it is far more terrible for women" (77). The captivity narrative's rhetoric of national reproduction backfires in the slave narrative into a decidedly antisentimental and ultimately antinationalist horror.

Clearly, the binary racial and national oppositions that captivity narratives invoked—between the Anglo-American captive and her readers, on the one hand, and Native American (or later, British) captors on the other—are confounded in slave narratives like Jacobs's just as they are in abolitionist fiction like *Uncle Tom's Cabin.* Chapter 5 argued that Stowe's turn to the project of African colonization works to reinscribe those very oppositions that the relations of sympathy between white readers and black slaves would appear to undo. *Incidents in the Life of a Slave Girl* also mobilizes sympathy in order to cross such boundaries, but it furthermore challenges those oppositions by exposing the permeability of the racial and national boundaries on whose presumed inviolability so much sentimental captivity literature depends. As a result, Jacobs's narrative also questions the valency and integrity of the categories those boundaries presumably divide. Jacobs highlights the fantasy of coherence on which these distinctions rely, as well as the violent cross-racial exchanges that fantasy must repress, when she urgently asks, "And then who *are* Africans? Who can measure the amount of Anglo-Saxon blood coursing in the veins of American slaves?" (44). The cautious unveiling promised by her preface and by Child's introduction of slavery's sexual violence gradually exposes the "tangled skeins [that] are the genealogy of slavery!" (78). Those "tangled skeins" impossibly complicate any schema that would cleanly and clearly distinguish black from white, "African" from "Anglo-Saxon." Even the one boundary within the nation itself on which this slave narrative seems to depend for its rhetorical and political effect—the opposition between North and South—collapses in upon itself by the end of the narrative, when "the bloodhounds of the north" become indistinguishable from "the bloodhounds of the south" (190–91). The result of this collapse is the representation of the United States as a slave nation—not a nation unified by slavery but one that resembles the self-divided households of slaveowners like the Flints, households in which the secrets colonizers try to keep from themselves return to haunt and betray them.

After insisting on the incalculable exchanges between "African" and "Anglo-Saxon" in her pointed questions about racial identity and integrity quoted above, Jacobs significantly concludes by qualifying slaves with the adjective "American." Ultimately, *Incidents* not only cuts racial identity loose from essence and coherence but destabilizes any essential coherence to national identity as well by exposing the ambivalence on which the seemingly absolute distinction between disenfranchised slave and free citizen is founded.[19] Jacobs dismantles this boundary through catachresis when she chooses to inhabit the position of an American citizen, to classify herself at once as a national subject and slave. When she returns to America from England, where she had experienced for the first time in her life the absence of "prejudice against color" (185), she remarks that "from the distance spectres seemed to rise up on the shores of the United States. It is a sad feeling to be afraid of one's native country" (186). Such fear is, for Jacobs, an outrage. But her narrative finally suggests that citizenship in antebellum America is more often than not characterized by precisely such an anger at and fear of one's own country. Indeed, her sentimental narrative of passive captivity and maternal suffering is underwritten by another kind of sensation entirely, by what Lauren Berlant eloquently calls Jacobs's "psychic rage at America for not even trying to live up to the conditions of citizenship it promises in law and in spirit" (466). This rage smolders within the sentimental proclamation of freedom with which her narrative ends.

Dr. Flint and Mrs. Flint, both of whom exercise tyrannical and abusive power over the slave Harriet Jacobs, are haunted by the limits of their own authority. Dr. Flint is constantly and frantically searching for his slave, both before and during the several stages of her escape, as well as for ways of asserting his dominance over her. Jacobs's acts of resistance are followed by sometimes bizarre and excessive acts on the part of Flint; he pursues her, for example, with "a pair of shears" in order to "cut every hair close to my head"

(77) after he learns of her pregnancy. Outbursts such as these read like desperate attempts to eliminate or conceal the rifts in his authority that she continually exploits. Like Mrs. Flint's paranoid nightly vigils over Jacobs's bedside or her murderous threats against her, Dr. Flint's actions resonate with the excesses of power that slaveholders performed in response to the slave rebellion of Nat Turner. Such scenes of panic disclose the ambivalence of colonial authority, betray the colonizers' desperate efforts to reinforce as impenetrable the hierarchical boundary that separates them from their subjects. Harriet Jacobs's text repeatedly moves to expose the loopholes that emerge at the imperfect suture where panic and tyranny coexist. By the close of *Incidents,* this portrayal no longer applies just to the South and slaveholders; instead, it characterizes the United States as a whole, as a place where national authority, obsessed with denying its own internal rifts and cracks, becomes paranoid and inspires a fearful anger in its subjects.

With the passage of the Fugitive Slave Law, Jacobs's residence in the North becomes suffused by the conditions of fear and furtiveness that dominated her existence as a southern slave. She repeatedly challenges, through scornful irony, the North's self-characterization as a site of freedom: "I was, in fact, a slave in New York, as subject to slave laws as I had been in a Slave State. Strange incongruity in a State called free!" (193). When she remarks, "What a disgrace to a city calling itself free, that inhabitants, guiltless of offence, and seeking to perform their duties conscientiously, should be condemned to live in such incessant fear, and have nowhere to turn for protection!" (191), she appears to be referring to herself and her status as a fugitive slave. But the open and imprecise reference to these guiltless "inhabitants" suggests what her narrative gradually makes clear: this fugitive condition might describe any U.S. citizen, even those who consider themselves free. Her employer, Mrs. Bruce, for example, through whose actions Harriet Jacobs gains her legal freedom, is forced to conform to the abhorrent laws of the slave system she despises by literally purchasing and thus commodifying her nurse before she is entitled to free her. Jacobs responds to the news of her now legal freedom with far more bitterness than gratefulness, absolutely refusing to accede to this scene's sentimental possibilities. Indeed, Jacobs's response suggests, against *Uncle Tom's Cabin,* that the sympathetic transference of agency from African Americans to Anglo-Americans was as likely to reinforce slavery's most central assumptions—like the classification and treatment of a human being as "an article of property" (199)—as it was to challenge them. Mrs. Bruce's magnanimous action nevertheless leaves the structure and assumptions of the slave system intact and validates the legal authority of slaveholders; it repeats the rules governing the institution of slavery but not with a difference.

Jacobs's horror at being "*sold* at last! A human being *sold* in the free city of

New York!" (200) is significantly not directed at her employer Mrs. Bruce, whom she represents as practicing what freedom she can within the confining limitations set for her as a member of a slave nation. Rather, Jacobs is angry at the national apparatus and "the legislators of the country" (194) who authorize such a system. That the father of her children is one of those legislators only serves to reinforce Jacobs's closing analysis of America as a nation whose noblest citizens struggle to act as agents *against* those who reputedly serve *as* their agents in Washington. Thus, Americans such as Mrs. Bruce tend to express the same emotions of fear and rage associated with the enslaved Jacobs. Even the senator whom Jacobs praises as one who "would not have voted for the Fugitive Slave Law, as did the senator in 'Uncle Tom's Cabin'" (194) is finally characterized by an overwhelming anxiety of detection, for he is too afraid of the very law he opposes to "hav[e] me remain in his house many hours" (194). Mrs. Bruce, whom Jacobs initially introduces to her readers as "an American" (190), responds with a scornful and angry expression—"Shame on my country that it is so!" (194)—when informed that she was "violating the laws of her country" by assisting the fugitive Jacobs.[20]

The deceptions slaveholders practice on those northerners who visit the South are, Jacobs suggests, being practiced daily by the men who represent America's citizens in the nation's capital. Like the institution of slavery, Congress is filled with secrets harbored by men like Mr. Sands: one congressman, she notes, wrote to ask that his six children borne by a slave mother be removed from the house upon his arrival, for "fear that friends might recognize in their features a resemblance to him" (142). Even the periodic elections that theoretically allowed America to renew its national virtue seem finally subject to the private obsessions of paranoid masters like Flint, a man who goes so far as to lobby for a particular congressional representative simply as a way of attempting to revenge the slave whose hair he once cut in a fit of rage. At the very end of her narrative, Jacobs implicitly contrasts enfranchised national subjects such as Flint with a moral, selfless, and brave individual like her Uncle Philip. The last page of *Incidents* quotes from Uncle Philip's obituary, which refers to him as "a *citizen*" even though, as Jacobs indicates with sarcasm, it is a legal misnomer to do so. Her readers, whether consciously or not, may have aligned themselves in these final chapters with the duped northerners who fail to recognize the veils deployed by their national representatives. Jacobs seems to suggest that in doing so those readers would be concealing from themselves their more anxious alignment with those other Americans called slaves.

There is one figure in Jacobs's *Incidents in the Life of a Slave Girl* who recalls the more aggressive agency deployed by captives like Hannah Dustan, Deborah Sampson, Magawisca, and even Cassy. Significantly, in Jacobs's text that aggression is directed at the nation, through its representatives. She illustrates the ignorance about the North in which southern slaveholders keep their slaves by recalling the gross misconceptions that she has heard slaves express:

> Some believe that the abolitionists have already made them free, and that it is established by law, but that their masters prevent the law from going into effect. One woman begged me to get a newspaper and read it over. She said her husband told her that the black people had sent word to the queen of 'Merica that they were all slaves; that she didn't believe it, and went to Washington city to see the president about it. They quarrelled; she drew her sword upon him, and swore that he should help her to make them all free. (45)

This fantastic figure of a sword-wielding American queen heroically freeing American slaves, not only from their masters but from the American president himself, might be seen as a moment in which the colonized imaginatively choose a different representative, one who is willing to transform their pervasive sense of angry betrayal into an act of physical agency. In her analysis of this anecdote, Jacobs both suppresses and validates that anger, first by noting with a sense of dismay the pathetic state of knowledge among slaves such as "[t]hat poor, ignorant woman [who] thought that America was governed by a Queen, to whom the President was subordinate." But she immediately goes on to legitimate that woman and her desire by expressing her own "wish [that] the President was subordinate to Queen Justice" (45).

Lauren Berlant has remarked on the monarchic leanings of this remarkable scene and its gestures toward what she calls "Diva citizenship," the impulse to "revitalize national identity" (471) through urgent, dramatic, and transgressive performances of national identity. The performance of citizenship displayed in Jacobs's anecdote repeats national authority with a difference, replacing a passive president with an active queen determined to "make them all free." Like the slaveholders whom this "ignorant" slavewoman believes position themselves above and against the law, the president is positioned here above and against justice. Importantly, however, the mimicry of authority that this scene performs reveals not only a royalist difference but cultural difference. As Yellin notes, among some African tribes certain decisions about tribal organization and rulership depended on the opinions of female leaders. The Ashanti, for example, reveal a matriarchal structure similar to that which characterized some Amerindian tribes. The choice of a new tribal chief among the Ashanti, for example, depended primarily on the "Queen Mother," whose questions, rebukes, and recommendations were of central influence on this important decision.[21] Thus, what may seem at first to be an anecdote characterized primarily by ignorance or fantasy is rather a moment of cultural difference. That difference emerges when national identity confronts its own self-division through mimicry, revealing what is perhaps the fundamental inequivalence exposed and exploited by *Incidents in the Life of a Slave Girl*, the gap between the profession and the practice of national virtue.

CONCLUSION

*A*T THE CENTER of the texts I have examined in *Captivity and Sentiment* are the bodies of women, bodies that engage in and prompt certain kinds of mobility precisely because they are held in confinement. The experience of captivity across cultural boundaries transports them to interstitial zones of contact, where dominant values, standards, and modes of representation fail, falter, or are brought to crisis. As a result, these captive figures transgress conventions that they continue to value and affirm even as—or especially as—they fail to conform to them. To this extent, narratives and novels of captivity consistently betray their own motives and undercut their own postures of nationalism and ethnocentrism, of sentimental motherhood and true womanhood, of domesticity and passivity. Furthermore, when readers respond with sympathy and tears to these stories, they are responding as much to these acts of cultural escape as they are to the oppressive experience of captivity that induces and legitimizes those acts. Thus, sympathy and captivity alike perform a double movement whose passive contours screen acts of escape and agency, acts that can have critical and revisionist force but that also can have violent and exploitative dimensions. The dynamics of cross-cultural exchange and of female agency—practices and processes that are both inscribed in and erased by each other in the genre-crossing texts I have examined—are ambivalent and elastic, as are the forms of sentiment they deploy. As a result, if these narratives and novels of captivity sometimes generate emergent feminist revisions of dominant ideologies, those revisions sometimes also deploy nationalist, imperialist, and racist representations of culture.

Those texts suggest as well that "America" as a political, cultural, and national category has in large part been articulated through the bodies, especially the reproducing bodies, of women.[1] As these captive women defend their virtue by arguing for the sustained integrity of their bodies, they argue also for the coherence of the cultural and national categories their bodies represent. But the affective stories relayed by the bodies and texts of these captive women contain and conceal other histories—of the tensions and exchanges between colonial America and Britain, between African Americans, Native Americans, and Euro-Americans—that subtend the coherence and stability of "America." As a way of gesturing toward the persistence of these rifts, fractures, and loopholes within the categories and the narratives through which we articulate identity, this conclusion moves in two very different directions: back to a colonial American narrative of male captivity and its eighteenth-century world of transatlantic contact and exchange, and forward, so to speak, to a popular 1991 film about the future and about tears. While these two texts fall to varying extents outside the scope of this project, they nevertheless point toward the possibilities and the limitations of cultural and literary border crossing.

Briton Hammon, author of the first work by a black writer published in English, begins his 1760 narrative, recorded by an amanuensis from Hammon's oral account, with his departure from Plymouth in 1747 on a ship headed to Jamaica. The narrative ends when he reunites with his "*good Master,*" a General Winslow of Massachusetts, nearly thirteen years later on board a ship scheduled to sail for Boston from London. Hammon's account of those intervening years is a remarkable one, not least of all for its record of his movement around and across the Atlantic world, much of it spent on board ships destined for Jamaica, Cuba, Florida, London, and Spain. But it is the various *restrictions* on his movement, the unceasingly multiplied events of captivity, that most characterize the narrative's content. Hammon is first taken captive en route to Jamaica by a party of Indians on the coast of Florida. He escapes on a Spanish schooner pursued by his captors; when the ship arrives in Havana, the governor purchases him for ten dollars. Hammon lives with the governor of Havana for a year, until he is kidnapped by a "Press-Gang" who imprison him for "almost five Years in a close Dungeon" after he refuses to board a ship for Spain (9). After two unsuccessful attempts to escape from jail, he is freed, with orders to help carry the bishop through the country for a period of seven months on a "Crimson velvet-lined chair" (10). When he finally succeeds in fleeing Havana, he serves on a series of ships as a soldier for the British army and as a cook, until he falls ill in London, where he is forced to remain "confin'd about 6 Weeks" (12).

The book's title, *A Narrative of the Uncommon Sufferings, and Surprizing Deliverance of Briton Hammon, A Negro Man,* resembles the titles of countless other eighteenth-century captivity narratives. Hammon's description of the Indian attack on the ship even recalls Mary Rowlandson's description of the violent attack on her Lancaster home: as the Indians kill members of the crew and set the ship on fire, Hammon jumps overboard, "chusing rather to be drowned, than to be kill'd by those barbarous and inhuman Savages." After he is "hawled . . . into the Canoe" and beaten "most terribly with a Cutlass," he watches his captors "making a prodigious shouting and hallowing like so many Devils" (6) around the burning ship. Yet when he goes on briefly to describe the five weeks he spent among the Florida Indians, he notes that "they us'd me pretty well, and gave me boil'd Corn" (7). Together these two moments recall the characteristic transcultural ambivalence that permeates Indian captivity narratives, despite their insistent maintenance of determinable boundaries between cultures. Hammon, like Rowlandson, generally identifies himself as an English subject and as a Christian and defines himself against the Indians, the Spanish, and the French, whose various forms of oppression toward him signal their barbarous difference from himself as well as from his Christian and English readers. But even while this narrative shares some of the strategies evident in earlier captivity narratives, it more forcibly reminds us of the ways in which captivity narratives tend to resist, in part by moving in those spaces between, traditional formal as well as social categories.

Clearly, Indian captivity is just the first of many successive layers and forms of entrapment represented in Briton Hammon's text; in retrospect, it even appears to have been perhaps his least oppressive experience of confinement. Therefore, one must ask whether Hammon's account, which might be considered a slave narrative as well as an autobiography or a travel narrative, is really a captivity narrative at all. The paired difficulties of categorizing this narrative and its author-figure might begin to explain the critical silence surrounding this extraordinary text, for surprisingly little has been written on Briton Hammon's *Narrative*.[2] Its publication predates James Albert Ukawsaw Gronniosaw's slave narrative by ten years, Phillis Wheatley's collection of poems by thirteen years, John Marrant's captivity narrative by twenty-five years, and Olaudah Equiano's slave narrative by nearly thirty years. Yet despite its status as the earliest of African American texts, *A Narrative of the Uncommon Sufferings, and Surprizing Deliverance of Briton Hammon* has gone largely ignored. While the circumstances of oral authorship and attendant anxieties of authenticity may account in part for this silence, the seemingly impossible task of classifying Hammon's text—not only in terms of literary genre but in terms of the national and racial identities implicit in the construction of genre—is more than likely responsible for critics' failure to pay attention to it. In his construction of the emergence of an African American literary tradition, for example, Henry Louis

Gates bypasses Hammon for Gronniosaw because, he claims, the latter's text "more clearly inaugurates the genre of the slave narrative" (133), even though Hammon's account is the first text authored by a slave.

Gates's leap over Hammon makes a great deal of sense: neither is the slave trade mentioned nor the narrator's racial identity discussed in Hammon's text, and nowhere does it engage in antislavery rhetoric; the narrative neither turns its autobiographical material to a polemical purpose nor does it mobilize those tropes, such as the talking book, that Gates identifies with the African American literary tradition. Instead, it concludes with Hammon's seemingly delighted, if not sentimental, reunion with "*My good master* [who] was exceeding glad to see me, telling me that I was like one arose from the Dead" (12). With an acknowledgment of "*the Providence of that GOD, who delivered his Servant* David out of the Paw of the Lion and out of the Paw of the Bear," a scriptural reference that likewise recalls Rowlandson's text, Hammon rejoices that "*I am freed from a* long *and* dreadful Captivity . . . *And am returned to my* own Native Land" (14). Hammon's celebration of freedom at the moment he reenters slavery resonates with an irony that contemporary readers may or may not have heard. For Gates, however, Hammon and his narrative apparently provide unstable ground from which to articulate "the beginning of the Afro-American literary tradition" (127), a tradition constituted in the process of sharing, exchanging, and revising tropes and strategies that serve to "create curious formal lines of continuity between the texts that together comprise the shared text of blackness" (128–29).

At best, Hammon's narrative seems to lurk on the remote edges of that tradition, just as it pushes against the confines of what might constitute a narrative of Indian captivity. In the same way, the figure of Hammon himself—a man of African descent who identifies himself as a British subject and who is literally the property of a presumably Anglo-American master who lives in colonial Massachusetts—seems perpetually fading out of view or just on the verge of coming into view at the corners of the categories within which identity gets traditionally defined. Briton Hammon's *Narrative of the Uncommon Sufferings* stands out therefore both as a text about various kinds of captivity and as a text that resists confinement within available social or literary categories. Any attempt to rescue this narrative from unreadability might begin by seeking the inherent rifts within those identities, rifts left behind by the inevitable exchanges between cultural, national, or literary traditions.

The difficulty posed by Hammon's text might be located in part, for example, with the emphasis on "continuity" in Gates's definition, which insists on a pattern of likeness that links texts together into a recognizable and coherent "tradition." Like those narratives of a national literature that construct Americanness around themes such as democracy or the frontier,[3] this narrative of an African American literary tradition depends on relations of resemblance. By employing the vexed figure of exchange and by focusing in particular on those sustained moments of negotiation and hybridity within the process of exchange, the readings of sentimental narratives and novels of captivity in this book have aimed not to construct another continuous tradition maintained by resemblance but to emphasize instead what gets left over, obscured, or retrodetermined in the very process by which traditions get narrated, to emphasize the disavowed persistence of difference on which narratives of resemblance or coherent identities are founded. This is not to dismiss the value of traditions or the existence of lines of continuity within them, but rather to insist on the movements along and across the borders of those traditions where difference and agency emerge. For Gates, Briton Hammon's narrative brings the coherence of an African American literary tradition into view precisely because it lacks the terms on which that coherence is founded. But it is necessary to read Hammon's text with and against that tradition in order to locate and potentially exploit the difference concealed within the tradition's ambivalent origins.

Cultural exchange is performed and inscribed at sites of often violent contestation, and it always generates an ambivalent surplus. It is with this sense of surplus and friction, rather than with associations of equivalence or consent, that I have used the term. Certainly, this use of cultural exchange bears little resemblance to the process Homi Bhabha refers to in his catalog of "liberal notions such as multiculturalism, cultural exchange or the culture of humanity," all of which he aligns with the category of "cultural diversity" (*Location* 34). As it has been elaborated in *Captivity and Sentiment,* the notion of cultural exchange aims to take advantage of the multiple, often self-contradictory gestures and recursive effects associated with the movements of exchange, and therefore it is more closely aligned with the notions of "cultural difference" or "cultural hybridity" to which Bhabha opposes these other concepts. Indeed, cultural exchange in this sense challenges the project of cultural diversity as Bhabha describes it: "the representation of a radical rhetoric of the separation of totalized cultures that live unsullied by the intertextuality of their historical locations, safe in the Utopianism of a mythic memory of a unique collective identity" (34).

But along with the essentialist, totalizationist, and culturally exceptionalist preoccupations against which Bhabha situates himself in this definition, I take it that his resistance to such "liberal notions" and their attendant "ethic of tolerance" (*Location* 24) is a resistance as well to what might be called their sentimentality. The sentimental narratives and novels examined in this book should indicate that to the extent that it is sentimental, any program of multiculturalism or cultural diversity assumes the coherence of in-

dividual cultures as well as the integrity of the borders that separate and distinguish them. But these same texts indicate as well what is at stake in such
border maintenance: any sentimental discourse of cultural diversity betrays
even while it overlooks culture's hybridity, defying the stability of the very
boundaries on which its affective appeal relies. Therefore, rather than dismiss such programs as multiculturalism, it would do to ask what forms of
agency, resistance, or even violence hide behind their moving elements.
Bhabha has claimed, for example, that "[i]t is from the affective experience
of social marginality that we must conceive of a political strategy of empowerment and articulation, a strategy outside the liberatory rhetoric of idealism and beyond the sovereign subject that haunts the 'civil' sentence of the
law" ("Postcolonial Authority" 56). This sentence suggests the possibility
that one place where this political strategy might emerge is from *inside* as
much as from outside that "liberatory rhetoric of idealism" that so often
makes of social marginality an "affective experience." The ideology of cultural diversity must, in these terms, be challenged by intercultural critique,
and multiculturalism must be sustained with interculturalism.

As a final example of sentimentality's persistent self-betrayal, I turn to a
text that, despite its extraordinary distance from the early American world
of transcultural and sympathetic exchange with which this book has been
concerned, shares much with the literature I have examined in *Captivity and
Sentiment*. The 1991 science fiction action film *Terminator 2* revolves around
the thesis that what makes humans human, what distinguishes humans from
the barbaric cruelty of machines, is the ability to cry. Early in the film, the
reprogrammed terminator (Arnold Schwarzenegger), who has been sent
back in time by John Connor in order to protect himself as a young boy,
looks at the tearful ten-year-old John (Edward Furlong) and coldly asks, in
the cyborg's flat and emotionless tone of voice, "What's wrong with your
eyes?" For all the ability of cybernetic machines of the future to emulate human beings, this unsympathetic query establishes a sentimental and impenetrable dividing line around which the film is based. It is precisely that distinction that also legitimates the extraordinary violence that propels the
film—much of it enacted, furthermore, by Sarah Connor (Linda Hamilton),
a woman who not only begins the film as a captive in a state mental hospi-
tal,[4] but whose aggressive rage and violent agency is subtended throughout
by her motherhood. Her young son, John Connor, is the future leader of
the resistance movement against the machines that, several decades in the
future, wage a genocidal war of extermination against humans. Therefore,
the very existence of humanity rests on Sarah Connor's ability to preserve
the body of her son, just as it was to preserve her own body for reproduction in the first *Terminator* film.[5]

But the few sentimental moments in *T2* all occur when the distinction between humans and machines cannot be preserved, when the seemingly inviolable border between them is crossed, exposed as an almost paradoxical hybridity. The otherwise enraged, aggressive, and unsentimental Sarah Connor cries at the moment when she finds herself unable to kill Miles Dyson (Joe Morton), the man who will become responsible for developing the self-regulating military computer that will initiate nuclear holocaust in the not too distant future. Sarah Connor is effectively paralyzed at the moment when she, like the viewer, suddenly confronts the series of paradoxes on which the film is based: she must both behave like a machine and use them to kill humans, all in order to ensure that humans will not be killed by the machines they create. Her tears and her subsequent, otherwise uncharacteristic profession of love to her son blur the inseparability of and the exchanges between machine and human exposed in this scene.[6] The terminator's expression at the end of the film of what is presumably a form of cross-cultural and transtemporal understanding—his claim that "I know now why you cry, but it is something I can never do"—both reasserts the distinction between himself and humans and movingly cedes them cultural superiority and therefore future dominance. As the machine allows himself to be lowered into a vat of molten steel where, for the good of humans, he will be terminated, John Connor cries on his mother's shoulder. Meanwhile, she holds down the button on the machine that destroys the only machine in the film that, her concluding narrative voiceover sentimentally notes, managed to "learn the value of human life."

The ambivalence of *T2*'s content is mirrored in the terms of its extraordinarily popular success. Much of the film's appeal, as the media coverage of its release indicated, depends on its use of special effects, which are enabled, of course, by the use of technology. And yet for all the technological performances the film enacts, its agenda is finally an antitechnological one; like captivity literature, the film permits audiences to indulge in that which they simultaneously disavow. The seeming opposition between humans and machines, like the one between captives and their captors, works to facilitate easy emotional alignments in viewers, even if the emotion works in part to mask exchanges that belie that opposition. If it is imperative that such identifications be problematized by exposing the cultural difference they conceal as well as the violence they propel, one way of doing so is to put such seemingly transparent texts into dialogic exchange with seemingly unreadable texts like Hammon's, for together they reveal the ways in which identity and identification both depend on and violate boundaries. Precisely by initiating such exchanges *Captivity and Sentiment* has sought to bring into focus the ambivalent colonial encounters obscured within sentimental narratives of American literary and national history.

Notes

Introduction

1. I am thinking in particular of ethnohistorical studies of cultural, national, and racial contact in colonial America, documented and discussed in the work of James Axtell, Colin Calloway, John Demos, and Neal Salisbury.

2. See Ernest Renan on the nation's obligation to forget, a concept that I develop within the more specific context of Jacksonian America in chapter 4.

3. This study concludes with Harriet Jacobs's slave narrative, published on the eve of the Civil War, but it does not suggest that this cultural tradition ends there. The discussion of the film *Terminator 2* in the conclusion, as well as more recent films such as *Not without My Daughter,* suggest its persistence, as does Christopher Castiglia's fascinating analysis of the Patty Hearst affair (87–105).

4. For an important reformulation of American literary and cultural studies within a more complex network of international and intercultural relations, see the introductory essays by editors Amy Kaplan and Donald E. Pease in the collection *Cultures of United States Imperialism.* See also Toni Morrison's *Playing in the Dark* for an analysis of the Africanist presence that functions within American literature as a support to its exceptionalist ideals of freedom and democracy.

5. My treatment of captivity narratives eschews the categorizations that have dominated discussions of the genre from early essays by Pearce and VanDer-Beets to recent books by Namias and by Derounian-Stodola and Levernier. These include gendered divisions between male- and female-centered narratives, divisions within women's narratives that distinguish varieties of response to captivity, and historical and stylistic divisions (traditionally between seventeenth-century narratives with religious or colonization agendas, eighteenth-century propaganda narratives, and nineteenth-century sentimentalized narratives and novels). My interest is rather in the sites of ambivalence and agency where these categories overlap and conflict and that such divisions therefore tend to obscure.

6. Castiglia's study shares with mine an interest in the female agency imagined in captivity narratives. Its only sustained consideration of sentimentality (108–10), however, does not examine its crucial role in validating and obscuring that agency, including its aggressively imperialist forms. As a result, I advocate a far more ambivalent framework for understanding the female agency that Castiglia celebrates.

7. Nancy Armstrong perceptively contends that Tompkins's analysis is sentimental because it "claims authority on the basis of exclusion" ("Why Daughters Die" 6).

8. Among these works, to which this study owes an enormous debt, are Baym (*Woman's* and *Novels*), Douglas, Kelley (*Private*), Tompkins, Davidson (*Revolution*), and Samuels ed.

9. Richard Poirier, for example, defines "the best American books" as "an image of the creation of America itself . . . of the expansion of national consciousness into the vast spaces of a continent and the absorption of those spaces into ourselves" (76). Philip Fisher likewise legitimizes novels like Stowe's through an exceptionalist appeal; sentimentalism represents a discourse through which is articulated one of the three "hard facts" that "[f]or America, . . . have had an unusual force" (10).

10. I would also argue that the critical turn of interest to women writers and sentimental fiction, a development of extraordinary value for American literary and cultural history, has at the same time served a redemptive function within that history that has gone largely unnoticed. The appealingly distinctive identity constructed for American literature by Fiedler and others foundered in later books —like Richard Slotkin's *Regeneration through Violence* and *The Fatal Environment* and Annette Kolodny's *Lay of the Land*—that powerfully exposed the exploitative and appropriative violence enshrined in classic American literature and the frontier myth. On the other hand, Kolodny's *The Land before Her,* which followed her earlier critique of masculinist empire building, emphasized the rather more appealing virtues of community and garden building in women's literary responses to the American wilderness. The rise of critical interest in Stowe's liberalism and abolitionism might bear a similarly redemptive relationship to the conservatism and imperialism increasingly associated with Cooper.

1.   Captivity, Cultural Contact, and Commodification

1. Unless otherwise noted, citations refer to the edition of Rowlandson's narrative in Lincoln, which follows the second New England edition printed in 1682 and includes the preface.

2. For accounts of King Philip's War emphasizing the impact of diminishing land available to the Indians and their increased dependence on trade controlled by European colonists, see Leach and also Sturtevant (92–94). See Vaughan for an account that rejects (too easily, in my view) the importance of land for King Philip's War. Note that Rowlandson, who dates the attack February 10, 1675, employed the Julian calendar. According to modern record keeping, the year was 1676.

3. These woodcuts appear in the 1771 Boston edition of Rowlandson's narrative, held in the Newberry Library's Ayer collection.

4. In the 1682 London edition of the narrative, the preface is signed "Per Amicum." For a discussion of seventeenth-century editions of Rowlandson's text, see Derounian "Publication."

5. Some recent studies that focus on issues of conflict and contradiction in Rowlandson's text include Howe, Breitwieser, Derounian-Stodola and Levernier, and Castiglia.

6. In a remarkable historical coincidence, the Rowlandsons' Indian servant was later killed by another captive Puritan woman, Hannah Dustan. Samuel Sewall, in a diary entry for 1697, records his meeting and discussion with the returned captive Dustan, and he describes Dustan's murdered Indian master as one who "formerly live[d] with Mr. Rowlandson at Lancaster" (372). See Griffin for a notation and brief discussion of this passage (47). For more on Dustan's captivity, see chapter 2.

7. The nearest towns to both the north and south of Lancaster were the praying towns of Nashobah and Marlboro, suggesting that Rowlandson's hostility was rooted in beliefs that preceded her entrance into captivity. See the map in Vaughan for these locations (217). Pulsipher's account of the 1677 murder of six Christian Indians provides additional evidence of anti-Christian Indian sentiment by Anglo-Americans in Massachusetts: one of the convicted men was from Lancaster, and another was the son of John Hoar, the Concord lawyer who appears near the end of Rowlandson's narrative to negotiate her ransom.

8. The other dominant perception of Indians by Puritans, exemplified by men such as John Eliot, was as members of the lost tribes of Israel for whom conversion and "civilization" would do the work of cultural (re)integration (Vaughan xv). But Rowlandson's hostility toward the "praying Indians" indicates her utter lack of sympathy for projects like Eliot's as well as for his perception of the Indians. For an account of Eliot's praying towns in the context of Puritan utopian thought and practice, see Holstun.

9. See, for example, Lincoln and *Present State*.

10. See also Brumm (esp. 20–33).

11. Roy Harvey Pearce's description of the genre emblematizes this approach: "The Puritan narrative is one in which the details of captivity itself are found to figure forth a larger, essentially religious experience; the captivity has symbolic value; and the record is made minute, direct, and concrete in order to squeeze the last bit of meaning out of the experience" (2). See also David L. Minter and Levernier and Cohen (xvii–xix).

12. Kathryn Zabelle Derounian usefully describes these two modes as "empirical narration (the 'colloquial' style)" and "rhetorical narration (the 'biblical' style)," a characterization that reflects the separation between the captive's participant status and her interpreter status ("Puritan Orthodoxy" 82). See also Derounian-Stodola and Levernier (101–2).

13. Breitwieser argues that Rowlandson's grief over the death of her daughter Sarah, who dies in her arms during captivity, marks an overvaluation of worldly ties that within orthodox Puritanism should be subordinate to spiritual concerns. Because Rowlandson resists that injunction, her grief exceeds the available typological interpretation of her experience, thus leading her "toward recognizing Indian society *as a society*, rather than as lawless animality" (148–49). See Derounian's "Puritan Orthodoxy" for another analysis of Rowlandson that emphasizes psychological sources for the text's inconsistencies.

14. John Demos likewise notes the frequency of exchanges between the Indians, the English, and the Dutch in colonial New England, and remarks on "the dailiness, the sense of familiarity, even the nonchalance, with which all parties met

and interacted" ("'Cannoe' Diplomacy"). Salisbury reminds us of the likely ways in which the European emphasis on trade for goods altered precontact economies, when exchanges between Indian bands were probably aimed at maintaining alliances more than acquiring products (*Manitou* 48–53); see Salisbury ("Indians' Old World") for an account of precontact exchange networks.

15. I take the reflective metaphor from Marx's claim that one commodity "acts as a mirror to the value" (*Capital* 59) of another commodity. Marx, of course, distinguishes as two modes of exchange the isolated act of direct barter from the circulation of commodities, but in the hybrid colonial economy that developed between natives and settlers, such distinctions were not so easy to maintain. As a result, I do not suggest that the exchange of Indian captives corresponds directly to either of these modes but rather that such exchange can be usefully informed by an understanding of the captive as an unusual commodity in a specifically colonial market.

16. For other accounts of these various sorts of exchange, see Salisbury (*Manitou*), Calloway (*Dawnland*), Sturtevant, and Vaughan.

17. Marx makes this analogy when he notes that "[i]n a sort of way, it is with man as with commodities. Since he comes into the world neither with a looking glass in his hand, nor as a Fichtian philosopher, to whom 'I am I' is sufficient, man first sees and recognizes himself in other men" (*Capital* n. 59).

18. My emphasis differs both from the anthropological economics of Marshall Sahlins and from Pierre Bourdieu's interest in cultural capital as it functions in the economics of social reproduction. As different as Sahlins's and Bourdieu's works are, they both focus on the reproduction—material or ideological—of single cultures, whereas my interest here is in that unknown quantity that is produced when two radically different cultures meet.

19. The sense I am giving to the term *surplus* renders it analogous to the term *supplement* as Derrida defines it, but I adopt the former for the more precise sense of excess that it conveys, as well as its association with economics and exchange. At the same time, I must distinguish my use of *surplus* from Marx's notion of "surplus value," which I mean, at most, only dissonantly to echo. For Derrida on the supplement, see *Of Grammatology*.

20. Vaughan and Clark suggest the usefulness of Turner's concept for the experience of the Indian captive but do not consider Rowlandson's narrative in its specificity. For an analysis of liminality that emphasizes race and gender in captivity narratives, see Castiglia (43–45).

21. This observation was first made, though not developed, by Kolodny (*Land* 18).

22. On adopted captives, see Heard, Calloway ("Uncertain Destiny"), VanDerBeets ("Indian Captivity"), and Axtell (*Invasion*). On Jemison, see Namias, and for an account of Williams, see Demos's *Unredeemed Captive*.

23. Anne Bradstreet's collection of poetry, published in New England in 1678, was a second edition of the volume first printed in London in 1650. Together, Bradstreet's and Rowlandson's books represent exactly half of all published works written by women in seventeenth-century New England. See Koehler 54.

24. Castiglia's analysis of Rowlandson's economic agency attributes to the captive a

gesture of "refusal" (51) toward Puritan society that, in my view, inadequately accounts for her self-definition within the terms of dominant Puritan ideology.

25. In Irigaray's model, the only other role for women allowed within patriarchy, besides those of the mother and the virgin, is that of the prostitute. In the case of the prostitute, Irigaray locates use value in "the qualities of woman's body" and claims, therefore, that "[p]rostitution amounts to *usage that is exchanged*" (*This Sex* 186). I distinguish what I have called Mary Rowlandson's revirginalization from what might incorrectly be perceived as her prostitution. For unlike the prostitute's use value, Rowlandson's use value does not reside in the qualities of her sexualized body, nor does she cease to be private property. Rather, for her Puritan husband, she returns to the state of usefulness *in potentia* that characterizes the virgin.

26. Only her final mention of an exchange is not followed by a visit to her son and by an expression of concern over his physical and spiritual well-being. That final record, near the end of her captivity, when she senses that her release is near, is followed instead by an outburst of tears and by a request for news about her husband (151).

27. See *Present State* for evidence of this claim.

28. Some editions of Rowlandson's narrative (1771, 1791, 1805) include what appears to be the name of another of Quinnapin's wives, Onux. However, other editions, both earlier and later, print "One, a Squaw" where these print "Onux, a Squaw"—indicating a printing error in one group of narratives or the other.

29. See especially VanDerBeets (*Held Captive*), Pearce, and Vaughan and Clark. The latter argue for multigenericism by describing the captivity narrative as a combination of elements from spiritual autobiography, the jeremiad, the sermon, and the adventure story. But any limit placed on such a listing comes to seem arbitrary by excluding the important influence of such genres as the travel narrative, which links personal and spiritual growth with geographic or spatial movement, and the accounts of Christian suffering and martyrdom popularized by John Foxe's *Acts and Monuments* ("Book of Martyrs").

30. See also Castiglia 5.

31. See Armstrong and Tennenhouse's important and provocative analysis of Rowlandson's narrative as an "origin" of the English novel and the national imagining made possible by that form. Other discussions of the relations between the captivity narrative and the novel, especially the sentimental novel, have assumed that the two forms developed separately and that eighteenth- and nineteenth-century captivity narratives change (always for the worse, in these critics' views) as a result of being influenced by novels of sensibility. My argument, developed in chapter 2, seeks a more dialectical and transnational account of exchanges between the two genres.

32. Breitwieser makes a brief but fascinating allusion to a possible connection between Rowlandson's narrative and the sentimentalism that would characterize so much of the literature of the eighteenth and nineteenth centuries, when he suggests that "sentimentalism is a reappearance of the Puritan sublimation of mourning" (n. 210).

2. Between England and America

1. Mott classifies both texts as best-sellers according to historically gauged sales figures. For the publication history of the four 1682 editions of Rowlandson's captivity narrative—three in New England and one in London—see Derounian ("Publication").

2. Armstrong and Tennenhouse's chapter in *The Imaginary Puritan*, titled "Why Categories Thrive," also appeared as "The American Origins of the English Novel." My citations refer to the former.

3. Lacan is describing the relation between these two modes of identification when he explains that symbolic identification "is not specular, immediate identification. It is its support. It supports the perspective chosen by the subject in the field of the Other, from which specular identification may be seen in a satisfactory light" and "from which the subject will see himself, as one says, *as others see him*" (268). My summary here relies on Lacan (244–58; 267–74) and on Žižek's lucid discussion of the Lacanian concept of identification (100–110). Žižek explains that "in symbolic identification we identify ourselves with the other precisely at a point at which he is inimitable, at the point which eludes resemblance" (109); without this relation of difference, identification itself dissolves. Furthermore, Žižek notes that identity, unlike the circular movement of identification, is constituted retroactively, through "the radical contingency of naming" (95). The name—a signifier such as "American" or "English," for example—works to transform differential relations into a homogeneous identity.

4. Teresa A. Toulouse has argued that Rowlandson's insistence on her "inviolate body" "points to her own need to be reintegrated into the community as the same body (mentally and physically) that was wrenched from it—that went out into the wilderness but remained the same" (655–56).

5. Levernier and Cohen, for example, call *The History of Maria Kittle* "a captivity narrative molded to fit the modes of the 'novel of sensibility'" (xxviii), and they associate sentimentalism with European influence on America (xxiv). Annette Kolodny, in her important early reading of "The Panther Captivity," calls it a successful attempt "to bend the outlines of an Indian fertility myth to the requirements of sentimental fiction" ("Turning the Lens" 338). My own argument resists the clear distinctions between genres on which these claims rely.

6. The narratives of Peter Williamson (1757) and John Marrant (1785), both reprinted in VanDerBeets (*Held Captive*), offer examples of such sentimentality. Although captivity narratives were increasingly written *by* men during the eighteenth century, the narratives they wrote were most often *about* women. Namias suggestively claims that this emphasis on female figures by male authors evidenced the latter's anxiety about protecting the family in the face of frontier dangers (264).

7. Calloway explains that the practice of separating captives into smaller groups was a strategy the Indians employed in an effort to elude their pursuers ("Uncertain Destiny" 199), although the captives themselves interpreted it as an inhumane act of dividing families.

8. The text here is taken from Drake's 1851 *Indian Captivities; or, Life in the Wigwam,* although Howe's narrative was first published as a pamphlet in 1793. She was taken captive in 1755/56, at the onset of the French and Indian War.

9. The translation is Lincoln's. Mather introduces these concluding lines with an anecdote about a "Petrified Man" whose body a traveler saw while visiting a ruined city in Italy. Mather virtually requires tears from his readers by claiming "That if thou canst Read these passages [about captivity] without Relenting Bowels, thou thyself art as really Petrified as the man at Villa Ludovisia" (*Decennium* 213).

10. Dustan's narrative first appeared in *Humiliations Followed with Deliverances* (Boston, 1697) and was subsequently included in *Decennium Luctuosum* (Boston, 1699) and in *Magnalia Christi Americana* (London, 1702).

11. The gauntlet ritual, Axtell notes, generally served the purposes of ritual adoption, since the captives who best survived this test were often chosen by tribal members to replace relatives who died in warfare (*Invasion Within* 312–14). Calloway more specifically suggests that the gauntlet served the symbolic function of "beat[ing] the whiteness out of the captive" in readiness for adoption and often consisted of only minor physical contact between the participants and the captive ("Uncertain Destiny" 204–5).

12. June Namias categorizes Dustan as the earliest example of the many "Amazons" who appear particularly in those captivity narratives published between 1764 and 1820 and whose aggressive acts of self-defense and escape she correctly aligns with nationalist purposes (33–34). My own analysis, however, challenges the separation between violent agent and passive victim on which types such as the "Amazon" and "Frail Flower" rely.

13. Hawthorne's version of Dustan's story, published in his *Magazine of Useful and Entertaining Knowledge,* significantly eliminates all possibility of a sympathetic response to the captive by portraying her as a "raging tigress" and a "bloody old hag" (136) who should either have drowned, sunk to her death in a swamp, or "starved to death in the forest, and nothing ever seen of her again, save her skeleton, with the ten scalps twisted round it for a girdle!" (137). By demonizing Dustan, Hawthorne eliminates the gap between an imaginary and a symbolic identification, effectively making identification with her impossible. Sympathy in Hawthorne's story is reserved for her strikingly maternal husband, "that tender hearted, yet valiant man" condemned to live with "[t]his awful woman" (137).

14. For a full account of Elizabeth Emerson's case in the context of Hannah Dustan's captivity experience, see Ulrich 184–201.

15. As Timothy Brennan points out, Bakhtin's notion of dialogism is not only textual but social (50). See Bakhtin's "Epic and Novel" in *The Dialogic Imagination.*

16. Like Hawthorne's version of Hannah Dustan's captivity narrative, Henry Fielding's rewriting of *Pamela* in *An Apology for the Life of Mrs. Shamela Andrews* makes sympathetic identification with the captive female impossible by eliminating the gap between her virtue and her agency.

17. Burr's father was Jonathan Edwards; her husband, Aaron Burr, was the president of what is now Princeton University; and her son was the future vice president of the United States. Her journal offers important insight into the con-

ditions of women's intellectual and daily life in the colonial eighteenth century. I thank Susan Howe for bringing this book to my attention.

18. See Baym for a discussion of reviewers' obsession with locating and defining a uniquely national literature in nineteenth-century America (*Novels* 241–48). Examples of exceptionalist theories of American literature based on themes like democracy, freedom, and the frontier include Lawrence, Matthiesen, Poirier, Henry Nash Smith, Bercovitch, and Reynolds. This brief list merely hints, however, at the persistence of exceptionalism within American literary criticism.

19. William Spengemann exposes the concealed tautology on which such definitions inevitably rely when he suggests that any definition of American literature operates by first selecting a group of texts and authors that are implicitly considered to be American. It is only second and on the basis of shared features or concerns (on the basis, precisely, of a shared identity based on resemblance) that these texts are explicitly labeled American (77–86). Because the second act of naming effectively obscures the first, the process of definition appears to fill in the term "American" only by, in effect, emptying it twice.

3. Republican Motherhood and Political Representation

1. See Vail for this publication history.

2. Sieminski mentions also that the number of Indians, their postures, and their rather European clothing all seem attempts to reproduce the artillery line of British soldiers in Revere's engraving.

3. Mary Beth Norton, an excellent source on women during the Revolution, comes closest to portraying the revolutionary era as the source for women's further emancipation, although she notes as well the increasing restrictions generated by the cult of republican motherhood. The collection of essays in Hoffman and Albert exemplify the argument that the status of women underwent no significant change during this era.

4. See also Denn for an analysis of the relation between this genre and the revolution. Denn focuses on prison narratives by men in his argument that such literature first articulated a distinctly American cultural character. As a result, he ignores the role of gender that is evident in any broader consideration of texts that employ the patterns of the captivity narrative, and he isolates a separate and distinct American culture and literature from other, predominantly British, influences.

5. See Bailyn's *Ideological Origins*. A pamphlet like Thacher's *Sentiments of a British American,* for example, might invoke the word *slavery* once, but it invokes the word *mother* five times. Stephen Hopkins's pamphlet *Rights of the Colonies Examined* likewise calls Britain "the mother state" ten times to its three references to slavery. These pamphlets are in Bailyn ed.

6. Bailyn *Ideological Origins* (58); quoted from Marchamont Nedham's *Excellincie of a Free State* (Richard Baron's 1767 ed.), 18–19.

7. See also Bloch for a discussion of the emergent distinction between private fe-

male virtue and public male virtue and the equation of chastity with female virtue (42, 52).

8. In the House of Commons, Edmund Burke denounced the British troops' use of Indian allies after hearing of this event. See Leary's "Introduction" 14.

9. See Namias for a good survey of various biographies and accounts of Jane McCrea (117–28).

10. Quoted in Leary, "Introduction" (9), from Hilliard's *Essais,* Vol. 2, trans. Eric LaGuardia, 267.

11. Although her father disapproves of her attraction, he cannot force Jane to renounce her new lover, for "the laws of the country did not allow her father to restrain her inclinations" (32). Such an absence of force is quite in contrast to Belton's blind pursuit of colonial defeat in the name of "what the nobles of England called duty" (20).

12. The fascination with Jane McCrea and her story apparently persisted well into the nineteenth century. An advertisement appearing in an 1853 retelling of her story offers "elegant Canes and Boxes" made out of the tree under which Jane was reportedly murdered. This ad promises that all Americans can own a piece of Jane as well as a piece of national history by purchasing "An Interesting Relic of the Revolution." By making these items available, George Harvey, who placed the ad, defends his act of "cutting down The Famous Jane McCrea Tree" and warns that "[a]ll other parties offering Canes for sale, representing them to be made from the renowned Jane McCrea Tree, are counterfeits, and will be dealt with accordingly." This remarkable ad, with its commercial refunctioning of the George Washington tree-chopping myth, appears at the conclusion of Wilson's account.

13. *Charlotte Temple* was published in England in 1791, one year before Wollstonecraft's manifesto but was published in America only in 1794, two years after the *Vindication* had its first American printing. Susanna Rowson, an Englishwoman who was a former resident of the colonies, would later repeat the westward transatlantic journey that her text and her heroine had already made and eventually become an American citizen.

14. For more on the publishing history of *Charlotte Temple* and audience reception of it, see Davidson's *Revolution and the Word.*

15. The association of both Betsy, the Irish servant, and LaRue, the French assistant, with Roman Catholic nations is significant here, particularly given these two works' reliance on earlier captivity narratives. Narratives written by or about captives who traveled to and lived in Canada before being ransomed often generated a culture of fear about the "papists" that was second only to their fear of the Indians. See, for example, John Williams's captivity narrative in Vaughan and Clark, eds.

16. See Douglas, "Introduction," *Charlotte Temple.*

17. As obscure as he may have been, however, biographical information does attest that Herman Mann—a former teacher, father of eleven children, and editor of a newspaper called *The Minerva*—was a man. See Levernier and Wilmes, eds., 939–40.

18. Although the single woman, or *feme sole,* had property rights, she nevertheless

could not "exercise the political rights that theoretically accompanied them" (Kerber, *Women* 120).

19. Quoted from *Martha Surtell* v. *William Brailford,* in Bay, *Cases in S.-C. Sup. Courts,* 2:163–65.

20. See Kerber's "Paradox" for a discussion of this case and its implications.

4. The Imperialist Audience

1. Ebersole's claim that Bleecker's "is a history of the heart, not a political history" (135) separates the interdependence of the emotional and the political to which Ellison points.

2. In addition to Barnett, see Dekker and Bell. Including writers like Bleecker and Rowson might position Sir Walter Scott and his 1814 *Waverly* as a later descendant of a transatlantic tradition of historical captivity fiction.

3. It is as though Rowson literalizes Herman Mann's symbolic 1797 claim that Deborah Sampson is the daughter of Columbia, who was figured in contemporary iconography as both the American nation and an Amerindian woman.

4. See also Castiglia on the role of women writers in this genre (112). The term *frontier romance* simply denotes a more specific type of historical romance, and since the texts on which I focus belong to both categories, I use the two terms more or less interchangeably in this chapter. Historians and anthropologists have critiqued the term *frontier* for its imperialist and ethnocentric assumptions, assumptions reproduced in most frontier romances. I follow June Namias in retaining a redefined notion of the frontier as a transcultural and transracial site of contact (12).

5. Doris Sommer outlines a model of the Latin American historical romance that similarly stresses the narrative interdependence of eroticism and nationalism, in which there is "a metonymic association between romantic love that needs the state's blessing and political legitimacy that needs to be founded on love" (41). Like the Latin American novels Sommer reads, nineteenth-century North American romances emphasize national and familial reproduction, but that narrative also depends on an Amerindian narrative of failed reproduction.

6. Castiglia's brief analysis of *A Peep at the Pilgrims* is the only critical work done on the book, to my knowledge, though he does not note its relation to *Hope Leslie. A Peep at the Pilgrims* was popular enough to be reprinted the year after its 1824 publication and to appear in a second edition in 1826. Its next American printing, in 1850, was also its last, although one London edition appeared in 1841. Cheney was the daughter of the early American novelist Hannah Webster Foster and sister of Eliza Lanesford Cushing, another writer of historical romances. Later Cheney and Cushing were co-editors of the *The Literary Garland,* a magazine published in Canada, where both women lived after marrying merchants who settled in Montreal. See Story (254) and MacDonald for biographical information on Cheney.

7. This captivity, which is briefly recounted in Underhill's 1638 narrative of the war, *Newes from America,* is the first documented captivity in North American

literature in English. Underhill's mention of it, however, is brief and utterly without details, so Cheney's reconstruction of it is conjectural, though no doubt based on other captivity experiences documented in narratives.

8. See, for example, Elizabeth Hanson's and Mary Jemison's narratives (Seaver).

9. For a concise account of the developing divisions that threatened social coherence in the Jacksonian era, see Smith-Rosenberg (*Disorderly Conduct* 79–89). Like Smith-Rosenberg, I take "the age of Jackson" to encompass a period extending from at least the early 1820s to the 1840s and beyond.

10. See Renan and Anderson for discussions of the crucial role of forgetting in the construction of a national memory.

11. See Horsman on the development of scientific racialism and removal attitudes.

12. Kelley first identified Cheney as this "sister labourer" (Sedgwick n. 358).

13. Alice Fletcher's kidnapping, for example, like the peculiar captivity of Sir Philip Gardiner's cross-dressed page, Rosa, suggests rather the confinement of women within a system of patriarchal authority, whereas Thomas Morton's imprisonment in the Boston jail suggests authority of a different kind.

14. See Dana Nelson on Sedgwick's revision of Puritan histories through the strategies of sympathy ("Sympathy").

15. Mary Kelley considers the similarity between Faith Leslie and Eunice Williams, who was captured by Indians as a child, remained among them, married a Caughnawaga Indian, converted to Catholicism, and resisted her family's effort to return to New England ("Introduction" xxxviii, n. 4). For an account of Eunice Williams's story, see John Demos, *The Unredeemed Captive.*

16. See Olson for discussions of these images in their revolutionary context.

17. I have relied on Rogin's study in my discussion of Jackson and debt.

5. Sympathetic Agency and Colonization in *Uncle Tom's Cabin*

1. Stephanie Smith concisely characterizes and questions this shift when she remarks that "such sentimental texts, once devalued as aesthetically void abolitionist propaganda, are now being devalued under the surprising rubric of the politically naïve" (39).

2. See, for example, Amy Schrager Lang's chapter titled "Feel Right and Pray" in her *Prophetic Woman.*

3. Of notable exception are the essays in the "Race and Slavery in *Uncle Tom's Cabin*" section of Lowance et al., eds., which engage Stowe's representation of race. But the separation of these essays from those on sentimentality in this collection still suggest an absence of dialogue between gender- and race-oriented critiques of the novel.

4. Citing slavery studies suggesting that the often impossible options of rebellion or escape left Christianity as the slave's primary mode of preserving a sense of self-worth, Douglas contends that the slave character Uncle Tom is a realistic representation rather than a degrading stereotype (Introduction, *Uncle Tom's Cabin* 25–26). Douglas's earlier critique of Stowe and nineteenth-century senti-

mentalism is in her *Feminization of American Culture*. For one characterization of the "Douglas-Tompkins debate" (9) on sentimental fiction, see Wexler.

5. James Forten, a wealthy black Philadelphian, is credited with influencing Garrison's anticolonizationist position and with supplying appended materials to Garrison's book. See Katz, i. Garrison's support for immediate emancipation and his opposition to colonization followed his earlier acceptance in the 1820s of colonization. Abraham Lincoln also, of course, held a procolonization position at least beyond the beginning of the Civil War. See Fehrenbacher for a discussion emphasizing Lincoln's strategic espousal of colonization, and see Schmitz for claims that Lincoln's support for colonization was more constitutive than strategic.

6. Baldwin describes novels like *Uncle Tom's Cabin* in terms that insist on their central colonizing impulse: "the aim of the protest novel becomes something very closely resembling the zeal of those alabaster missionaries to Africa to cover the nakedness of the natives, to hurry them into the pallid arms of Jesus and thence into slavery" (20).

7. Rogin notes that "Jackson opposed every action that challenged slavery" (298).

8. I borrow the notion of imperial prosthetics from Bill Brown's study of science fiction, technology, and American empire in the early twentieth century.

9. Stowe's paraphrase of Sterne comes from his *Sentimental Journey*.

10. For a discussion of Stowe's use of slave narratives, see Stepto, in Sundquist ed. 135–53. See also Henry Bibb. Critics consistently refer to the "Indian captivity" segment of Bibb's narrative; strictly speaking, however, Bibb is not a captive but a slave since he was sold by his former master to a wealthy Cherokee Indian slaveholder (139).

11. Sundquist's reformulation of the American Renaissance emphasizes the important tradition of slave rebellions and white Americans' ambivalent relation to their revolutionary and emancipatory ideals. Sundquist also specifically notes the role that the insurrectionary threat plays in *Uncle Tom's Cabin* and Stowe's own resistance to such violence in any antislavery campaign (*To Wake* 79).

12. VanDerBeets measures this popularity in terms of the number of editions printed (*Held Captive* 177). The only other more popular narratives were those of Peter Williamson and Mary Jemison.

13. The full title of Marrant's narrative is *A Narrative of the Lord's wonderful Dealings with John Marrant, a Black, (Now gone to Preach the Gospel in Nova-Scotia) Born in New-York, in North-America, Taken down from his own Relation, arranged, corrected and published, By the Rev. Mr. Aldridge*. Publication history of the narrative is supplied by VanDerBeets (*Held Captive* 177).

14. William Lloyd Garrison's review of *Uncle Tom's Cabin* in *The Liberator* criticized not only Stowe's "objectionable sentiments respecting African colonization" but her distinction between "one law of submission and non-resistance for the black man, and another law of rebellion and conflict for the white man" (Cain 131).

15. The phrase "romantic racialism" is George Frederickson's label for the ideology of race in Stowe's novel.

16. This example suggests the cultural function that Eric Lott attributes to black-

face performances. The white performer who donned blackface as well as the white spectator who watched such shows were "ascribing [their own] excess to the 'degraded' other *and indulging it*"; through such transferential exchange "one conveniently and surreptitiously takes and disavows pleasure at one and the same time" (482).

17. For a compelling reading of Cassy's gothic motherhood and its articulation of maternal affect as that which supports and threatens Legree's social subjectivity, see Cherniavsky, esp. 55–60.

18. Stephanie Smith observes more generally the tendency of criticism on sentimentalism to imitate the strategies of its subject when she notes that "critical discourse on the sentimental frequently employs, if it does not exploit, the highly charged images it seeks to censure as sentimental practice. Such critical readings 'suture' over conflict and indeed bury the traces and remains of conflict, thereby reproducing the phenomenon they examine" (62). In Smith's terms, what I am emphasizing here is the "conflict" that accompanies exchanges between the public and private spheres, between imperialist policy and domestic practice.

19. Quoted in Stephanie Smith (54).

20. Garnett significantly prefaced his defense of colonization with a characterization of Henry Clay, a founding member of the ACS and Speaker of the House of Representatives, as "a hardened sinner—a cruel and murderous persecutor of my people, and of late, a baptized and confirmed hypocrite" (qtd. in Kinshasa 79). His response illustrates, of course, the vastly different motives of ACS members and proemigrationists like Martin R. Delany, who supported the movement to Africa as a way of countering the white racial domination that many colonizationists sought to maintain. For information contained in this paragraph, I have relied on Kinshasa's study of African American responses to debates about colonization and emigration. See also Nesbit and Williams for two opposed positions on the Liberian project.

21. Marrant's vision, of course, should not be confused with material conditions in Nova Scotia at the time, where black loyalists were often subject to segregation and cheated of land claims and where legal and political decisions in general hardly favored these three groups equally. See James W. St. G. Walker for more on black loyalists in Nova Scotia and later in Sierra Leone as well as for a brief discussion of Marrant.

6. Loopholes of Resistance

1. Gayatri Spivak elaborates a postcolonial strategy of catachresis that shares some of the same tactics as Bhabha's colonial mimicry. For Spivak, catachresis enables the (re)claiming of "concept-metaphors for which no historically adequate referent may be advanced from postcolonial space" (60).

2. Joanne Braxton has pointed to Jacobs's many uses of disguise and concealment, including keeping secret her literacy, her pregnancy, her love for a black man, and the identity of her white lover. See Painter's "Representing Truth" for a fas-

cinating discussion of Sojourner Truth's use of silence and secrecy and her attendant "apprehension of trust" (462) and "preoccupation with credibility" (463)—strategies and anxieties echoed in Jacobs's life and work.

3. This exchange reveals the divide, the impossibility of translation, between the discourse of the slave and that of the master, despite the fact that they both speak the same language. It recalls Homi Bhabha's reference to that "strategic space of enunciation" described by Lacan and Benveniste "where to say 'I am lying' is strangely to tell the truth or vice versa" (*Location* 134).

4. Elizabeth Fox-Genovese has suggested that this tension "between exhibitionism and secrecy, between self-display and self-concealment" (166) may be especially marked in the autobiographies of African American women.

5. A missal, in addition to being a prayer book, is an obsolete variant of *missile* according to the *OED*. In a slight twist on the Derridean postal system in which letters always potentially fail to arrive at their destination, these letters successfully reach their addressee only to misrepresent utterly their origin and sender. Alan Bass's glossary suggests the fascinating possibility of an association between the postal system and the loophole in his analysis of the term *trier*, which "means 'to sort,' especially in the postal sense of sorting letters for distribution. . . . The false link between sorting and death is contained in the word *meutrière*, which means both murderess, and *the vertical slot in a fortress wall through which one can project weapons* [viz., a loophole]" (xxviii; emphasis added). I thank Eileen Godollei for suggesting that the word *missive*, which means both letter and missile, speaks as well to the particular strategies of Jacobs's loophole condition.

6. In addition to Bhabha's notion of colonial mimicry, I am using mime here in the sense that Luce Irigaray gives it as a feminist strategy in which "[o]ne must assume the feminine role deliberately. Which means already to convert a form of subordination into an affirmation, and thus to begin to thwart it. . . . To play with mimesis is thus, for a woman, to try to recover the place of her exploitation by discourse, without allowing herself to be simply reduced to it" (*This Sex* 76).

7. This arrangement is roughly analogous to Nancy Armstrong's reading, in *Desire and Domestic Fiction,* of domestic novels and the Victorian domestic sphere, in which female power is able to operate precisely because it is hidden in the home, where its operation is so unlikely.

8. In fact, and almost as though to prove the point, Bentham's original panopticon design contained its own inadvertent loophole. As Alan Liu has noted, "Bentham's totalitarian vision . . . had a loophole," for "Bentham discovered after drawing up his plans that a blank space had inadvertently been left in the central tower in the area of the chapel" (103). Liu's short and limited discussion of that space focuses on the vision of the tourists with whom Bentham proposed to fill the space, rather than on the implications that empty space might have for the inmates themselves. I thank Deidre Lynch for bringing this note to my attention.

9. See Elkins and Lane. For studies that counter Elkins's, see Genovese and Gutman. One more recent intervention in these debates is Painter's call for an accounting of the psychological effects of slavery—its perpetuation of what she calls soul murder—that has been avoided in the aftermath of Elkins's controver-

sial and flawed thesis. One effect of the resistance to Elkins's psychological analysis has been a refusal to envision "slaves as people who developed psychologically" and to examine more closely "the culture of violence in which they matured" ("Soul Murder" 131). I thank Mary Kelley for bringing Painter's essays to my attention.

10. Walker's larger agenda is to urge a shift away from class-oriented Marxist analyses of race relations in nineteenth-century America and toward a theoretical model that would not conflate race with or reduce it to economic categories.

11. William L. Andrews has similarly argued that the spiritual autobiographies of black women justify their transgression of cultural conventions against women preachers only by invoking and obeying theological conventions such as sanctification (Andrews, ed., *Sisters* 16).

12. Lacan makes precisely such a connection between mimicry and camouflage when he writes that "[t]he effect of mimicry is camouflage in the strictly technical sense. It is not a question of harmonizing with the background, but against a mottled background, of becoming mottled—exactly like the technique of camouflage practiced in human warfare" (99).

13. Valerie Smith identifies in Jacobs's narrative "linguistic spaces—verbal equivalents analogous to the garret in which she hides" (xxxiii) that are similar in conception to my notion of a textual or discursive loophole. Smith's focus, however, is on Jacobs's *revision* of the male slave narrative and the sentimental novel, while I am emphasizing Jacobs's far more tactical *attack* on the latter.

14. Valerie Smith notes the similarity between Harriet Jacobs's story and Samuel Richardson's novel (xxxi–ii). It is especially striking that Flint, like Mr. B, seems as obsessed with obtaining his servant's consent as he is with achieving her seduction.

15. See Fuss on Fanon's location of politics at the site where identification and imitation fail to meet (153).

16. Though the use of sentimentality is by no means limited to female writers and feminocentric plots, discussions of the politics of sentimentality are generally, and curiously, limited to just such texts. Karen Sánchez-Eppler, in her essay "Bodily Bonds," convincingly demonstrates that feminist-abolitionist discourse in its sentimental mode appropriates and bleaches the body of the black slave in its represention of slavery as sexual oppression, thus constructing images and plots with which white feminist writers and readers could identify. Ann Douglas insists that sentimental fiction supports the developing capitalist system in *The Feminization of American Culture,* while Jane Tompkins and Gillian Brown claim, respectively, that sentimental fiction stages a critique of traditional economic and domestic orders.

17. Rousseau's depiction of compassion is a scene with remarkable parallels to and intriguing differences from this moment in Jacobs's text: "the tragic image of an imprisoned man who sees, through his window, a wild beast tearing a child from its mother's arms, breaking its frail limbs with murderous teeth, and clawing its quivering entrails" (qtd. in Fisher 105). As Fisher notes, Rousseau borrows the image from Mandeville's *Fable of the Bees.* The scenario Rousseau describes is, of course, also appropriate for the sentimental relation between

readers and captivity narratives that present images of Indian violence against captive children.

18. For more background on this editorial change, see Bruce Mills.

19. For an excellent analysis of the uncanny national subject, see Wald.

20. By designating Mrs. Bruce as "an American," Jacobs is of course distinguishing her from the first Mrs. Bruce, who was English. But given her later observations on the second Mrs. Bruce's relation to her own national identity, this initial characterization takes on far greater significance.

21. I take this detail of Ashanti tribal structure from Yellin (n. 267), who in turn relies on and quotes from Ratray's *Ashanti* (81–84).

Conclusion

1. Although this project works with many of the popular texts given early critical treatment in Leslie Fiedler's *Love and Death in the American Novel* and *The Return of the Vanishing American,* my conclusions work against theories of American literature that, like Fiedler's, offer what Nina Baym calls "melodramas of beset manhood" as the defining material of what makes such literature "American." See also Baym.

2. Even Rafia Zafar's essay on African American captivity narratives gives relatively scant treatment to Hammon's text.

3. In the conclusion to chapter 2, I briefly discuss such national narratives of American literature and the fundamental but repressed ambivalence on which they depend.

4. One might argue that Sarah Connor manipulates the systems of surveillance in the institution that confines her in ways analogous to those of Harriet Jacobs, but the central loophole in both *Terminator* films is the loop in time that generates a site of resistance capable of literally changing the future.

5. For discussions of the maternal emphasis in the portrayal of Sarah Connor in *The Terminator* (1984), see Penley (77) and Goscilo (50). Both essays mention also the representation of Ripley (Sigourney Weaver) as surrogate mother in *Aliens,* another film directed by James Cameron. These films reflect, and certainly helped to inaugurate, a continuing trend in filmic depictions of aggressive female agency, including, among others, *The Burning Bed, Thelma and Louise,* and *The Silence of the Lambs.* In these films, that agency is often legitimated in the same ways that it is in colonial American captivity narratives, as a revenge for rape or through a discourse of motherhood (a strategy both enacted and spoofed in John Waters's *Serial Mom*). In many ways, *Terminator 2,* which begins and ends with a sequence showing the transformation of a Los Angeles playground into the killing fields of a postnuclear twenty-first century, is all about children.

6. J. P. Telotte points toward the hybridity between machine and human in the film, noting that John Connor's initial portrayal as a lawless antisocial youth aligns him with the terminator, and his mother's concern with physical conditioning and her emotional repression make her seem somewhat cyborg-like in her very effort to destroy cyborgs (31).

Works Cited

Affecting History of the Dreadful Distresses of Frederic Manheim's Family. Philadelphia, 1800.

The Affecting History of the Dreadful Distresses of Frederic Manheim's Family. 1794. VanDerBeets, *Held Captive* 202–42.

Aldridge, Rev. Mr. *A Narrative of the Lord's wonderful Dealings with John Marrant, a Black.* VanDerBeets, *Held Captive* 177–201.

Ammons, Elizabeth. "Stowe's Dream of the Mother-Savior: *Uncle Tom's Cabin* and American Women Writers before the 1820s." Sundquist, ed. *New Essays* 155–69.

Anderson, Benedict. *Imagined Communities: Reflections on the Origin and Spread of Nationalism.* Rev. ed. London: Verso, 1991.

Andrews, William L., ed. *Sisters of the Spirit: Three Black Women's Autobiographies of the Nineteenth Century.* Bloomington: Indiana UP, 1986.

———. *To Tell a Free Story: The First Century of Afro-American Autobiography, 1760–1865.* Urbana: U of Illinois P, 1986.

Appiah, Anthony. "Tolerable Falsehoods: Agency and the Interests of Theory." *The Consequences of Theory.* Ed. Jonathan Arac and Barbara Johnson. Baltimore: Johns Hopkins UP, 1990.

Armstrong, Nancy. *Desire and Domestic Fiction: A Political History of the Novel.* Oxford: Oxford UP, 1987.

———. "Why Daughters Die: The Racial Logic of American Sentimentalism." *Yale Journal of Criticism* 7.2 (1994): 1–24.

Armstrong, Nancy, and Leonard Tennenhouse. "The American Origins of the English Novel." *American Literary History* 4 (1992): 386–410.

———. *The Imaginary Puritan: Literature, Intellectual Labor, and the Origins of Personal Life.* Berkeley: U of California P, 1992.

An Authentic Narrative of the Seminole War and of the Miraculous Escape of Mrs. Mary Godfrey, and her four female children. New York, 1836. Rpt. in *The Garland Library of Narratives of North American Indian Captivities.* Sel. and arr. Wilcomb E. Washburn. Vol. 52. New York: Garland, 1978.

Auerbach, Eric. *Mimesis: The Representation of Reality in Western Literature.* Princeton: Princeton UP, 1953.

Axtell, James. *The European and the Indian: Essays in the Ethnohistory of Colonial North America.* New York: Oxford UP, 1981.

———. *The Invasion Within: The Contest of Cultures in Colonial North America.* New York: Oxford UP, 1985.

Bailyn, Bernard. *The Ideological Origins of the American Revolution.* Cambridge: Harvard UP, 1967.

———, ed. *Pamphlets of the American Revolution 1750–1776*. Cambridge: Belknap P of Harvard UP, 1965.

Bakhtin, M. M. *The Dialogic Imagination*. Ed. Michael Holquist. Trans. Caryl Emerson and Michael Holquist. Austin: U of Texas P, 1981.

Baldwin, James. *Notes of a Native Son*. Boston: Beacon P, 1955.

Barnett, Louise. *The Ignoble Savage: American Literary Racism, 1790–1890*. Westport: Greenwood Press, 1975.

Bass, Alan. "Translator's Introduction: L before K." *The Post Card: From Socrates to Freud and Beyond*. By Jacques Derrida. Trans. Alan Bass. Chicago: U of Chicago P, 1987. ix–xxx.

Baym, Nina. "Melodramas of Beset Manhood: How Theories of American Fiction Exclude Women Authors." *The New Feminist Criticism: Essays on Women, Literature, and Theory*. Ed. Elaine Showalter. New York: Pantheon Books, 1985. 63–80.

———. *Novels, Readers, and Reviewers: Responses to Fiction in Antebellum America*. Ithaca: Cornell UP, 1984.

Bell, Michael Davitt. *Hawthorne and the Historical Romance of New England*. Princeton: Princeton UP, 1971.

Bercovitch, Sacvan. *The American Jeremiad*. Madison: U of Wisconsin P, 1978.

Berlant, Lauren. "The Queen of America Goes to Washington City: Harriet Jacobs, Frances Harper, Anita Hill." *Subjects and Citizens: Nation, Race, and Gender from Oroonoko to Anita Hill*. Ed. Michael Moon and Cathy N. Davidson. Durham: Duke UP, 1995. 455–80.

Bhabha, Homi K. "DissemiNation: Time, Narrative, and the Margins of the Modern Nation." Bhabha ed. *Nation and Narration* 291–322.

———. *The Location of Culture*. New York: Routledge, 1994.

———, ed. *Nation and Narration*. London: Routledge, 1990.

———. "Postcolonial Authority and Postmodern Guilt." *Cultural Studies*. Ed. Lawrence Grossberg, Cary Nelson, and Paula Treichler. New York: Routledge, 1992. 56–66.

Bibb, Henry. *Narrative of the Life and Adventures of Henry Bibb, an American Slave*. In *Puttin' on Ole Massa*. Ed. Gilbert Osofsky. New York: Harper and Row, 1969. 51–171.

Bleecker, Ann Eliza. *The History of Maria Kittle*. Hartford, 1797.

Bloch, Ruth. "The Gendered Meanings of Virtue in Revolutionary America." *Signs* 13 (1987): 37–58.

Bourdieu, Pierre. *Distinction: A Social Critique of the Judgement of Taste*. Trans. Richard Nice. Cambridge: Harvard UP, 1984.

Braxton, Joanne. "Harriet Jacobs' *Incidents in the Life of a Slave Girl*: The Re-definition of the Slave Narrative Genre." *Massachusetts Review* 27 (1986): 379–87.

Breitwieser, Mitchell. *American Puritanism and the Defense of Mourning: Religion, Grief, and Ethnology in Mary White Rowlandson's Captivity Narrative*. Madison: U of Wisconsin P, 1990.

Brennan, Timothy. "The National Longing for Form." Bhabha, ed. *Nation* 44–70.

Brown, Bill. "Science Fiction, the World's Fair, and the Prosthetics of Empire, 1910–1915." Kaplan and Pease 129–63.

Brown, Gillian. *Domestic Individualism: Imagining Self in Nineteenth-Century America*. Berkeley: U of California P, 1990.

Brown, William Hill. *The Power of Sympathy*. Ed. William S. Osborne. Albany: New College and University Press, 1970.

Brumm, Ursula. *American Thought and Religious Typology*. 1963. Trans. John Hoaglund. New Brunswick: Rutgers UP, 1970.

Burke, Edmund. *A Philosophical Enquiry into the Origin of our Ideas of the Sublime and the Beautiful*. 1757. New York: Oxford UP, 1990.

Burr, Esther Edwards. *The Journal of Esther Edwards Burr, 1754–1757*. Ed. Carol F. Karlsen and Laurie Crumpacker. New Haven: Yale UP, 1984.

Cain, William E., ed. *William Lloyd Garrison and the Fight Against Slavery: Selections from* The Liberator. New York: Bedford Books, 1995.

Calloway, Colin. *Dawnland Encounters: Indians and Europeans in Northern New England*. Hanover: UP of New England, 1991.

———. "An Uncertain Destiny: Indian Captivities on the Upper Connecticut River." *Journal of American Studies* 17 (1983): 189–210.

Castiglia, Christopher. *Bound and Determined: Captivity, Culture-Crossing, and White Womanhood from Mary Rowlandson to Patty Hearst*. Chicago: U of Chicago P, 1996.

Caverly, Robert B. *Heroism of Hannah Duston, Together with the Indian Wars of New England*. Boston, 1874.

Cheney, Harriet V. *A Peep at the Pilgrims in Sixteen Hundred Thirty Six: A Tale of Olden Times*. Boston, 1824. 2 vols.

Cherniavsky, Eva. *That Pale Mother Rising: Sentimental Discourses and the Imitation of Motherhood in 19th-Century America*. Bloomington: Indiana UP, 1995.

Child, Lydia Maria. *Hobomok and Other Writings on Indians*. Ed. Carolyn L. Karcher. New Brunswick: Rutgers UP, 1986.

Complete Description of the Duston Statue, Contoocook Island, Fisherville, N.H. Also full Account of Hannah Dustan's Adventure with the Indians. Franklin, N.H., 1874.

Copjec, Joan. "The Orthopsychic Subject: Film Theory and the Reception of Lacan." *October* 49 (1989): 53–71.

Corning, Charles R. *An Exploit in King William's War 1697, Hannah Dustan; Address Delivered before the New Hampshire Historical Society Feb. 10 1890*. Concord, 1890.

Cowper, William. "The Task." *The Poetical Works of William Cowper*. 3rd ed. Ed. H. S. Milford. London: Oxford UP, 1926.

Cronon, William. *Changes in the Land: Indians, Colonists, and the Ecology of New England*. New York: Hill and Wang, 1983.

Davidson, Cathy N. "Ideology and Genre: The Rise of the Novel in America." *Proceedings of the American Antiquarian Society* 96 (1986): 295–321.

———. Introduction. *Charlotte Temple*. By Susanna Rowson. New York: Oxford UP, 1986. xi–xxxiii.

———. *Revolution and the Word: The Rise of the Novel in America*. New York: Oxford UP, 1986.

Davis, Margaret H. "Mary White Rowlandson's Self-Fashioning as Puritan Goodwife." *Early American Literature* 27 (1992): 49–60.

Dekker, George. *The American Historical Romance.* Cambridge: Cambridge UP, 1987.

de Lauretis, Teresa. *Technologies of Gender: Essays on Theory, Film, and Fiction.* Bloomington: Indiana UP, 1987.

Demos, John. "'Cannoe' Diplomacy." *New York Times* 23 Nov. 1995: A27.

———. *The Unredeemed Captive: A Family Story from Early America.* New York: Knopf, 1994.

Denn, Robert J. "Captivity Narratives of the American Revolution." *Journal of American Culture* 2 (1980): 575–82.

Derounian, Kathryn Zabelle. "The Publication, Promotion, and Distribution of Mary Rowlandson's Indian Captivity Narrative in the Seventeenth Century." *Early American Literature* 23 (1988): 239–61.

———. "Puritan Orthodoxy and the 'Survivor Syndrome' in Mary Rowlandson's Indian Captivity Narrative." *Early American Literature* 22 (1987): 82–93.

Derounian-Stodola, Kathryn Zabelle, and James Arthur Levernier. *The Indian Captivity Narrative, 1550–1900.* New York: Twayne, 1993.

Derrida, Jacques. *Of Grammatology.* Trans. Gayatri Chakravorty Spivak. Baltimore: Johns Hopkins UP, 1974.

Dimock, Wai-chee. *Empire for Liberty: Melville and the Poetics of Individualism.* Princeton: Princeton UP, 1989.

Dodd, Stephen, ed. *Revolutionary Memorials, Embracing Poems by the Rev. Wheeler Case, Published in 1778.* New York, 1852.

Douglas, Ann. *The Feminization of American Culture.* New York: Alfred A. Knopf, 1977.

———. Introduction. *Charlotte Temple and Lucy Temple.* By Susanna Rowson. New York: Penguin, 1991. vii–xliii.

———. "Introduction: The Art of Controversy." *Uncle Tom's Cabin.* By Harriet Beecher Stowe. New York: Penguin, 1981. 7–36.

Downing, David. "'Streams of Scripture Comfort': Mary Rowlandson's Typological Use of the Bible." *Early American Literature* 15 (1980/1): 252–59.

Drake, Samuel. "A Particular Account of the Captivity of Mrs. Jemima Howe." *The Indian Captivity Narrative: A Woman's View.* Ed. Frances Roe Kestler. New York: Garland, 1990.

Ebersole, Gary L. *Captured by Texts: Puritan to Postmodern Images of Indian Captivity.* Charlottesville: UP of Virginia, 1995.

Elkins, Stanley M. *Slavery: A Problem in American Institutional and Intellectual Life.* 3rd ed., rev. Chicago: U of Chicago P, 1976.

Ellison, Julie. "Race and Sensibility in the Early Republic: Ann Eliza Bleecker and Sarah Wentworth Morton." *American Literature* 65 (1993): 445–74.

Erkkila, Betsy. "Revolutionary Women." *Tulsa Studies in Women's Literature* 6 (1987): 189–223.

Fanon, Frantz. *Black Skin, White Masks.* Trans. Charles Lam Markmann. New York: Grove P, 1967.

Fehrenbacher, Don E. "The Deep Reading of Lincoln." *Lincoln in Text and Context.* Stanford: Stanford UP, 1987. 214–27.

Fiedler, Leslie A. *Love and Death in the American Novel*. Rev. ed. New York: Dell, 1966.

——. *The Return of the Vanishing American*. New York: Stein and Day, 1968.

Fielding, Henry. *Joseph Andrews with Shamela and Related Writings*. Ed. Homer Goldberg. New York: Norton, 1987.

Fisher, Philip. *Hard Facts: Setting and Form in the American Novel*. New York: Oxford UP, 1987.

Fitzpatrick, Tara. "The Figure of Captivity: The Cultural Work of the Puritan Captivity Narrative." *American Literary History* 3 (1991): 1–26.

Fliegelman, Jay. *Declaring Independence: Jefferson, Natural Language, and the Culture of Performance*. Stanford: Stanford UP, 1993.

——. *Prodigals and Pilgrims: The American Revolution against Patriarchal Authority, 1750–1800*. Cambridge: Cambridge UP, 1982.

Foucault, Michel. *Discipline and Punish: The Birth of the Prison*. New York: Vintage, 1979.

——. *The History of Sexuality: An Introduction*, Vol. 1. New York: Vintage, 1980. 3 vols.

——. "The Subject and Power." *Michel Foucault: Beyond Structuralism and Hermeneutics*. Ed. Hubert L. Dreyfus and Paul Rabinow. 2nd ed. Chicago: U of Chicago P, 1983.

Foxe, John. *The Acts and Monuments of John Foxe*. New York: AMS P, 1965.

Fox-Genovese, Elizabeth. "To Write My Self: The Autobiographies of Afro-American Women." *Feminist Issues in Literary Scholarship*. Ed. Shari Benstock. Bloomington: Indiana UP, 1987.

Frederickson, George M. *The Black Image in the White Mind: The Debate on Afro-American Character and Destiny, 1817–1914*. New York: Harper and Row, 1971.

Frost, John. *Heroic Women of the West*. 1854. Rpt. ed. Wilcomb E. Washburn. New York: Garland, 1976.

Fuss, Diana. *Identification Papers*. New York: Routledge, 1995.

Garrison, William Lloyd. *Thoughts on African Colonization*. New York: Arno P, 1968.

Genovese, Eugene D. *Roll, Jordan, Roll: The World the Slaves Made*. New York: Vintage, 1976.

Goscilo, Margaret. "Deconstructing *The Terminator*." *Film Criticism* 12.2 (1987–1988): 37–52.

Greene, David L. "New Light on Mary Rowlandson." *Early American Literature* 20 (1985): 24–38.

Griffin, Edward M. "Women in Trouble: The Predicament of Captivity and the Narratives of Mary Rowlandson, Mary Jemison, and Hannah Dustan." *Für eine offene Literaturwissenschaft: Erkundungen und Erprobungen am Beispiel US-amerikanischer Texte*. Ed. Leo Truchlar. Salzburg: W. Neugebauer, 1986. 41–51.

Gutman, Herbert G. *The Black Family in Slavery and Freedom, 1750–1925*. New York: Pantheon, 1976.

Habermas, Jürgen. *The Structural Transformation of the Public Sphere: An Inquiry into a Category of Bourgeois Society*. Trans. Thomas Burger. Cambridge: MIT P, 1989.

Hambrick-Stowe, Charles E. *The Practice of Piety.* Chapel Hill: U of North Carolina P, 1982.

Hamilton, Alexander, James Madison, and John Jay. *The Federalist Papers.* New York: New American Library, 1961.

Hammon, Briton. "A Narrative of the Sufferings and Deliverances of Briton Hammon." [Original title: *A Narrative of the Uncommon Sufferings, and Surprizing Deliverance of Briton Hammon, A Negro Man*]. Boston, 1760. Rpt. in *The Garland Library of Narratives of North American Indian Captivities.* Sel. and arr. Wilcomb E. Washburn. Vol. 8. New York: Garland, 1978.

Hanson, Elizabeth. *God's Mercy Surmounting Man's Cruelty.* Vaughan and Clark 229–244.

Harbison, Massy. *A Narrative of the Sufferings of Massy Harbison, from Indian Barbarity....* Pittsburgh, 1825.

Hawthorne, Nathaniel. "The Duston Family." *Hawthorne as Editor: Selections from His Writings in* The American Magazine of Useful and Entertaining Knowledge. Ed. Arlin Turner. University: Louisiana State UP, 1941. 131–37.

Heard, Norman J. *White into Red: A Study of the Assimilation of White Persons Captured by Indians.* Metuchen: Scarecrow P, 1973.

Hedrick, Joan. *Harriet Beecher Stowe: A Life.* New York: Oxford UP, 1994.

Hilliard d'Auberteuil, Michel René. *Miss McCrea: A Novel of the American Revolution.* Trans. Eric LaGuardia. Gainesville: Scholars' Facsimiles & Reprints, 1958.

Hoffman, Ronald, and Peter J. Albert, eds. *Women in the Age of the American Revolution.* Charlottesville: UP of Virginia, 1989.

Holstun, James. *A Rational Millennium: Puritan Utopias of Seventeenth-Century England and America.* New York: Oxford UP, 1987.

Hopkins, Stephen. *The Rights of the Colonies Examined.* 1765. Bailyn, *Pamphlets* 499–530.

Horsman, Reginald. *Race and Manifest Destiny: The Origins of American Racial Anglo-Saxonism.* Cambridge: Harvard UP, 1981.

Howe, Susan. "The Captivity and Restoration of Mrs. Mary Rowlandson." *Temblor* 2 (1985): 113–21.

Irigaray, Luce. *Speculum of the Other Woman.* Trans. Gillian C. Gill. Ithaca: Cornell UP, 1985.

——. *This Sex Which Is Not One.* Trans. Catherine Porter. Ithaca: Cornell UP, 1985.

Jacobs, Harriet A. *Incidents in the Life of a Slave Girl.* Ed. L. Maria Child. Ed. and intro. Jean Fagan Yellin. Cambridge: Harvard UP, 1987.

JanMohamed, Abdul R. "The Economy of Manichean Allegory: The Function of Racial Difference in Colonialist Literature." *"Race," Writing, and Difference.* Ed. Henry Louis Gates, Jr. Chicago: U of Chicago P, 1985. 78–106.

Jefferson, Thomas. *Notes on the State of Virginia.* Ed. William Peden. Chapel Hill: U of North Carolina P, 1954.

Jennings, Francis. *The Invasion of America: Indians, Colonialism, and the Cant of Conquest.* New York: Norton, 1975.

Kaplan, Amy. "'Left Alone with America': The Absence of Empire in the Study of American Culture." Kaplan and Pease, eds. 3–21.

Kaplan, Amy, and Donald E. Pease, eds. *The Cultures of United States Imperialism.* Durham: Duke UP, 1993.

Katz, William Loren. "Earliest Responses of American Negroes and Whites to African Colonization." Garrison i–xiv.

Kelley, Mary. Introduction. *Hope Leslie.* By Catharine Maria Sedgwick. New Brunswick: Rutgers UP, 1987. ix–xxxix.

——. *Private Woman, Public Stage: Literary Domesticity in Nineteenth-Century America.* New York: Oxford UP, 1984.

Kerber, Linda K. "The Paradox of Women's Citizenship in the Early Republic: The Case of *Martin vs. Massachusetts,* 1805." *American Historical Review* 97 (1992): 349–78.

——. "The Republican Mother: Women and the Enlightenment—an American Perspective." *American Quarterly* 28 (1976): 187–205.

——. *Women of the Republic: Intellect and Ideology in Revolutionary America.* Chapel Hill: U of North Carolina P, 1980.

King Philip's War Narratives. March of America Facsimile Series. No. 29. Ann Arbor: University Microfilms, 1966.

Kinshasa, Kwando M. *Emigration vs. Assimilation: The Debate in the African American Press, 1827–1861.* Jefferson, N.C.: McFarland & Company, 1988.

Koehler, Lyle. *A Search for Power: The "Weaker Sex" in Seventeenth-Century New England.* Urbana: U of Illinois P, 1980.

Kolodny, Annette. *The Land before Her: Fantasy and Experience of the American Frontiers, 1630–1860.* Chapel Hill: U of North Carolina P, 1984.

——. *The Lay of the Land: Metaphor as Experience and History in American Life and Letters.* Chapel Hill: U of North Carolina P, 1975.

——. "Turning the Lens on 'The Panther Captivity': A Feminist Exercise in Practical Criticism." *Critical Inquiry* 8 (1981): 329–45.

Lacan, Jacques. *The Four Fundamental Concepts of Psychoanalysis.* Ed. Jacques-Alain Miller. Trans. Alan Sheridan. New York: Norton, 1971.

Landes, Joan. *Women and the Public Sphere in the Age of the French Revolution.* Ithaca: Cornell UP, 1988.

Lane, Ann J., ed. *The Debate over Slavery: Stanley Elkins and His Critics.* Urbana: U of Illinois P, 1971.

Lang, Amy Schrager. Introduction to Mary Rowlandson. "A True History of the Captivity and Restoration of Mrs. Mary Rowlandson." *Journeys in New Worlds: Early American Women's Narratives.* Ed. William L. Andrews. Madison: U of Wisconsin P, 1990.

——. *Prophetic Woman: Anne Hutchinson and the Problem of Dissent in the Literature of New England.* Berkeley: U of California P, 1987.

Lawrence, D. H. *Studies in Classic American Literature.* New York: Penguin, 1923.

Leach, Douglas Edward. *Flintlock and Tomahawk: New England in King Philip's War.* New York: Norton, 1966.

Leary, Lewis. Introduction. *Miss McCrea: A Novel of the American Revolution.* By Michel René Hilliard d'Auberteuil. Trans. Eric LaGuardia. Gainesville: Scholars' Facsimiles & Reprints, 1958.

Levernier, James, and Hennig Cohen, eds. and comps. *The Indians and Their Captives*. Westport: Greenwood P, 1977.

Levernier, James A., and Douglas R. Wilmes, eds. *American Writers before 1800: A Biographical and Critical Dictionary*. Westport: Greenwood P, 1983.

Lincoln, Charles H., ed. *Narratives of the Indian Wars, 1675–1699*. New York: Charles Scribner's Sons, 1913.

Liu, Alan. *Wordsworth: The Sense of History*. Stanford: Stanford UP, 1989.

Lott, Eric. "White Like Me: Racial Cross-Dressing and the Construction of American Whiteness." Kaplan and Pease 474–95.

Lowance, Mason I., Jr., Ellen E. Westbrook, and R. C. DeProspo, eds. *The Stowe Debate: Rhetorical Strategies in* Uncle Tom's Cabin. Amherst: U of Massachusetts P, 1994.

Lowry, Jean. *A Journal of the Captivity of Jean Lowry and her Children . . . .* Philadelphia, 1760. Rpt. in *The Garland Library of Narratives of North American Indian Captivities*. Sel. and arr. Wilcomb E. Washburn. Vol. 8. New York: Garland, 1977.

Lynch, Deidre. "Overloaded Portraits: The Excesses of Character and Countenance." *Body and Text in the Eighteenth Century*. Ed. Veronica Kelly and Dorothea von Mücke. Stanford: Stanford UP, 1994. 112–43.

MacDonald, Mary Lu. "Harriet Vaughan Cheney." *Canadian Writers before 1890*. Ed. W. H. New. Vol. 99 of *Dictionary of Literary Biography*. Detroit: Gale Research, 1990.

Manley, Mary de la Rivière. "Preface to *The Secret History of Queen Zarah . . .* (1705)." *Novel and Romance, 1700–1800: A Documentary Record*. Ed. Ioan Williams. London: Routledge and Kegan Paul, 1970. 33–39.

Mann, Herman. *The Female Review; or, Life of Deborah Sampson*. New York: Arno P, 1972.

Marx, Karl. *Capital*. Ed. Frederick Engels. Trans. Samuel Moore and Edward Aveling. Vol. 1. New York: International Publishers, 1967. 3 vols.

———. *Pre-Capitalist Economic Formations*. Ed. E. J. Hobsbawm. Trans. Jack Cohen. New York: International Publishers, 1964.

Mather, Cotton. *Decennium Luctuosum*. Lincoln 169–300.

———. *Magnalia Christi Americana*. New York: Russell and Russell, 1967. 2 vols.

Matthiesen, F. O. *American Renaissance: Art and Expression in the Age of Emerson and Whitman*. London: Oxford UP, 1941.

Mills, Bruce. "Lydia Maria Child and the Endings to Harriet Jacobs' *Incidents in the Life of a Slave Girl*." *American Literature* 64 (1992): 255–72.

Minter, David L. "By Dens of Lions: Notes on Stylization in Early Puritan Captivity Narratives." *American Literature* 45 (1973–74): 335–47.

Montgomery, Benilde. "Recapturing John Marrant." *A Mixed Race: Ethnicity in Early America*. Ed. Frank Shuffleton. New York: Oxford UP, 1993. 105–15.

Moretti, Franco. *Signs Taken for Wonders*. Trans. Susan Fischer et al. London: Verso, 1983.

Morrison, Toni. *Playing in the Dark: Whiteness and the Literary Imagination*. New York: Vintage, 1992.

Mott, Frank Luther. *Golden Multitudes: The Story of Best Sellers in the United States*. New York: Macmillan, 1947.

Namias, June. *White Captives: Gender and Ethnicity on the American Frontier.* Chapel Hill: U of North Carolina P, 1993.

Narrative of Mrs. Scott and Capt. Stewart's Captivity. Boston, 1786; Newburyport, 1799. Both rpt. in *The Garland Library of Narratives of North American Indian Captivities.* Sel. and arr. Wilcomb E. Washburn. Vol. 16. New York: Garland, 1978.

Nelson, Dana. "Sympathy as Strategy in Sedgwick's *Hope Leslie.*" Samuels 191–202.

Nesbit, William, and Samuel Williams. *Two Black Views of Liberia.* New York: Arno P and the *New York Times,* 1969.

A New and Further Narrative of the State of New England. King Philip's War Narratives. Original pagination.

Norton, Mary Beth. *Liberty's Daughters: The Revolutionary Experience of American Women, 1750–1800.* Boston: Little, Brown, 1980.

Olson, Lester C. *Emblems of American Community in the Revolutionary Era: A Study in Rhetorical Iconology.* Washington: Smithsonian Institution P, 1991.

Oxford English Dictionary. 1971 ed.

Paine, Thomas. *Common Sense: Political Writings.* Ed. Bruce Kuklick. Cambridge: Cambridge UP, 1989. 1–38.

Painter, Nell Irvin. "Representing Truth: Sojourner Truth's Knowing and Becoming Known." *Journal of American History* 81 (1994): 461–92.

——. "Soul Murder and Slavery: Toward a Fully Loaded Cost Accounting." *U.S. History as Women's History: New Feminist Essays.* Ed. Linda K. Kerber, Alice Kessler-Harris, and Kathryn Kish Sklar. Chapel Hill: U of North Carolina P, 1995. 125–46.

Panther, Abraham. *A surprising Account of the Discovery of a Lady who was taken by the Indians in the year 1777, and after making her escape, she retired to a lonely Cave, where she lived nine years.* Norwich, Conn., 1787.

Pearce, Roy Harvey. "The Significances of the Captivity Narrative." *American Literature* 19 (1947): 1–20.

Pease, Donald E. "New Perspectives on U.S. Culture and Imperialism." Kaplan and Pease, eds. 22–37.

Penley, Constance. "Time Travel, Primal Scene, and the Critical Dystopia." *Camera Obscura* 15 (1986): 67–85.

Plummer, Rachel. *Narrative of the Capture and Subsequent Sufferings of Mrs. Rachel Plummer, Written by Herself.* VanDerBeets, *Held Captive* 333–66.

Pocock, J. G. A. *The Machiavellian Moment: Florentine Political Thought and the Atlantic Republican Tradition.* Princeton: Princeton UP, 1975.

——. *Virtue, Commerce, and History: Essays on Political Thought and History Chiefly in the Eighteenth Century.* Cambridge: Cambridge UP, 1985.

Poirier, Richard. *A World Elsewhere: The Place of Style in American Literature.* Madison: U of Wisconsin P, 1985.

Pratt, Mary Louise. *Imperial Eyes: Travel Writing and Transculturation.* London: Routledge, 1992.

The Present State of New-England. King Philip's War Narratives. Original pagination.

Pulsipher, Jenny Hale. "Massacre at Hurtleberry Hill: Christian Indians and English Authority in Metacom's War." *William and Mary Quarterly* 3d ser. 53 (1996): 459–86.

Ratray, Captain R. S. *Ashanti*. Oxford: Clarendon P, 1923, 1969.

Renan, Ernest. "What Is a Nation?" Trans. Martin Thom. Bhabha, ed. *Nation* 8–22.

Reynolds, David S. *Beneath the American Renaissance: The Subversive Imagination in the Age of Emerson and Melville*. Cambridge: Harvard UP, 1989.

Richardson, Samuel. *Pamela or, Virtue Rewarded*. Ed. T. C. Duncan Eaves and Ben D. Kimpel. Boston: Houghton Mifflin, 1971.

Rogin, Michael Paul. *Fathers and Children: Andrew Jackson and the Subjugation of the American Indian*. New Brunswick: Transaction, 1991.

Rowlandson, Joseph. *The Possibility of God's Forsaking a People Who Have Been Near and Dear to Him*. Boston, 1682.

Rowlandson, Mary. *Narrative of the Captivity of Mary Rowlandson*. 1682. Lincoln 107–67.

———. *A Narrative of the Captivity, Sufferings and Removes of Mrs. Mary Rowlandson*. Boston, 1771.

Rowson, Susanna. *Charlotte Temple*. Ed. Cathy N. Davidson. New York: Oxford UP, 1986.

———. *Reuben and Rachel; or, Tales of Old Times: A Novel*. Boston, 1798.

Ruttenberg, Nancy. "George Whitefield, Spectacular Conversion, and the Rise of Democratic Personality." *American Literary History* 5 (1993): 429–58.

Ryan, Mary P. *The Empire of the Mother: American Writing about Domesticity, 1820–1860*. New York: Institute for Research in History and Haworth P, 1982.

Sahlins, Marshall. *Stone Age Economics*. New York: Aldine de Gruyter, 1972.

Salisbury, Neal. "The Indians' Old World: Native Americans and the Coming of Europeans." *William and Mary Quarterly* 3d ser. 53 (1996): 435–58.

———. *Manitou and Providence: Indians, Europeans, and the Making of New England, 1500–1643*. New York: Oxford UP, 1982.

Samuels, Shirley, ed. *The Culture of Sentiment: Race, Gender, and Sentimentality in 19th Century America*. New York: Oxford UP, 1992.

Sánchez-Eppler, Karen. "Bodily Bonds: The Intersecting Rhetorics of Feminism and Abolition." Samuels 92–114.

Schmitz, Neil. "Refiguring Lincoln: Speeches and Writings, 1832–1865." *American Literary History* 6 (1994): 103–18.

Scott, Sir Walter. *Waverley; or, 'Tis Sixty Years Since*. Ed. Claire Lamont. New York: Oxford UP, 1986.

Sedgwick, Catharine Maria. *Hope Leslie; or, Early Times in the Massachusetts*. 1824. Ed. Mary Kelley. New Brunswick: Rutgers UP, 1987.

Seaver, James E., ed. *The Narrative of the Life of Mrs. Mary Jemison*. Syracuse: Syracuse UP, 1990.

Sewall, Samuel. *The Diary of Samuel Sewall, 1674–1729*. Ed. M. Halsey Thomas. Vol. 1. New York: Farrar, Straus and Giroux, 1973. 2 vols.

Sheehan, Bernard W. *Seeds of Extinction: Jeffersonian Philanthropy and the American Indian*. Chapel Hill: U of North Carolina P, 1973.

Sieminski, Captain Greg. "The Puritan Captivity Narrative and the Politics of the American Revolution." *American Quarterly* 42 (1990): 35–56.

Singley, Carol J. "Catharine Maria Sedgwick's *Hope Leslie*: Radical Frontier Romance." *Desert, Garden, Margin, Range: Literature on the American Frontier.* Ed. Eric Heyne. New York: Twayne, 1992. 110–22.

Slotkin, Richard. *Regeneration through Violence: The Mythology of the American Frontier, 1600–1860.* Middletown: Wesleyan UP, 1973.

———. *The Fatal Environment: The Myth of the Frontier in the Age of Industrialization, 1800–1890.* Middletown: Wesleyan UP, 1985.

Smith, Henry Nash. *Virgin Land: The American West as Symbol and Myth.* New York: Vintage, 1950.

Smith, Stephanie A. *Conceived by Liberty: Maternal Figures and 19th Century American Literature.* Ithaca: Cornell UP, 1994.

Smith, Valerie. "Introduction." *Incidents in the Life of a Slave Girl.* By Harriet Jacobs. New York: Oxford UP, 1988.

Smith-Rosenberg, Carroll. *Disorderly Conduct: Visions of Gender in Victorian America.* New York: Knopf, 1985.

———. "Subject Female: Authorizing American Identity." *American Literary History* 5 (1993): 481–511.

Some Indian Events of New England. Boston: State Street Trust Company, 1934.

Sommer, Doris. *Foundational Fictions: The National Romances of Latin America.* Berkeley: U of California P, 1991.

Spengemann, William. *A Mirror for Americanists: Reflections on the Idea of American Literature.* Hanover: UP of New England, 1989.

Spivak, Gayatri. *Outside in the Teaching Machine.* New York: Routledge, 1993.

Staudenraus, P. J. *The African Colonization Movement, 1816–1865.* New York: Columbia UP, 1961.

Steele, Ian K. *The English Atlantic, 1675–1740: An Exploration of Communication and Community.* New York: Oxford UP, 1986.

Stepto, Robert B. "Sharing the Thunder: The Literary Exchanges of Harriet Beecher Stowe, Henry Bibb, and Frederick Douglass." Sundquist, ed. *New Essays* 135–53.

Sterne, Laurence. *A Sentimental Journey through France and Italy.* In *Three Sentimental Novels.* Ed. Albert J. Kuhn. New York: Holt, Rhinehart, and Winston, 1970. 1–114.

Stewart, Susan. *On Longing: Narratives of the Miniature, the Gigantic, the Souvenir, the Collection.* Durham: Duke UP, 1993.

Story, Norah. *The Oxford Companion to Canadian History and Literature.* Toronto: Oxford UP, 1967.

Stowe, Harriet Beecher. *A Key to* Uncle Tom's Cabin. Port Washington: Kennikat P, 1968.

———. *Uncle Tom's Cabin; or, Life Among the Lowly.* New York: Penguin, 1981.

Sturtevant, William C., gen. ed. *Handbook of North American Indians.* Vol. 15: *Northeast.* Ed. Bruce G. Trigger. Washington: Smithsonian Institution, 1978.

Sundquist, Eric J., ed. *New Essays on* Uncle Tom's Cabin. Cambridge: Cambridge UP, 1988.

———. *To Wake the Nations: Race in the Making of American Literature.* Cambridge: Belknap P of Harvard UP, 1993.

Telotte, J. P. "*The Terminator, Terminator 2*, and the Exposed Body." *Journal of Popular Film and Television* 20.2 (1992): 26–34.

Terminator. Dir. James Cameron. Orion Pictures. 1984.

Terminator 2: Judgment Day. Dir. James Cameron. TriStar Pictures. 1991.

Thacher, Oxenbridge. *The Sentiments of a British American*. 1764. Bailyn, *Pamphlets* 483–98.

Tompkins, Jane. *Sensational Designs: The Cultural Work of American Fiction, 1790–1860*. New York: Oxford UP, 1985.

Toulouse, Teresa A. "'My Own Credit': Strategies of (E)Valuation in Mary Rowlandson's Captivity Narrative." *American Literature* 64 (1992): 655–76.

Turner, Victor. *Dramas, Fields, and Metaphors*. Ithaca: Cornell UP, 1974.

Ulrich, Laurel Thatcher. *Good Wives*. New York: Knopf, 1982.

Underhill, John. *Newes from America*. London, 1638.

Vail, R. W. G. *The Voice of the Old Frontier*. New York: U of Pennsylvania P, 1949.

Vaughan, Alden T. *New England Frontier: Puritans and Indians, 1620–1675*. Rev. ed. New York: Norton, 1979.

Vaughan, Alden T., and Edward W. Clark. "Cups of Common Calamity: Puritan Captivity Narratives as Literature and History." Vaughan and Clark, eds. 1–28.

——, eds. *Puritans among the Indians: Accounts of Captivity and Redemption, 1676–1724*. Cambridge: Belknap P of Harvard UP, 1981.

VanDerBeets, Richard, ed. *Held Captive by Indians: Selected Narratives, 1642–1836*. Knoxville: U of Tennessee P, 1973.

——. "The Indian Captivity Narrative as Ritual." *American Literature* 43 (1972): 548–62.

Wald, Priscilla. *Constituting Americans: Cultural Anxiety and Narrative Form*. Durham: Duke UP, 1995.

Walker, Clarence E. *Deromanticizing Black History: Critical Essays and Reappraisals*. Knoxville: U of Tennessee P, 1991.

Walker, James W. St. G. *The Black Loyalists: The Search for a Promised Land in Nova Scotia and Sierra Leone, 1783–1870*. New York: Africana, 1976.

Warner, Michael. *The Letters of the Republic: Publication and the Public Sphere in Eighteenth Century America*. Cambridge: Harvard UP, 1992.

Wexler, Laura. "Tender Violence: Literary Eavesdropping, Domestic Fiction, and Educational Reform." Samuels 9–38.

Williams, John. *The Redeemed Captive Returning to Zion*. Vaughan and Clark, eds. 167–226.

Wilson, D. *The Life of Jane McCrea*. New York, 1853.

Winter John, ed. *A Narrative of the Sufferings of Massy Harbison, from Indian Barbarity . . . .* 4th ed. Beaver, 1826.

Winthrop, John. "A Modell of Christian Charity." *Winthrop Papers*. Vol. 2. Boston: Massachusetts Historical Society, 1943. 282–95.

Wollstonecraft, Mary. *Vindication of the Rights of Woman*. Middlesex: Penguin Books, 1982.

Yellin, Jean Fagan. Introduction. *Incidents in the Life of a Slave Girl*. By Harriet Jacobs. Cambridge: Harvard UP, 1987. xiii–xxxiv.

Yarborough, Richard. "Strategies of Black Characterization in *Uncle Tom's Cabin* and the Early Afro-American Novel." Sundquist, ed. 45–84.

Zafar, Rafia. "Capturing the Captivity: African Americans among the Puritans." *MELUS* 17.2 (1991–1992): 19–35.

Žižek, Slavoj. *The Sublime Object of Ideology*. London: Verso, 1989.

Index

abolitionism, 119, 120–21, 144, 160

African colonization, 120–22, 134, 136, 142–44, 146

agency, 7, 8, 78–79, 123, 168; of Amerindians, 107, 113, 117, 156–57; of colonists, 67, 72; and coverture, 90–91; grammatical construction of, 93, 104, 110; in *Hope Leslie*, 113, 116–17; in imperialist discourse, 94, 98, 101–2, 106; and maternal influence, 121, 139–40, 143; national, 167–68; in the new historicism, 156–57; in *Pamela*, 58, 59; and political virtue, 82; and race, 122, 124, 127, 135–41, 145–48; and typology, 129; and violence, 48, 49, 52, 62; of women, 3–4, 68, 88, 151–52, 170, 192 n.5

Aldridge, Rev., *Narrative of the Lord's Wonderful Dealings with John Marrant*, 125–33, 145–46

Algonquin Indians, 19, 32; Christianized, 179 nn.7&8. *See also* King Philip (Metacom); Quinnapin; Weetamoo

America. *See* exceptionalism; nation; national literature; nationalism; republican motherhood; virtue, national

American Colonization Society (ACS), 120–22, 125, 128, 134, 143–44, 189 n.20

American revolution, 60, 61, 62; rhetoric of, 67, 68, 85; women in, 67–68, 89. *See also* captivity, as revolutionary trope; family, as revolutionary trope; freedom and power; independence; slavery, as revolutionary trope; violence, and revolution

Anderson, Benedict, 44, 45

Andrews, William L., 154, 160

Appiah, Anthony, 156–57

Armstrong, Nancy, 190 n.7; and Leonard Tennenhouse, 44–45, 57

Ashanti, 168–69

Auerbach, Erich, 16

Bailyn, Bernard, 69, 70, 86

Bakhtin, M. M., 34–35, 37, 56, 62

Baldwin, James, 118–19, 121

Baym, Nina, 6, 62

Berlant, Lauren, 168

Bhabha, Homi: on cultural difference, 21, 174–75; on interstitiality and agency, 3, 8, 153; on mimicry, 109, 148; on national narrative, 44, 47, 62

Bibb, Henry, 123

Bleecker, Ann Eliza, *History of Maria Kittle*, 49, 92–96, 112, 125

Bloch, Ruth, 68, 82, 91

Breitwieser, Mitchell, 17, 181 n.32

Brent, Linda. *See* Jacobs, Harriet

Brown, Gillian, 120

Brown, John, 162

Brown, William Hill, *The Power of Sympathy*, 61

Burgoyne, General, 73, 77

Burke, Edmund, 2, 5

Burr, Esther Edwards, diary of, 59–60

captivity: and adoption, 24, 183 n.11; and commodification, 11, 13, 18, 28, 33, 180 n.15; in domestic sphere, 86, 89–91, 99; erotics of, 105; and escape, 48–49, 52, 86, 96, 170; and female transgression, 26, 37; in frontier romances, 98; and historical narrative, 106; and liminality, 17, 18, 20, 21; and nationalism, 68, 127; and rape, 71, 73, 75, 85; as revolutionary trope, 69, 70, 86, 89, 91

captivity narrative: as escape literature 2, 3, 14, 39; and genre, 34–35, 172, 177 n.5, 181 n.29, 182 n.5; and novels, 68, 72, 95,

207

UNIVERSITY PRESS OF NEW ENGLAND publishes books under its own imprint and is the publisher for Brandeis University Press, Dartmouth College, Middlebury College Press, University of New Hampshire, Tufts University, and Wesleyan University Press.

LIBRARY OF CONGRESS CATALOGING-IN-PUBLICATION DATA
Burnham, Michelle.
    Captivity and sentiment : cultural exchange in American literature, 1682–1861 / Michelle Burnham
    p.   cm. — (Reencounters with colonialism — new perspectives on the Americas)
    Includes bibliographical references (p.   ) and index.
    ISBN 0–87451–818–0 (cl. : alk. paper)
    1. American literature — Colonial period, ca. 1600–1775 — History and criticism.
2. American literature — Revolutionary period, 1775–1783 — History and criticism.
3. American literature — 19th century — History and criticism. 4. Intercultural communication in literature. 5. Sentimentalism in literature. 6. Imprisonment in literature.
7. Imperialism in literature. 8. Colonies in literature. 9. Slavery in literature. 10. Slaves in literature.
    I. Title. II. Series.
PS186.B87   1997
810.9'358 — dc21   96-49268